Social Security in Contemporary Japan

The present study analyzes the livelihood security system of contemporary Japan in international comparison from a historical and gender perspective. It posits 'livelihood security systems' rather than 'welfare states' or 'welfare regimes' as its object of analysis to enter the role of non-governmental institutions and of governmental policies reaching beyond income transfers into vision.

Based on rich statistical materials, the evolution of Japan's livelihood security system in recent decades is traced to reveal a rigid male breadwinner orientation increasingly out of step with social realities. The need for remedying the gender bias built into Japan's social insurance schemes has been politically highlighted since the late 1990s, but legislative action has continued to be deferred.

The author argues that at present the livelihood security system of Japan is not only dysfunctional, but actually functioning in reverse, in a sense of furthering social exclusion. The study concludes with suggestions for a possible reconstruction of Japan's social security system, arguing for an increased role of the 'third sector' or 'social economy' in livelihood security and care provision.

This book will appeal to scholars and students with an interest in social policy, welfare economics and gender studies, as well as Japanese politics and society.

Mari Osawa is Professor at the Institute of Social Science at the University of Tokyo.

Routledge / University of Tokyo Series
Editorial Board

Editor-in-Chief:
Masashi Haneda, Professor, Institute for Advanced Studies on Asia, University of Tokyo

Associate Editors:
Jun Furuya, Professor, Graduate School of Arts and Sciences, University of Tokyo. Shinsaku Iwahara, Professor, Graduate School of Law and Politics, University of Tokyo. Hiroshi Mitani, Professor, Graduate School of Arts and Sciences, University of Tokyo. Shōgo Takegawa, Professor, Graduate School of Humanities and Sociology, University of Tokyo. Ryōko Tsuneyoshi, Professor, Graduate School of Education, University of Tokyo. Susumu Yamakage, Professor, Graduate School of Arts and Sciences, University of Tokyo. Hiroshi Yoshikawa, Graduate School of Economics, University of Tokyo

Managing Editor:
Michael Burtscher, Associate Professor, Division of International Affairs and Institute of Social Science, University of Tokyo

1. **Koizumi and Japanese Politics**
   Reform strategies and leadership style
   Yu Uchiyama, Translated by Carl Freire

2. **Social Security in Contemporary Japan**
   A comparative analysis
   Mari Osawa, Translation edited by Michael Burtscher

Social Security in Contemporary Japan
A comparative analysis

Mari Osawa

Translation edited by Michael Burtscher

LONDON AND NEW YORK

First published 2011
by Routledge
2 Park Square, Milton Park, Abingdon, Oxon OX14 4RN

Simultaneously published in the USA and Canada
by Routledge
711 Third Avenue, New York, NY 10017

Routledge is an imprint of the Taylor & Francis Group, an informa business

© 2011 The University of Tokyo

First issued in paperback 2013

The right of The University of Tokyo to be identified as authors/editors of this work has been asserted by them in accordance with the Copyright, Designs and Patent Act 1988.

All rights reserved. No part of this book may be reprinted or reproduced or utilised in any form or by any electronic, mechanical, or other means, now known or hereafter invented, including photocopying and recording, or in any information storage or retrieval system, without permission in writing from the publishers.

Trademark notice: Product or corporate names may be trademarks or registered trademarks, and are used only for identification and explanation without intent to infringe.

British Library Cataloguing in Publication Data
A catalogue record for this book is available from the British Library

Library of Congress Cataloging in Publication Data
Osawa, Mari, 1953-
Social security in contemporary Japan : a comparative analysis of its livelihood security system / by Mari Osawa ; translation edited by Michael Burtscher.
    p. cm. — (Routledge/University of Tokyo series ; 2)
  Includes bibliographical references and index.
  1. Social security—Japan. I. Title.
  HD7227.O734 2011
  361.952—dc22   2010051276

ISBN 978-0-415-55940-9 (hbk)
ISBN 978-0-415-85551-8 (pbk)

Typeset in Times New Roman by
Pindar NZ, Auckland, New Zealand

Contents

List of illustrations — vii
List of abbreviations — ix
Editorial note — xi

Introduction: the aims and structure of this book — 1

1 From welfare regimes to livelihood security systems — 7

Characteristics of the 20th century welfare state 8
Esping-Andersen's threefold typology of welfare states and its critics 13
The limits of welfare states and the theory of livelihood security systems 22

2 The livelihood security systems approach — 26

The production and distribution of goods and services and the livelihood security system 26
Economic globalization and social exclusion 36
The functioning of livelihood security systems 45
Structural components of Japan's rigid male breadwinner model 47

3 The 1990s – Japan's lost decade — 55

Locating Japan along the 'three routes' of welfare state transition 55
Clinging to the male breadwinner model: from The Five-Year Plan for Building a Lifestyle Superpower *to Hashimoto's 'Six Major Reforms'* 57
The restructuring of employment and marriage 69

4 Japan in international comparison at the turn of the century   85

Quantitative and qualitative interrelations between the four relations of production 86
Employment performance 94
Main features of Japan's small welfare government 102

5 Taking stock of the Koizumi reforms   124

The social policy reforms of the Koizumi administration 126
Real-life consequences of the 'muscular economic structure' 135
Hollowing out and reverse functioning of the social insurance system 140
Summary 153

6 Beyond exclusion – building a cohesive society   157

The National Commission on Social Security's failure to face realities 158
Universal services and a unified pension plan 164
Learning from 'livelihood cooperation' practices in Italy 173
Social inclusion as key to market viability 181

Notes   185
Bibliography   191
Index   215

Illustrations

Figures

2.1	Estimated length of crisis (recovery time) and gross output loss (in per cent of GDP)	39
2.2	Comprehensive process model of gendering social policy	45
3.1	Proportion of non-regular employees, female, by age group	73
3.2	Proportion of non-regular employees, male, by age group	73
4.1	Percentage of self-employed and their family workers, by gender	89
4.2	Daily time use of married couples with at least one child aged six and under (aged five and under for Japan and the US) (weekly averages for husbands and wives)	92
4.3	Labour market regulations in 1990, 1999 and 2003	97
4.4	Pension benefit levels by type of household (earnings replacement rates in per cent)	112
4.5	Percentage reduction of poverty rates among the working-age population, operated by net social transfers, mid-2000s	122
4.6	Child poverty rates, before and after taxes and transfers, in the 1980s, mid-1990s and around 2000	123
5.1	Change in pension benefit levels by the 2004 reform	130
5.2	Changes in corporate earnings and employee income (bottom of the recession=100)	136
5.3	Trends in proportions of non-regular employees, by gender	137
5.4	Trends in duration of unemployment in Japan, by gender	138
5.5	Coverage of employees' social insurance schemes, proportion of insured to number of employees, by scheme and gender	141
5.6	Coverage of Employees' Pension Insurance and mutual aid pension, by gender and age group, years 1995, 2000 and 2004	142
5.7	Coverage of the public pension scheme for those aged 20–9, by class and gender, in 1997, 2002 and 2006	143
5.8	Persons receiving unemployment benefit and the number of unemployed, by gender	147
5.9	Cost of social security benefits (per cent of national income)	154

viii *Illustrations*

6.1 Schematic image of the system of three welfare governments 164
6.2 Pension benefit formula 172

Tables

2.1 Classification of relations of production of goods and services according to commoditization 31
2.2 Classification of relations of production of goods and services according to commoditization, the case of Japan 54
3.1 Average monthly labour cost per ordinary employee (yen) 76
3.2 Labour costs other than cash earnings (average monthly labour cost per ordinary employee, in yen) 77
3.3 Legally mandated welfare expenditures (average monthly labour cost per ordinary employee, in yen) 78
4.1 Comparison of social security contributions as percentage of labour costs, 1998 and 2004 100
4.2 Public pension schemes in Japan, the US, the UK and Germany (from the perspective of women's lifestyle choice) 105
4.3 Summary indicators of work/family reconciliation policies and relevant flexible work arrangements 117
4.4 Japan's ranking for Gini coefficient and relative poverty rate among 14 OECD countries (around 2000) 121

List of abbreviations

ALMP	Active Labour Market Policy
CDPC	Central Disaster Prevention Council
CEDAW	Convention on the Elimination of All Forms of Discrimination Against Women
CEFP	Council on Economic and Fiscal Policy
CGM	Consorzio Gino Mattarelli
CIRIEC	International Centre of Research and Information on the Public, Social and Cooperative Economy
CSR	Corporate Social Responsibility
DPJ	Democratic Party of Japan
EHI	Employees' Health Insurance
EPA	Economic Planning Agency
EPF	Employees' Pension Fund
EPI	Employees' Pension Insurance
EPSI	Employment Protection Security Index
ESI	Economic Security Index
ESRI	Economic and Social Research Institute
FILP	Fiscal Investment and Loan Program
FTE	Full-time Equivalents
FY	Fiscal Year
GATT	General Agreement on Tariffs and Trade
GDP	Gross Domestic Product
GPIF	Government Pension Investment Fund
ICA	International Co-operative Alliance
ILO	International Labour Organization
IMF	International Monetary Fund
ISTAT	Istituto nazionale di statistica
JILPT	Japan Institute for Labour Policy and Training
LDP	Liberal Democratic Party of Japan
METI	Ministry of Economy, Trade and Industry
NCSS	National Commission on Social Security
NEET	Not in Employment, Education or Training
NGO	Non-governmental Organization

NHI	National Health Insurance
NIPA	National Income and Product Accounts
NIPSSR	National Institute for Population and Social Security Research
NIRA	National Institute for Research and Advancement
NLI	Nippon Life Insurance Company
NPO	Non-profit/Not-for-profit Organization
NRI	Nomura Research Institute
OECD	Organisation for Economic Co-operation and Development
PARC	Policy Affairs Research Council (LDP)
PCD	Policy Coherence for Development
SAP	Structural Adjustment Program
SERPS	State Earnings Related Pension (UK)
SMD	Single-Member District
SME	Small and Medium-sized Enterprise
SNA	System of National Accounts
SPC	Social Protection Council
S2P	State Second Pension (UK)
TFR	Total Fertility Rate
WTO	World Trade Organization

Editorial note

The present book is a substantially revised and updated translation of the author's *Gendai Nihon no seikatsu hoshō shisutemu: Zahyō to yukue* 現代日本の生活保障システム―座標とゆくえ, published by Iwanami Shoten 岩波書店 in 2007. The translation of this book was funded by the University of Tokyo in the framework of its English-Language Monograph Publications Program.

Translations were provided by Keith Casner (Chapters 1, 2, 3, and 5), Margaret Gibbons (Chapter 4 and Bibliography) and Lingua Guild Inc., Tokyo (Introduction and Chapter 6). The final version of the translation was prepared by Michael Burtscher and checked by the author.

Japanese names are given in the English order, that is, personal name first, followed by the family name. Apostrophes indicating syllable separation after final n before vowel or y have been omitted in names in the main text, but are retained in the bibliography and transcriptions of Japanese. Macrons over vowels indicate lengthened pronunciation. In the case of terms well established in English usage, they are omitted (Tokyo instead of Tōkyō).

Introduction
The aims and structure of this book

The global financial crisis that began with the collapse of the subprime mortgage market in the United States spread to real economies across the world at an unprecedented pace. In Japan, too, as 2009 began, people lost their jobs and often homes with a suddenness and on a scale previously unknown, leaving them at a loss as to where to turn. This situation continues today. At a time when societal sustainability is increasingly seen as being under threat, an unprecedented degree of instability has been laid bare within the globalized economy. Against this backdrop, in the general election of 30 August 2009, the coalition government headed by the Liberal Democratic Party (LDP) was replaced by a coalition led by the Democratic Party of Japan (DPJ) in an historic change of administration.

Tarō Asō, the last prime minister of the outgoing LDP government, declared in his New Year's Day 2009 comments that 'Japan will be the first country in the world to extricate itself from this recession'. In his Special Address to the World Economic Forum Annual Meeting in Davos at the end of January, Asō went on to emphasize that to put the world economy back onto a stable growth trajectory, countries (including Japan) with overall trade balance surpluses must shed their reliance on external demand, to achieve economic growth by increasing internal consumption instead. Restoration of vitality to the Japanese economy, the second-largest in the world, was Japan's foremost duty. However, as also recognized by the government's *Annual Report on the Japanese Economy and Public Finance*, the view at mid-2009 was that the slump in the Japanese economy was clearly the most severe among all the advanced industrialized countries. Since then, economic revival has continued to stall. Far from Japan performing its duty, there was, to the contrary, fear that it could thwart recovery of the world economy.

The economy and society of Japan, as discussed particularly in Chapter 5 of this volume, were deliberately restructured from the latter half of the 1990s, and especially after 2000, to base economic growth on external demand as opposed to domestic consumption. To defeat the crisis and avoid its recurrence, it became necessary to reverse trends that had prevailed for more than 15 years. The leaders of the outgoing government failed to recognize the implications of this and to formulate adequate policy responses.

This study presents a comparative gender analysis of livelihood security systems with a focus on Japan. From a gender perspective and historical as well as internationally comparative viewpoints, it analyzes the trajectory of livelihood security provision in contemporary Japan with the aim of assessing its future direction. Two scenarios present themselves: one deeply worrisome, and one more promising.

The term 'livelihood security system' will here be used to refer to the totality of economic and social structures involved in economic production, distribution and consumption, as it relates to the livelihood of individuals. 'Livelihood security' can be restated to mean that vital needs are sustainably met. The primary concern of the 'livelihood security system' approach adopted in this book is with the 'capability' of individuals to lead decent lives and participate in society as realized human beings. Deficiencies in this capability constitute livelihood 'needs'. Sustained satisfaction of livelihood needs presupposes a suitable living environment and opportunities for earning an income. Engaging in income-raising and community activities is in itself vital for gaining recognition as an equal participant in society.

To guarantee a sustainable decent livelihood and opportunities for social participation, it is essential that government social policies and non-governmental institutions or social practices such as the family, community, corporations and not-for-profit organizations, finely interact with each other. In Japan as elsewhere, there can be no doubt that the welfare state (in the sense of measures and policies enacted by the central government) has played an important role in securing livelihood. However, if this book were to limit its scope to the welfare state, it would run the risk of overlooking various conditions that affect the stability of livelihood and chances for social participation at the beginning of the 21st century, and will continue to do so in the future. Especially in its final chapter, this study will therefore close in on options for livelihood security provision based on spontaneous cooperation at the meso level of society, suggesting the concept of 'livelihood cooperation' as a more promising way of approaching the problem.

Of course, like the term 'livelihood security system' relied on in this volume, the term 'welfare state' may also be used in senses that include the livelihood security functions of non-governmental institutions such as the family or corporations in their interaction with government policies. Within the framework of my own approach, however, I will use the term 'welfare government' instead where I specifically refer to government-enacted welfare policies.

The welfare state of the latter half of the 20th century typically regarded inadequate livelihood as a situation in which the income of a male provider was insufficient to cover the living expenses of a family due to his unemployment, sickness, injury or old age. Income transfers in the form of social insurance benefits (and in exceptional cases public assistance) were considered the mainstay of social security. In other words, it was income transfers to a 'male breadwinner' in which the 20th century welfare state found its purpose. The 20th century welfare state was thus founded on a (socially constructed) gender relation in which a husband was considered the main provider of a household's income, while the wife was expected to bear the main burden of housework and child-rearing. As long as a man was able to obtain sufficient income from employment during his productive years, he would be able to maintain a household with a wife and children, raise the next generation and be assured an income after retirement.

However, from the last quarter of the 20th century, as economies became increasingly globalized and post-industrialization mainly in the advanced industrial countries deepened, the livelihood security system of the conventional welfare state reached an impasse. Welfare states in their existing form proved unable to respond to new social risks, furthering 'social exclusion' on a widening scale instead. Increasing numbers of people have been faced with serious difficulties in securing a livelihood and fully participating in society.

This volume centrally relies on the concept of social exclusion/inclusion, set into relation with the functioning of the livelihood security system. That is, social inclusion is here seen as the result (outcome) of the proper functioning of a livelihood security system, while social exclusion is explained as the result (outcome) of a 'dysfunction' or 'reverse functioning' of the latter. 'Reverse functioning' refers to a situation in which a system that is supposed to secure livelihoods actually works to threaten the latter, producing social exclusion in turn.

The argument of this book is that the livelihood security system of Japan in its present form is not merely dysfunctional but functioning in reverse. It succeeds to comparative research on welfare states and welfare regimes (Chapter 1), at the same time that it is indebted to feminist and gender analyses of labour and the economy (Chapter 2). Naturally, as touched on below, gender-based analyses have been introduced to comparative research on welfare states and welfare regimes already. These two currents can by now be said to intersect. Nonetheless, there have been few attempts so far to bring this combination of perspectives to an investigation of the situation in Japan. The comparative gender analysis offered in the present volume endeavours to fill this gap.

Chapter 1 begins by recalling that in the blueprint for the 20th century welfare state, the needs for livelihood security were reduced to the single dimension of loss of income-earning capability by a 'male breadwinner'. It then retraces the development of comparative research on welfare states and welfare regimes by following the lead of Gøsta Esping-Anderson's work and of critiques that have been raised against it, with a view not least to the limitations inherent in these approaches. Livelihood security systems, as taken to be the proper object of comparative analysis in this book, will be distinguished into three different types: the 'male breadwinner' model, the 'work/life balance' model and the 'market-oriented' model. What differentiates the threefold typology adopted in this work from prior approaches is its application of a gender perspective, emphasis on labour market regulation through law as well as collective bargaining, and the fact that the role of the 'social economy' in livelihood security, comprising not-for-profit organizations, is brought into view.

Chapter 2 undertakes a theoretical examination of livelihood needs and their satisfaction. Scrutinizing the various relations governing the production of goods and services necessary for daily life and generation of income under a market economy can make not only the logic behind the evolution of government social policy stand out, but also limitations in its conventional forms. Under conditions of economic globalization, livelihood security systems based on the idea of the welfare state have fallen into dysfunction and awareness of social exclusion as a problem is spreading. Of the three models contrasted in this volume, the 'male breadwinner' model in particular is at an impasse regarding the need to respond to post-industrialization. Chapter 2 will conclude with a survey of the structural components of Japan's livelihood security system, revealing a 'male breadwinner' orientation that is even more rigid than in comparable countries.

Chapter 3 looks back at changes that occurred in Japan's livelihood security system during the 1990s when the economy entered a period of prolonged stagnation. Since the early 1990s, there were continual calls for reform in various policy arenas, including social policy, but it was not until the Koizumi administration took office in 2001 that the need for a *structural* reform of the livelihood security system, which would extend to a reconfiguration of the very *model* on which it was based, was addressed by a government's basic policy. Meanwhile, economic stagnation and the demographic trend of an aging population and declining birth rate forced upon corporations and families inevitable change. Japanese corporations began to withdraw from their role as livelihood security providers, while excessive expectations placed on the role of the family, including the expectation that a male household head support his wife and children and that the wife should bear the entire burden of caring and housework, have left people hesitant not only about having and rearing children, but caused many to even shy away from marriage.

Chapter 4 situates Japan's livelihood security system at the turn of the century in an international comparative framework. In Japan, commercial enterprises command an overwhelming share in the relations governing the production of goods and services and the generation of income, while employment arrangements continue to presuppose a male breadwinner. The Japanese government, although a 'small welfare government', is a 'large construction government'. And, while small, its welfare government is heavily weighted toward income transfers to male breadwinners. As families become increasingly diverse, not only have the functions of Japan's livelihood security system to support the nurturing and raising of the next generation declined. Its functions to guarantee a minimum livelihood have also been eviscerated. Closer inquiry into the effects of redistribution through taxation and the social security system reveals that they have in fact caused the poverty rate to rise, directly affecting large numbers of people. Japan's livelihood security system is clearly functioning in reverse.

The Koizumi administration was marked by a strong aspiration towards neo-liberalism, expressed by the slogan 'From the public to the private sector'. However, it should not be overlooked that a disassociation of Japan's livelihood security system from its focus on the male breadwinner to make it more 'gender-neutral' and a strengthening of work/life balance were included among the Koizumi administration's basic policies. Chapter 5 examines to what extent these signboard policies were given real substance by focusing on pension reform. To state my conclusion ahead, an actual breakaway from the 'male breadwinner' model ended up being postponed. Under the 'muscular economic structure' the Koizumi reforms were set to achieve, employment of women and young men has been non-regularized, income gaps have widened and the relative poverty rate has risen. As corporations are evading their responsibilities under the social insurance system by extra-legal means, social insurance in present-day Japan has turned into a mechanism for social exclusion.

As mentioned at the beginning of Chapter 6, the post-Koizumi governments included review of the social security system among their top priorities. In the end, however, they stopped short of looking squarely at the critical state of Japan's livelihood security system, and proved unable to carry through required reforms. This volume seeks a breakthrough from this impasse to a more promising scenario by projecting an increased role for livelihood cooperation undertaken by not-for-profit cooperative organizations in conjunction with welfare government guided by the principle of universalization. This may evoke association with the social democratic model. However, whereas traditional social democracy has been mainly concerned with redistribution of income, the prescription laid out by this volume calls for a shift of emphasis in social policy away from income transfers to service provision, and as concerns income transfers, a clear commitment to the principle of cooperation in risk sharing. The potentials of livelihood cooperation rooted in the community have been evinced in actual practice by the social cooperatives of Italy.

Insofar as universal social inclusion functions as a brake on runaway markets such as seen in the current global financial and economic crisis, it is also a precondition for a market economy to be stably sustained. Expressed in everyday terms, social inclusion signifies a society in which everyone, regardless of gender, age, origin, education or disability, has a role to play and can make a fresh start – in other words: a society where those that have stumbled are not simply written off. It is my hope that this volume can make a contribution to the realization of such a society in the future.

Several limitations of this study should also be noted. The argument of this book is developed chronologically, departing from the observation that Japan's livelihood security system in the 1980s was far more rigid in its 'male breadwinner' orientation than that of other countries. Despite continual calls for structural reform of corporations and of social policy during the prolonged economic stagnation of the 1990s, the need to break away from the 'male breadwinner' model was not realized in governmental basic policy. The Koizumi administration included a departure from the male breadwinner model among its basic policies, but, failing to look squarely at the dysfunction, or indeed reverse functioning, of the system in its present form, it ultimately deferred action.

Naturally, there arises the question of why things have turned out this way. However, I will not discuss the broader historical and political reasons for the formation and strengthening of the male breadwinner model in Japan, or for why it has failed to be reformed despite obvious dysfunction, here. Likewise, several issues central to the problem of social inclusion, such as disparities in health and education as well as political participation, could not be covered in this volume.

Margarita Estévez-Abe, in her brilliant study on *Welfare and Capitalism in Postwar Japan* published in 2008, seeks the reasons for the existence of the Japanese-style welfare state and social protection system from the 1950s up to the end of the 1990s largely in the Japanese election system. She argues that under the old system where the LDP as the party in power would run or endorse multiple candidates in multi-seat electoral districts, constituents were casting votes for individual candidates rather than political parties. For this reason, there was a tendency to adopt non-universalistic policy measures that gave favourable treatment to particular interest groups in an electoral district (Estévez-Abe 2008). I very much hope that the reader will refer to this work in combination with the present volume.

The proofs for this book were received on 10 March 2011. On 11 March, the Great Eastern Japan Earthquake and Tsunami struck Japan, causing unprecedented loss of lives and livelihoods. At the time of this writing, workers at the Fukushima nuclear power plant are desperately trying to contain a nuclear catastrophe, while power shortages are crippling production and vital infrastructure is destroyed. The long-term consequences of these devastating events are incalculable while immediate crisis response is taking precedence. However, the 'muscular' economic structure that the Koizumi administration announced has proven particularly vulnerable to crisis and weak in recovery in the past. In the current support activities in Eastern Japan, paring support between organizations on the meso level of society, such as municipalities, consumer cooperatives and corporations, is performing a pivotal role and proving to be both reliable and effective.

1 From welfare regimes to livelihood security systems

Livelihood security, in the so-called advanced or developed countries, is at present provided through government-enacted 'social policies' in close interlock with the role of non-governmental institutions and social practices, such as families, corporations, labour unions and not-for-profit organizations (NPOs). In this book, social policy will be understood as encompassing not only social security measures (social insurance and welfare/public assistance), the tax system and social services (such as child care, education, health care and long-term care for the aged or disabled), but also employment policy and labour market regulation. The latter include direct measures such as minimum wage systems, working hour regulations and occupational health and safety standards, as well as state-enacted legislation pertaining to the regulation of work conditions through collective bargaining between labour unions and employers (or federations of employers). An additional indirect but important component of employment policy is economic growth policy insofar as it serves to maintain and increase economy-wide employment.

Among these institutions and policies, social security and the tax system along with social services are most frequently cited as the core elements of the welfare state. As we will see, employment policy and labour market regulation are included because they frequently serve as 'functional equivalents' for welfare policies in the more narrow sense (Bonoli 2003a; Miura 2003).

Families and corporations constitute the micro level, institutions such as community organizations and cooperatives the meso level, and systems instituted by the central government the macro level. Social services provided independently by local governments, however, belong to the meso level. The multilayered articulation between government legislation and policies on the one hand, and non-governmental institutions and social practices on the other, will be referred to as 'livelihood security system' in this book.[1]

The several stages traversed by the industrialized countries of the developed world with regard to the problem of livelihood security during the modern era could be summed up, in a pointedly schematic manner, as follows. Originally, the individual's only safety net against falling into deprivation or a state of social exclusion were the family and the community. Inclusion in the family and community was not a matter of individual choice, but a station in life occupied by the individual due to accident of birth. As the market economy developed and society urbanized, the range of choices available to individuals broadened while traditional extended family and communal structures broke down, if not to the extent of eliminating the family's function in providing livelihood security entirely. With regard to livelihood security as well, local authorities took over providing public assistance based on coercive means such as taxation, while in some cases cooperative organizations such as labour unions and friendly societies facilitated mutual aid for workers in the event of sickness or job loss. Since these self-organized small-scale mutual aid activities were dogged by financial weakness, however, they ultimately gave way to social insurance systems that made participation and contribution compulsory. In past eras, receiving public assistance could carry with it a loss of civil rights such as suspension of the right to vote, but as the voting franchise widened, public assistance came by all intents and purposes to be regarded a citizen's right itself. This marked the advent of the welfare state.

This chapter will begin by broadly retracing the development of comparative research on 'welfare states' and 'welfare regimes' to date. The limitations inherent in these approaches will be emphasized to clarify my reasons for choosing to speak of 'livelihood security systems' instead.

Section 1 considers the Beveridge Plan in the United Kingdom which laid out the blueprint for the creation and development of the welfare state during the latter half of the 20th century. Livelihood security needs are by nature varied and individual. Never the less, the 20th century welfare state zeroed in on a single dimension: loss of income-earning capability by a 'male breadwinner'. The political and economic power relations that drove this development need to be clarified first.

Section 2 will review Gøsta Esping-Andersen's initial typology of welfare states, along with four lines of criticism that have been raised against it. Esping-Andersen himself responded to these critiques by improving his welfare state typology into a theory of 'welfare regimes'. However, as of this writing, the so-called 'third sector' or 'social economy' remains to be accounted for in this framework. Accordingly, in Section 3 the social economy will be brought into the picture, and three types of livelihood security systems will be identified: the *male breadwinner* model, the *work/life balance* model and the *market-oriented* model. What distinguishes the typology adopted in this book is its application of a gender perspective, an emphasis on labour market regulations through law as well as collective bargaining, and attention to the contributions to livelihood security made by the 'social economy' consisting of not-for-profit organizations.

Characteristics of the 20th century welfare state

The Beveridge Plan's account of needs and blueprint for security

If one looks back on the welfare state of the second half of the 20th century, its reduction of the varied spectrum of livelihood needs down to the single dimension of inadequate income is the characteristic that stands out. The problem of inadequate income, furthermore, was reduced to the question of whether a male head of household was in employment or not. In other words, the 20th century welfare state was characterized by income-centric, male-centric and employment-centric biases.

The term 'welfare state' originated in the UK during World War II, to designate the objective for post-war reconstruction on the Allied side in pointed contrast to the militaristic, totalitarian 'warfare state' of Nazi Germany. Its background was formed by reflection on the experience of two horrific wars in the first half of the 20th century, and the realization that the Great Depression and mass unemployment between the wars had given fascism a foothold, thus paving the road to World War II. The British government established a Committee on Reconstruction Problems in early 1941, with the war in Europe in full swing, assigned to investigate what international and national order should prevail in the arenas of economy, polity and society after the war's eventual end. This Committee on Reconstruction Problems formed a subcommittee to consider 'social insurance and allied services', headed by Sir William Beveridge.

Beveridge was reputed as an official with expertise in matters of unemployment and social insurance reaching back decades. In late November 1942, the subcommittee issued the white paper *Social Insurance and Allied Services*, officially subtitled as 'Report by Sir William Beveridge'. The Beveridge Report not only provided the blueprint for the British social security system, it also exercised considerable influence internationally. The Beveridge Plan can be regarded as containing the archetype for the design of the 20th century welfare state.

The Beveridge Plan defined social security as 'security of income up to a minimum' to provide for material 'want' (Beveridge 1942: para. 300). 'Want', in turn, was defined as 'families and individuals ... lack[ing] the means of healthy subsistence' (Beveridge 1942: para. 11). The Beveridge Plan also pronounced that 'very few men's wages are insufficient to cover at least two adults and one child' (Beveridge 1942: para 417), indicating that the model it envisioned was a household headed by a male breadwinner as the family's primary wage earner. In the view of the report, such households would experience 'want' in the event of loss of earning power by the male breadwinner due to unemployment, sickness or injury, or retirement due to old age, loss of means for a wife and children through the death of the male breadwinner, or 'exceptional expenditures, such as those connected with birth, death and marriage'.

The 'main instrument' of social security was to be social insurance covering 'any risk so general or so uniform that social insurance can be justified', such as unemployment, inability to work due to illness or injury, retirement due to old age, funerals and so on. Included among these 'basic needs' were also the 'marriage needs of a woman', but these remained confined to marriage and maternity, 'interruption or cessation of husband's earnings', widowhood and 'incapacity for household duties' (Beveridge 1942: paras 308, 311).

Social insurance is a means of pooling and redistributing risk. 'Involuntary' or 'incidental' risks to which everyone has a certain degree of exposure and that are difficult for the afflicted individual to avoid are regarded as 'legitimate'. In the case of retirement due to old age, however, the 'risk' of living long beyond the loss of one's income-earning capability is covered by insurance, although longevity itself can hardly be considered 'involuntary'. Moreover, since longevity is a result of improved living standards and health, it has come to be universal rather than incidental.

The Beveridge Plan further specified, separately from social insurance, 'children's allowances' to assist households in meeting the clothing, food and fuel needs of children beyond the second, to prevent want arising from large family size, as well as 'comprehensive health and rehabilitation services' to meet medical needs in the event of disease (irrespective of interruption of income). Another major precondition for the social security system to function was believed to be 'avoidance of mass unemployment' (Beveridge 1942: para. 301; Ōsawa 1999a: Section 3).

To address the 'basic needs' described above, the Beveridge Plan proposed to provide 'security of income up to a minimum' (para. 300) by means of cash payments from social insurance funds. Needs of the so-called working poor, on the other hand, who work full time but at wages too low to cover subsistence living expenses, or of the underemployed, who can only find work half of the week, were largely ignored as causes of want. Nor did the plan evince any awareness of needs in the case of men who have an income but lack time to perform housework or care for family members, or recognize as a need the need of married women to manage housework and child-rearing while pursuing employment at the same time.

Blind spots and contrivances of the 20th century welfare state

It may be that such needs were not recognized because they are not strongly typical of 'involuntary' or 'incidental', and thus 'legitimately' insurable risks. Yet the Beveridge Plan assumed, as we have seen, that a man's income should ordinarily enable him to provide for himself, his wife and one child. That is, as long as a man was in employment, his earnings were thought sufficient to support a wife and child (the family wage hypothesis), whereas child-rearing or nursing care as well as housework could easily be performed by the wife, with no need for the government to get involved.

To sum up, the 20th century welfare state treated 'want' one-dimensionally as a lack of financial resources, and with regard to the latter's causes, its question boiled down to whether a male head of household was employed or not, as if that was self-understood. However, the phenomenon of the working poor already had a long history at the time, stretching back even to prior to the Industrial Revolution. It had been one of the defining themes of social reform ever since the late 19th century. Skill obsolescence, which occurs when mechanization causes workers' acquired skills to lose their value, had emerged as a pressing issue with the Industrial Revolution. And as women took work in factories, the problem of reconciling employment with family life had become a focus of debate already in the struggles over the Factory Acts of the 1830s and 1840s (Bruce 1968; Thane 1996). Under the post-war welfare state, poverty among employed persons (the working poor), especially if they were heads of households with children, repeatedly cropped up as a policy issue as well (Ōsawa 1999a).

In the realm of social insurance as an approach carried over from the 19th century, the area most in need of overhaul by the post-war welfare state was income security after retirement. One of the problems with old-age pensions was that life expectancy after retirement increased more than anticipated, and, under a fully funded pension finance regime, funds would become insufficient to pay out entitlements barring contribution rate hikes. In a fully funded pension regime the capital and interest from an individual's contributions are accumulated and drawn down after retirement.

An additional problem was that the long economic boom and fixed exchange rate regime of the years after World War II exerted an upward pressure on wages and prices, causing the real value of past contributions to plunge and depressing benefit levels accordingly. Against this background, West Germany and Sweden carried out pension system reforms around 1960, abandoning the fully funded pension financing regime in favour of pay-as-you-go regimes under which benefits are adjusted to changes in prices and wages (Shakai hoshō kenkyūsho 1987: Ch. 7; Shakai hoshō kenkyūsho 1989, Ch. 4). In a pay-as-you-go system, the majority of contributions by pension insurants still in the workforce are paid out as benefits to present retirees. There is no large pool of accumulated funds. The introduction of pay-as-you-go financing and price or wage indexation of benefits further strengthened the notably income transfer-centred character of the welfare state during the latter half of the 20th century.

The three power relationships behind the development of the welfare state and their transition

Political scientist Tarō Miyamoto has pointed out that the development of the welfare state in the years after World War II was driven by three power relationships in the political and economic sphere: the power relationship between labour and management within the developed countries, the power relation between developed and developing countries, and power relationships based on gender in the developed and the developing countries (Miyamoto 2003: 3–5).

First, concerning the labour-management power relationship within developed countries, the labour movement, which organized primarily around heavy industries, made forceful demands not only for wage increases and employment security, but also redistribution by the state in the form of income transfers and social services. The interests of capital on their part accommodated labour's demands by fostering mass consumption to complement mass production. An historic rapprochement was reached that drove the formation and development of the welfare state. In Japan's case, the first time that the welfare state was publicly advanced as a policy goal was in the 1955 party merger that created the Liberal Democratic Party (LDP). The welfare state was considered necessary at that time to stave off socialism in the mould of the Soviet Union (Tōkyō daigaku shakaikagaku kenkyūsho: 1984–5).

Second, the problem of the power relations obtaining between developed and developing countries calls attention to the Bretton Woods system of fixed exchange rates and liberalized international trade managed by institutions such as the International Monetary Fund (IMF) and the General Agreement on Tariffs and Trade (GATT). This system essentially regulated international capital flows, thus allowing each developed country to set its own autonomous economic policy and pursue full employment without fear of currency instability. In the developed countries, high priority was placed on preventing mass unemployment. Moreover, in spite of the free trade-oriented regime, the developed countries were permitted to enact restraints on trade on grounds of public policy, at the same time that they could import raw materials from developing countries at low prices. Even as they were enmeshed in Cold War confrontation with the socialist planned economies of the Soviet Union and Eastern Europe, the developed countries of the West thus revelled in a long run of economic growth that lasted until the early 1970s. This long boom also made the historic rapprochement between capital and labour interests discussed above possible.

Third, power relationships based on gender in the developed countries on the one hand and the developing countries on the other were a precondition for the existence of the welfare state in developed countries. The cheap goods of developing countries were made possible by the unpaid work of women in subsistence primary sector production and the urban informal sector. In the developed countries, families and households were structured around gender-based role expectations and norms according to which the husband was the primary earner of household income while the wife would perform the housework and child-rearing. It was taken for granted that this division of labour did in fact prevail. Consequently, the target of employment security and social security was the male full-time worker supporting a wife and children, whereas the wife provided unpaid labour for child rearing and nursing care. This was the model on which the design of social services was predicated (Miyamoto 2002: 3–5).

In other words, the welfare state in developed countries typically defined an inadequate livelihood as a family's inability to meet its living expenses due to risks involving the income of a breadwinning man, i.e. unemployment, sickness or injury, and retirement due to old age. Accordingly, livelihood security was provided mainly via income transfers taking the form of social insurance benefits (or in exceptional cases public assistance). This welfare state centred on income transfers for male breadwinners was intended to foster stable social reproduction according to the following pattern: if a man is able to obtain sufficient income from employment during his 'productive years', he can maintain a household with a wife and children, raise the next generation with proper education and training and will be assured an income after retirement. Gender relations are thus one of the three power relations that shaped and propelled the development of the post-war welfare state. And shifts in these three power relations were to determine its trajectory.

Unquestionably, these three power relations have undergone change from the early 1970s onward. The US experienced budget and trade deficits, partly as a result of expenditures on the Vietnam War, that triggered the collapse of the Bretton Woods system in 1973 and a switch to an international currency regime with floating exchange rates. In the same year, the first oil shock heralded an end to the long spell of economic growth that the developed countries had enjoyed. From the mid-1970s onward it became clear that unemployment, inflation, fiscal policy strictures and other socio-economic problems, as well as government responses to them, took rather different forms in the various capitalist countries.

On the Cold War front, China adopted the slogan of 'reform and opening up' and began its move towards a market economy in 1978, and in 1991 the Soviet Union collapsed. As the former Soviet republics and Eastern Bloc countries adopted the 'big bang approach' to transition to a market economy and China's reforms embarked on their next stage in 1992, the world economy entered an era of 'megacompetition' on the global scale. Capitalism was no longer in need to demonstrate its superiority over socialist planned economies. Meanwhile, in the sphere of labour-management relations, the union density of the workforce fell (although not in the Nordic countries, where unionization remained steady or even rose) as the service sector came to occupy a growing proportion of the economy, concomitant to the post-industrial transition that began in the developed countries in the 1970s.

Gender relations were also changing as the labour force participation rate of women rose (the 'feminization of labour'). Immediately after World War II, the male breadwinner norm had been firmly entrenched all over Europe (Esping-Andersen 2002: 20, 68; Fukazawa 2003: 223–5). However, not all 20th century welfare states were structured alike. In comparing the US, the UK, Canada and Sweden, Sainsbury found that in Sweden the imprint of the male breadwinner model had been relatively light to begin with, and expunged by the 1970s (Sainsbury 1996: Ch. 3).

The present book adopts a threefold typology of livelihood security systems with the situation in the developed countries circa 1980 in mind: the 'male breadwinner model', the 'work/life balance model' and the 'market-oriented model'. The motivation for dividing livelihood security systems into these types will become clear as we review developments in comparative research on welfare states and welfare regimes over recent decades.

Esping-Andersen's threefold typology of welfare states and its critics

The advent of the threefold typology

Gøsta Esping-Andersen, as is widely known, proposed in *The Three Worlds of Welfare Capitalism* (1990) a typology of welfare states or welfare regimes that distinguishes a 'liberal' (Anglo-Saxon), 'conservative' (Continental European) and 'social democratic' (Scandinavian) type. This threefold typology, based on the situation circa 1980, has attracted interest throughout the world, and established Esping-Andersen as the standard bearer in a surge of comparative welfare state research that extends into the present.

Let us begin with a basic overview of the typology at its inception. The first cluster consists of the *liberal* welfare states (the US, Canada, Australia) 'in which means-tested [i.e. targeted] assistance, modest universal transfers or modest social-insurance plans predominate' (Esping-Andersen 1990: 26). Public welfare benefits are held to a minimum level and bear the stigma of deprivation and social failure. Private welfare schemes such as company benefits or individual pensions, on the other hand, are subsidized. The terms 'universalistic' and 'targeted' express contrasting welfare philosophies; the defining criterion of universalism is the absence of restriction, or differentiation, of benefit eligibility on the basis of occupation, place of residence, family relationships and, above all, income.

The second cluster consists of the *conservative* welfare states, which include Austria, France, Germany and Italy. In this model, preservation of status differentials is stressed. Rights, therefore, depend on class and status and the redistributive effects of state benefits are negligible (although the magnitude of benefits is not). This model seeks to preserve the family in its traditional form. Non-working wives are excluded from social insurance, family services are underdeveloped, and there is a strong commitment to the principle of 'subsidiarity', meaning, in Esping-Andersen's definition, that 'the state will interfere only when the family's capacity to service its members is exhausted' (Esping-Andersen 1990: 27).

The third cluster encompasses the *social democratic* (Scandinavian) regime-type characterized by universalistic welfare programmes with a high degree of de-commodification. Manual workers, white-collar employees and civil servants all participate in a unified social insurance system. Under this model, the costs of maintaining a family are socialized to maximize the individual's capacity for independence. Since the state grants income transfers directly to children (substantial child allowances and scholarships) and 'takes direct responsibility of caring for children, the aged and the helpless', this model empowers individuals, especially women, to opt for work rather than the household. The social democratic welfare state undertakes a commitment to full employment. At the same time, it depends on actual attainment of full employment to maximize the number of income earners whose social insurance contributions and taxes support the system (Esping-Andersen 1990: 28).

Regarding gender Esping-Andersen pointed out the following: the ideal of the social democratic system was to maximize the potential for the individual to be autonomous (including economic independence for women) rather than depend on the family. In this sense, it is a 'peculiar fusion of liberalism and socialism'. In contrast, under the conservative model women's employment is constrained, but under the liberal model consideration of gender remains secondary to the 'sanctity of the market' (Esping-Andersen 1990: 28). Esping-Andersen thus emphasized gender and family aspects in his characterization of the various types, but as we will see, he did not include gender and family among the indicators actually determining his typology as such.

As the foregoing makes clear, Esping-Andersen's threefold typology of welfare states revolves around the concept of 'de-commodification'. The scoring criteria for de-commodification are (1) the degree to which social insurance (pension, unemployment insurance and medical insurance) benefits 'approximate normal expected earnings-levels' (the income replacement rate); (2) the number of years of contributions required to qualify; and (3) the share of benefit financing borne by individuals (Esping-Andersen 1990: 49–50). In a capitalist society, workers depend for their livelihood upon selling their labour power on the market. In this sense, people are 'commodified'. A high degree of de-commodification means that even if people are prevented from selling their labour power either temporarily or permanently due to unemployment, sickness or injury, or retirement due to old age, they continue to be guaranteed an adequate income by the social insurance system, and that the costs of the latter are borne to a greater degree by the government and employers than by contributions of the insured person.

By having society assume responsibility for the risk of income interruption due to individuals' inability to 'sell' their labour power, and moreover by considering this a right, the 'pure commodity status' of labour power is attenuated. In his introduction to the Japanese edition of *The Three Worlds of Welfare Capitalism*, Esping-Andersen restated his definition of de-commodification as the degree to which 'individuals (and families) can maintain income and consumption without reliance on the market' (Esping-Andersen 2001: iv).

Esping-Andersen also accounted for social stratification in his typology. His indicators for the conservative welfare state were *corporatism*, measured by the number of occupationally distinct public pension schemes, and *etatism*, measured by the share of GDP devoted to pension expenditures for government employees. For the liberal regime type, the indicators were the relative weight of means-tested public assistance and the importance of the private sector in health care and pension provision. The indicators for socialist regime types, finally, were the degree of programme universalism and the degree of equality in the benefit structure (Esping-Andersen 1990: 73). Esping-Andersen's typology thus pays close attention to the relationship between state (social insurance benefits) and market (wage income), as well as to inequalities of social class, but it does not account for the role of the family and gender.

Moreover, this typology did not yield consistent results. Japan and Switzerland, for example, are ranked close to conservative welfare states such as France and Germany by their de-commodification score. But as regards their systems of social stratification, they cluster with the liberal welfare states (Esping-Andersen 1990: 52, 76). Not only is there lack of consistency with regard to Japan and Switzerland, but the de-commodification score for Japan itself must be viewed as inconsistent (Esping-Andersen 1990: 52; Ōsawa 1996a: 88).[2] As of 1980, the Japanese welfare state had among the lowest social spending levels in the OECD and applied a selectivist social policy, while its family support orientation was weak. Its low degree of de-commodification, compelling individuals to participate in the market, makes Japan typical of a liberal welfare regime. Yet, the occupational fragmentation and stratification of Japan's social insurance system (e.g. disparities based on the size of the company the individual works for) are characteristic of a conservative welfare state regime.

Critiques of The Three Worlds of Welfare Capitalism

Its difficulties in accounting for certain countries like Japan and Switzerland notwithstanding, Esping-Andersen's typology of welfare states has exerted a far-reaching influence on comparative social policy research. It is thus no surprise that it also elicited a variety of critiques. Let us take a closer look at four kinds of criticism that have been directed against it.

The first line of critique came on feminist grounds. Lewis (1992), Orloff (1993) and Sainsbury (1994) argued that although Esping-Andersen was employing a gender-neutral terminology in his description and analysis, his analytical concepts and units of analysis often presume men as their point of reference. His concept of de-commodification failed to reflect that commodification of one's labour can be impeded not just by retirement, unemployment and sickness, but also by family responsibilities such as rearing children or caring for the aged. Also, where Esping-Andersen writes of 'individuals (and families)', as in his introduction to the Japanese edition of his work quoted above, 'individual' is implicitly taken to mean 'a male head of household'. 'Individuals' and 'families' thus tend to be used interchangeably. Of course, the feminist response did not confine itself to criticism; new gender-sensitive typologies of the welfare state were offered in its course. As will be discussed later on, Esping-Andersen himself has responded to this feminist critique since the latter half of the 1990s by including the family's relationships with the state and the market among his indicators, and thus developing his welfare state typology into a typology of welfare regimes (Miyamoto 2003; Igami 2003).

A second line of criticism based itself on the logic that primary distribution was more important than redistribution in providing livelihood security for able-bodied persons. This approach does not deny the necessity of redistribution by means of ex post income transfers in the case of individuals 'unable to sell' their labour power. It rather argues that redistribution will become secondary in importance if workers are protected against unemployment or underemployment, employment at inadequate wages, and the caprice of employers as far as working conditions and employment security are concerned. From this perspective, provision of sufficient employment opportunities by means of economic growth and employment maintenance policies, a minimum wage system, regulation of working hours and workplace health and safety, as well as the maintenance and improvement of working conditions through the agency of labour unions are key. Such labour-market policies are seen as 'functional equivalents to the welfare state' in the sense that the redistributive role of the welfare state is thereby minimized (Bonoli 2003a; Miura 2003). Mari Miura has defined varying patterns of unemployment risks and income maintenance by sex and age more specifically as 'employment performance' as a tool for investigating the possibility of substitution of such policies for provision of income security by the welfare state (Miura 2001).[3]

If in the West scholars' attention was directed to labour market regulation as a substitute for welfare by an upswing in comparative welfare state research, in Japan the order was reversed. Kazuo Ōkōchi, who, after serving as the chair of the University of Tokyo's economics department and later as the University's president, was chairman of the Prime Minister's Advisory Council on the Social Security System from 1973 to 1984, may well be called the founder of social policy studies in Japan. Ōkōchi postulated legislations and regulations that prevent exploitative employment at inadequate wages and ensure minimum decent conditions of work and employment as the defining feature of a genuine social policy that could be considered economically rational. More specifically, such a policy had to comprise worker protection laws (limiting working hours, ensuring adequate wages, limiting the employment of children and women and regulating workplace health and safety) and labour union 'emancipation legislation' (securing legal recognition of unions and their right to engage in collective bargaining and industrial disputes) (Ōkōchi 1963; Ōsawa 1996b).

The argument that such a concept of social policy could not include social security and welfare services at the same time began to surface during the first half of the 1980s (Okada 1981; Takegawa 1985). And although the term 'functional equivalent' was not yet in use, by the beginning of the 1980s it had become standard to observe that Japan had 'substituted growth for welfare' (Shibagaki 1985: 168). Tarō Miyamoto and Takafumi Uzuhashi later pointed out 'substitution' effects also in the case of public works projects in Japan's non-metropolitan areas (Miyamoto 1997; Uzuhashi 1997).

Four worlds of welfare capitalism?

A third line of criticism objected that welfare states ought not to be clustered into three types, but four or more. Thus the nations of Oceania, Southern Europe and East Asia have been variously proposed to constitute a 'fourth world'.

The earliest critique along these lines came in 1991, with the publication of Deborah Mitchell's *Income Transfers in Ten Welfare States*, followed by further work by Mitchell and Francis Castles (Mitchell 1991; Castles and Mitchell 1993). These scholars have emphasized a distinction between two groups within the Anglo-Saxon world: one consisting of countries with a labour party tradition, such as the UK, Australia, New Zealand and Ireland, and the other of countries like Canada and the United States, which lack such a tradition. The former are referred to as wage earners' or 'lib lab' welfare states. Especially Mitchell based this on the grounds that in the UK and similar countries policy outcomes from income transfers though taxation and social insurance measured by the incidence of poverty (percentage of households in poverty and poverty gap) or the degree of inequality (Gini coefficient) were close to those found in the conservative Continental European countries (Mitchell 1991: 187–9; Ōsawa 1999a: 128–33). According to Mitchell, Esping-Andersen's typology exhibited a tendency to 'divorce the outcomes of different welfare states from their production characteristics and use the latter to make judgments about what a "good" welfare state does ... as opposed to a "bad" welfare state' (Mitchell 1991: 187).

Ferrera (1996), on the other hand, proposes to distinguish the Southern European countries from the conservative Continental European ones as a fourth type of welfare states on the basis of pronounced dualism in the labour market. Labour market dualism refers to a structure in which a core market with high employment performance (i.e. a favourable pattern of unemployment risk and income maintenance) and generous social security exists side by side an essentially separate labour market for peripheral workers, from which it is difficult to return to the core labour market once one has dropped out. Corresponding to such dual labour markets, the income security systems of these societies are characterized by segmented structures as well. In addition, Ferrera lists the following characteristics to differentiate the Southern European countries from the countries of Continental Western Europe: a low degree of state penetration of the welfare sphere, a collusive mix between public and non-public actors and institutions, strong influence of the Catholic church and the persistence of clientelism, i.e. patron-client dependencies for the selective distribution of cash subsidies.

There also have been attempts to categorize the newly industrializing countries (NICs) of East Asia, including Japan, as a 'fourth world' of welfare capitalism with Confucianism as a shared heritage, under headings such as 'Confucian capitalism' or 'Confucian welfare states' (Jones 1993). This approach has been rejected by White and Goodman (1998) as well as Takegawa (2005), among others, as 'welfare orientalism' reflecting a shallow understanding of East Asian societies on the part of Western scholars. Subsequently, East Asian welfare states have been described in such terms as 'oikonomic', 'productivist', 'developmental' and 'late-starting' (Peng 2004; Suehiro 2006; Kim 2006).

Esping-Andersen responded to these arguments for various 'fourth worlds' with a book titled *Social Foundations of Postindustrial Economies* in 1999, defending his threefold typology. He did concede in his rebuttal to the arguments of Castles and Mitchell that the UK and countries in Oceania may have belonged to the social-democratic regime type during the 1960s and 1970s, but only to emphasize that liberalization from the 1980s onward made them come close to 'prototypical liberalism' (Esping-Andersen 1999: 90).

The present work, on the other hand, rejects the 'lib lab' type as a separate category because it acknowledges the merit of Mitchell's argument. Indeed, as far as the outcomes of income transfer policies are concerned, the UK and Australia may have been closer to the countries of Continental Europe than to the US and Canada. However, the instruments used by these two countries to achieve these outcomes were different. The fact that Mitchell ranked Australia first among ten countries evaluated in terms of their 'efficiency' in either reducing poverty or mitigating inequality, while the UK remained below the median, makes this difference clear. The UK is as difficult to be included under the same type with Australia as with the US and Canada (Ōsawa 1999a: 131–3).

Esping-Andersen challenged assertions of either Southern Europe or East Asia constituting a 'fourth world' by questioning the explanatory power of 'familialism'. A simple inquiry into levels of welfare state servicing to families and the share of aged living with their children as well as employment rates for women (the 'male breadwinner bias' variable) reveals that the countries of Southern Europe and Japan show no major differences from the countries of Continental Western Europe in these regards (Esping-Andersen 1999: 92–4). Katrougalos and Lazaridis (2003) have argued on the basis of a very detailed investigation that the Southern European variant should be seen as merely a sub-category of the conservative welfare regime, as opposed to a different model entirely.

Toshimitsu Shinkawa, on the other hand, has combined the results of previous research (including the above) with Esping-Andersen's own de-commodification and social stratification indices to propose that Southern Europe along with Japan and Switzerland ought to be considered a fourth 'familialist' type (Shinkawa 2005: 272–4). The present book does not adopt Shinkawa's fourfold typology either, because, as Shōgo Takegawa has pointed out, social stratification cannot be regarded as an independent variable relative to de-commodification (Takegawa 2006: 95).

Welfare regime theory and 'de-familialization'

In *Social Foundations of Postindustrial Economies* (1999), Esping-Andersen newly introduced the concept of 'de-familialization' into his analysis and proposed to recalibrate the debate by speaking of 'welfare regimes' instead of 'welfare states'. De-familialization refers to 'the degree to which households' welfare and caring responsibilities are relaxed – either via welfare state provision, or via market provision'; or the degree to which social policy (and perhaps markets) give autonomy to women. Autonomy in this context means the autonomy of women to commodify their labour, or to set up independent households. Indicators of de-familialization are (1) public spending on family services (excluding health services) as a percentage of GDP; (2) the combined value of family allowances and tax deductions for child families; (3) diffusion of day care for children less than three; and (4) percentage of those aged 65-plus receiving home-help services (Esping-Andersen 1999: 51, 61).

The theory of welfare regimes clarifies that it is the relative importance of the state, the market and the family in the management of social risks that determines the institutional structure of a welfare regime as 'the combined, interdependent way in which welfare is produced and allocated' between these three actors (ibid.: 34–6). Under the social-democratic (Scandinavian) regime, the government (the welfare state in its narrow definition) assumes a large share of the welfare provision burden. Under the liberal (Anglo-Saxon) regime, on the other hand, the market (corporations) internalizes functions such as welfare (employee fringe benefits) and job training. Under the conservative (Continental European) regime, finally, families bear the ultimate responsibility for their members' welfare (the principle of subsidiarity), and the social protection system evinces a male breadwinner bias. They are therefore referred to as 'familialistic' (Esping-Andersen 1999: Ch. 5). Welfare regime theory was thus a reconfiguration of the welfare state typology, again taking the situation circa 1980 as a basis.

But as Miura has pointed out, in this approach labour market regulations are treated separately, and their relationships to the various welfare regime types remain unclear (Miura 2003: 111). Also, even in a welfare regime typology that incorporates de-familialization indicators, Japan remains a difficult case to classify, given its degree of internalization of welfare functions by large corporations corresponding to the liberal model, combined with an emphasis on the role of the family that is typical of conservative welfare regimes. Miyamoto has cautioned that the configuration of the Japanese regime, in which family welfare and company welfare undergird each other, has no corollary among Western welfare states (Miyamoto 2003: 17).

The missing dimension: the social economy/third sector

A fourth line of criticism directed toward Esping-Andersen's typology originated with researchers studying not-for-profit organizations on the grounds that his theory failed to account for the social economy or 'third sector' (Salamon and Anheier 1998; Lewis 2004: 170). The social economy or third sector encompasses the economic activities of cooperatives, mutual societies and associations. These organizations are considered to operate on the principle of 'generating collective wealth rather than a return on individual investment', to be 'self-governing, in the sense that they have their own regulations and decision making bodies' and are barred from distributing profit 'to either their members, directors, or a set of "owners"' (Borzaga and Defourny 2001: 4–8; Evers and Laville 2004: 13). Two typologies addressing the qualitative and quantitative links between the NPO/third sector and welfare regimes have been proposed.

One of these is the fourfold typology offered by Lester M. Salamon as director of the Johns Hopkins Comparative Nonprofit Sector Project and his colleagues. Salamon *et al.* applied Esping-Andersen's typology to a data set covering initially seven, and subsequently 22 countries. In grouping these country data, the scale of government social welfare spending (government social spending as per cent of GDP) was used as one axis, and the scale of the non-profit sector (paid employment in the NPO sector as per cent of non-agricultural employment) as another. This generated four types of non-profit regime: *liberal* (the US, the UK), in which the scale of non-profit activity is large while government social welfare spending is low; *social democratic* (Sweden, Italy), with a small scale of non-profit activity and high government social welfare spending; *corporatist* (Germany, France), in which the scale of non-profit activity is large and government social welfare spending is high; and *statist* (Japan), with both non-profit activity and government social welfare spending at low levels (Salamon and Anheier 1996: 32).[4]

However, when applied to European contexts, the approach of the Johns Hopkins Comparative Nonprofit Sector Project faced serious limitations. Because the American understanding of 'non-profit' as applying only to organizations that are 'not profit-distributing' was used as a standard, the NPO sector in the Project's definition does not include cooperatives and mutual societies. However, in Europe, cooperatives and mutual associations form the heart of the social economy. What matters here is that they are 'not-for-profit' in the sense that profit generation is not the organizational objective and profit distribution is constrained.

Against this, Evers and Laville proposed the following three types of relationships between associations and welfare regimes with the situation circa 1980 in mind.[5] Their first type is the universal or social democratic system of the Scandinavian countries, where the field of social services is under government responsibility and gender equality is an official objective. Their second type combines the liberal system as typified by the UK with the dual systems of the Southern European countries. Here the role of the third sector as a goods and services provider remains limited. Their third type, finally, corresponds to the corporatist regimes of Continental Western Europe, where the third sector plays a major role in social service delivery, while governments contribute funding and regulations for enterprises (Evers and Laville 2004: 27–8).

Evers and Laville did not provide quantitative data, and Japan is not included in their analysis. Incidentally, Spear *et al.* have estimated the scale of employment in the social economy of 15 European countries for the years 1995–7 in a report based on studies conducted by the International Centre of Research and Information on the Public, Social and Cooperative Economy (CIRIEC). According to their analysis, neither the UK nor Continental Western European countries such as Germany and France have social economy sectors on a significantly larger scale than the Nordic and Southern European countries. Comparing the rankings by Salamon *et al*'s indicators and Spear *et al*'s estimates, the only change is that Germany and France are switched with Spain and Finland. This suggests that even though Spain and Finland have a smaller scale of non-profit organizations under the American definition (non-distribution of profits), the scale of their cooperatives and mutual associations, considered crucial to social economy in Europe, is large. (Spear, Thiry and Vivet 2000)

Particularly in the Continental Western European countries, third sector entities have consistently played an important part as a provider of social services. Consequently, it is difficult to deny the validity of the critique made by Lewis (2004: 170) that 'the third sector is conspicuous by its absence' from Esping-Andersen's welfare regime theory as based on the situation circa 1980. In fact, in a note to his book *Social Foundations of Postindustrial Economies*, Esping-Andersen acknowledged that 'we should rightfully add the "third sector" of voluntary, or non-profit, welfare delivery' to the triad of state, market and family. Citing Salamon and Anheier (1996) he also laments that the paucity of international comparisons hinders systematic investigation (Esping-Andersen 1999: 35). But in terms of his argument as a whole, the third sector remains unaccounted for by his triadic structure of family, state and market.

According to Defourny, the idea of a distinct third sector in the sense of 'enterprises and organisations which are not primarily seeking profit, and which are not part of the public sector, really began to emerge in the mid 1970s' (Borzaga and Defourny 2004: 3). International comparative scholarship on this point took off with the launching of the Johns Hopkins Comparative Nonprofit Sector Project in the early 1990s. This 'rediscovery' of the role of NPOs came with an increasing sense that the welfare state in its existing form had reached an impasse or even become dysfunctional. For Esping-Andersen's theory of welfare regimes, institutionalized welfare capitalism at its peak had provided the point of reference. Even while acknowledging the importance of the third sector, his approach remained incapable of incorporating it into the state-market family triad that formed its basis.

The limits of welfare states and the theory of livelihood security systems

New social risks and dysfunction of the welfare state

Awareness of the limitations inherent in theories based on the concepts of the welfare state or welfare regimes rose as dysfunctionality of livelihood security systems centred on income transfers became increasingly manifest. The impasse of the welfare state in its existing form concerns first of all difficulties faced in responding to 'new social risks' brought about by post-industrialization (Bonoli 2003b; Taylor-Gooby 2004).

As Bonoli has shown, the so-called new social risks are attributable above all to socio-economic change, in particular a shift of employment to tertiary (i.e. service) industries and the massive entry into the workforce of women. As examples of new social risks, Bonoli cites inability to reconcile work and family life, single parenthood, having an aged or disabled relative requiring care, possessing low job skills or skills that have become obsolete, and following an 'atypical' career pattern resulting in diminished social security coverage (Bonoli 2003b). Clearly, demographic transition to a low-fertility, aging population must also be seen as a relevant factor. (To be sure, skill obsolescence and inability to reconcile factory work and family life surfaced as problems already during the industrial revolution. In this sense, these risks cannot really be said to be new.)

A second circumstance behind the dysfunction of the welfare state is globalization. Financial liberalization spearheaded the globalization of economies, constricting the capacity of sovereign states to exercise autonomous economic and social policy. Faced with the need to cover imbalances in international payments, individual countries found themselves at the mercy of short-term capital flows beyond the control of domestic fiscal and monetary policies. Meanwhile, a free trade regime under the aegis of the WTO demanded that even education and welfare services be opened up to market competition (Miyamoto 2002: 12–13; Scharpf 2005).

As we will see in Chapter 2, it is not so much that sovereign states lost free reign in policymaking as that, under economic globalization, domestic economies are set on a perpetual roller-coaster ride of economic crises, with market bubbles alternating with market crashes. Faced with this bind, an approach has emerged that addresses welfare governance rather than welfare states. It stresses the governance of livelihood security supplied by a different set of principals: supranational regional governance entities such as the EU (Johnson 2005), non-governmental actors such as social economy institutions, and devolution of authority to local communities (Miyamoto 2006).

In summary, it has proven difficult to accommodate the role of non-governmental institutions or social practices such as families, companies, labour unions and not-for-profit organizations (NPOs) within the theoretical framework of the welfare state. Esping-Andersen's theory of 'welfare regimes' is based on 'decommodification' as its central concept, just as his earlier welfare state typology had been. In other words, for all practical purposes state-provided welfare as measured by social insurance coverage and benefit levels continues to serve as his indicator distinguishing regime types. Esping-Andersen has responded to critique from a gender perspective by introducing the concept of de-familialization into his theory, but even so, it is the magnitude of outlays to families and social services coverage – in short, state-provided welfare – that forms the basis of his analysis.

State-provided welfare is taken as the key variable in this fashion, because welfare is effectively understood as synonymous with public sector income transfers or state provision of goods and services. For that reason, the concept of welfare regimes cannot contribute much to the discussion of eras and societies in which state-provided welfare is undeveloped, or where its preponderance and role decline. His theory's failure to incorporate the social economy or third sector is due not only to comparative research in this area still being in its infancy, but also to the fact that Esping-Andersen identifies welfare with public sector income transfers and state provision of goods and services.

Three types of livelihood security systems

Both welfare state theory and welfare regime theory may have been effective in analyzing the developed countries in the third quarter of the 20th century, when the scope of state-provided welfare soared (which is not to say that companies and families were not playing major roles, too). However, the heuristic value of these theories is limited when it comes to explaining other eras and societies. In welfare state theory as well as welfare regime theory, Japan tends to be labelled as a 'hybrid' of more than one type, or an exception. This is not unrelated to Japan's history as a late developing country in terms of both industrialization and welfare state formation. As already noted, Esping-Andersen himself, in his preface to the Japanese edition of *The Three Worlds of Welfare Capitalism*, has acknowledged that Japan's welfare system is still a work in process and a challenging case to classify.

The object of comparative analysis in this book is conceived of as 'livelihood security systems' to set a focus on the articulation between non-governmental institutions or social practices such as families, corporations, labour unions and NPOs on the one hand, and government-maintained tax and social security systems, employment maintenance policy and labour market regulation, on the other. As previously stated, the livelihood security systems of the developed countries will be discussed in terms of a threefold typology based on the situation circa 1980, distinguishing a *male breadwinner* model, a *work/life balance* model and a *market-oriented* model.

In livelihood security systems of the male breadwinner type, the labour market is regulated to secure stable employment for men (although not all men) in their working prime, at which they can earn a 'family wage' sufficient to support a wife and children. On that premise, the social insurance system is set up to deal with the risk of interruptions to men's income-earning ability. Women and children receive security through membership in a household headed by such a man. Women are expected to devote their full time to household duties. Support for these responsibilities in the form of child care, nursing care and other such services, is restricted to 'exceptional' cases of low-income households or children 'in need of care'. The typical male breadwinner model countries are those of Continental Europe along with Japan. Within this group, the role played by the third sector or social economy in livelihood security can be thought of as rather modest in the case of the Southern European countries and of Japan. In the Western European countries by contrast, NPOs linked to the Church, the Red Cross, political parties and similar institutions, are part of the fabric of welfare service provision.

The Nordic countries during the 1970s and 1980s on the other hand, pursued an active labour market policy, expansion of social welfare services and policies of gender equalization informed by the view that both women and men should be able to balance work and family, in addition to becoming involved in their communities; in other words, that people should be able to work and care. Every individual, man or woman, receives treatment commensurate with actual work performed in addition to social insurance coverage and public social services for supporting families. Under this work/life balance model of livelihood security, support for families in the form of child allowances, child care services from infancy onward, aged care services, parental leave and similar programmes, was institutionalized in close conjunction with regulations to promote gender equality in employment. The individual – rather than the family – was taken as the unit for tax and social security contribution purposes, while tax breaks for families were trimmed and survivors' benefits eliminated. Under this model, the proportion of social services provided by government agencies is high. Non-profit associations are active mainly in the domains of civic activism and rights advocacy.

The market-oriented model for which the Anglo-Saxon countries are typical places little weight on public policy to support family formation, and keeps labour market regulation at a minimum. Wages are expected to reflect performance and a commitment to livelihood security is not in effect. Workers that are valued by their companies, however, are often provided with generous employee benefits. The scope of activity by NPOs and cooperatives can be said to be at an intermediate level. The US was exceptional among the Anglo-Saxon countries in not offering public health insurance that covers all citizens.

These types correspond to templates of workplace and family that are encoded with gender roles, expectations and stereotypes. In short, they are structured around gender. Adopting a concept of livelihood security system based on a gender perspective in this fashion will thus also enable analyses of the historical transformation of welfare systems and comparative research on recent developments in Asian countries. There is rapidly growing interest in the social economy as it pertains not only to Europe, but also to countries such as Japan and South Korea. At the same time, there is a pressing need to theoretically account for the activities of various forms of NPOs that contribute to livelihood security in various fashions. Even the social enterprise theory of Borzaga and Defourny, which represents the forefront of research on the social economy today, has yet to incorporate the dimension of gender.

From welfare regimes to livelihood security systems 25

In the present book, the meaning of 'welfare' will not be restricted to public sector income transfers or state provision of goods and services. Taking its cue from feminist and gendered analyses of labour and the economy, it seeks to bring into view income flows connected with the production and distribution of goods and services in all areas of the economy. The framework for such an analysis will be laid out in Chapter 2.

2 The livelihood security systems approach

Life has needs which must be met. In Chapter 1, we saw how 20th century welfare states reduced livelihood needs to the single dimension of income insufficiency, and the cause of income insufficiency to lack of employment of a male household head. Section 1 of this chapter will reiterate that livelihood needs are inherently individual and multidimensional. What is more, recognition and fulfilment of needs requires 'cooperation' – in the form of social participation and third-party contributions – as an essential moment.

In exercising their various functions, people utilize various kinds of goods and services. A closer examination of the social and economic relations that govern the production of goods and services under a market economy will make the logic behind the evolution of government social policy, as well as its inherent limitations, stand out. Section 2 of this chapter demonstrates that, under economic globalization, livelihood security systems based on the conventional welfare state have fallen into dysfunction, causing social exclusion to become widespread. In the developing countries and in Japan, particular attention must be paid to the fact that social exclusion affects even insiders in the labour market. Section 3 then models the process according to which livelihood security systems function, distinguishing modes of functioning, dysfunction and reverse functioning. Taking this framework as a basis, Section 4 finally proceeds to identify the structural components of Japan's livelihood security system circa the 1980s.

The production and distribution of goods and services and the livelihood security system

Capabilities and needs

Needs are intrinsically diverse and individual

In the well-known capability approach pioneered by economist Amartya Sen, the set of interrelated 'beings' and 'doings' of which an individual's 'living' consists, and that are constitutive of that individual's quality of life or 'well-being', are referred to as her or his 'functionings'. The set of 'functionings' from which an individual can choose, on the other hand, is her or his 'capability'. In other words, an individual's capability reflects her or his 'freedom to lead one type of life or another', and as such forms a constitutive part of her or his 'well-being' (Sen 1992: 39–40).

People who cannot get enough food to eat and people who choose to limit the amount of food they eat on a purely voluntary basis resemble each other in their 'functioning', in the sense of being on an empty stomach. But the former is constrained in her ability to choose another functioning due to inadequate income, whereas the latter can choose to be in a state of having a full stomach at any time. Their 'capabilities' are therefore vastly different.

The livelihood security systems approach adopted in this volume is concerned with the capability to earn a livelihood and participate in society as a realized human being. It defines needs as deficiencies in this capability. Needs must therefore be distinguished from demand. Demand is desire backed up by purchasing power. In not a few cases consumers spend considerable amounts of money on articles of taste that actually are harmful to their health, due to a perceived 'utility' they derive from them.

To achieve their various functionings, people rely on all kinds of goods and services. However, in societies where a market economy prevails, large numbers of goods and services are commoditized. An income is necessary to procure them. And the primary means of obtaining such income has become not so much sale of own produce (as a small producer) as sale of one's labour power (as a wage worker). In earlier history, those directly engaged in production were often in an unfree status, such as the slaves of the ancient or the serfs of the medieval world. But with the penetration of the market economy, wage labourers who can be hired and fired at will came to constitute the majority of the working population. Below, we will observe how the unfolding of this employment relation called forth social policy.

A 'service' – as opposed to a 'good', which is a material object invested with potential for *exchange* – has been defined as 'a *change* in the condition of one economic unit ... realised by the activity of another economic unit'. Production of a service then refers to 'a process by which the condition of the consumer, or the goods which he owns, is changed in some way which the consumer requests'. The important point in distinguishing whether or not an activity constitutes the production of a service is whether the 'change that is brought about in the person of some economic unit or in the goods belonging to that unit' is 'capable of being effected by another unit' (Hill 1979: 32–3). Studying and pastime pursuits, or the meeting of physiological needs such as sleeping and eating, are not activities that could be performed by someone else hired for that purpose. These activities do not constitute service production, but fall under the rubric of 'enjoyment' of goods or services.

In many cases, 'needs' simply refers to a lack of goods and services necessary to a 'decent' life. The cause of such lack may be income too low to procure needed goods or services at the required prices to the same degree as people not in need ('average' people representing the 'norm') or lack of opportunity to procure them (for lack of an automobile or access to online commerce, for example). In such cases needs can be met by augmenting the income of, or providing goods and services to those in need. As research on poverty and relative deprivation has shown, in each society and historical period there is a broadly if loosely maintained consensus about what goods and services or opportunities are considered indispensible for maintaining a decent life (Abe 2006). As social and economic conditions are transformed, the list of indispensible items changes as well.

Of course, not all goods and services are commoditized, even in societies with highly developed market economies. And not are all of them are procurable through purchase. Human beings exist within a cultural matrix. To have one's individual worth and social contributions valued can also be considered a 'service' essential to leading a fulfilled life. Obviously, it is difficult to procure the respect and goodwill of others through sheer purchasing power.

Sen was mostly concerned with the fact that individuals are often unable to meet their needs despite having a decent income in addition to opportunities to procure goods and services. Even if people are equipped with the same primary goods (such as income and talents, for example), the functionings they are able to achieve may vary on grounds of personal diversity. In other words, their possibility of *converting* primary goods into achievements of well-being may be affected by a variety of additional factors.

Factors that may intervene in the conversion of primary goods into achieved functionings include individual attributes such as gender, age, health status, existence (as well as degree and type) of disability, ethnicity, and so on, in addition to external factors such as access to transport, health care and care services, or also climatic conditions. Sen cites the case of 'a pregnant woman who may have to overcome disadvantages in living comfortably and well that a man at the same age need not have, even when both have the exact same income and other primary goods ... With the same bundle of primary goods, a pregnant woman or one with infants to look after has much less freedom to pursue her goals than a man not thus encumbered would be able to do so' (Sen 1992: 27).

The 'norm' has so far tended to be identified with those occupying a privileged position in society, such as healthy men in their prime with an above-average education and earning potential and belonging to the dominant ethnic group or religion. Gender and other biases conspire to make additional needs for goods and services or opportunities in people who do not correspond to the 'norm' appear not as genuine needs, but 'indulgence' or 'luxury' instead.

Recognition and fulfilment of needs through cooperative activity

It is important to keep in mind that needs are not always or necessarily recognized and voiced by the concerned individuals themselves. When an individual has a need but is not aware of this, a third party can spur recognition of it. In the case of lack of purchasing power or non-commoditization of a good or service, livelihood security can be achieved by meeting needs through governmental or non-governmental provision. Third party provision may be private and informal, as when undertaken by family members, friends or volunteers. But it also may be formal, either as private-sector provision through nursing care personnel or medical employees, or as public-sector provision undertaken by civil servants implementing government welfare policies. (Cases of mixed provision, as when the government delegates tasks to the private sector, also exist.) Although needs are intrinsically diverse and individual, recognition and fulfilment of needs is a social process that presupposes 'cooperation', in the form of social participation by the individual and third-party contribution, as an essential moment.

Individual attributes such as gender and age, and external factors such as access to public transit, climatic circumstances and so forth intervene in the possibility of converting goods and services, or opportunities, into achieved functionings. Of special concern in this regard is the factor of gender. Even though limitations on the availability of statistical data may be part of the problem, in mainstream economic theory individuals have been equated with households or household budgets. The male head of household has been taken to represent the interests and welfare of all household members, as if this were self-understood. Unlike other attributes or factors such as age and ethnicity, gender is strictly binary. The household of a modern family is considered constituted by the 'nucleus' of a man and a woman forming a couple linked by mutual bonds of affection. If individuals are equated with households and a household is taken to be represented by its head, the interests and voices of women become unheard.

Sen's capability approach is built around a fundamental critique of the utility approach of mainstream economics. 'Utility', needless to add, is the most fundamental concept of the neoclassical school dominating contemporary economic theory. Utility is at times restated to mean 'happiness' or 'well-being', but the important point is that it refers to a subjective (mental) state of desire-fulfilment. The individual (or rather the household budget) is presumed to possess a clearly articulated and consistent rank preference of utility (perceived satisfaction) regarding all goods and services. Needs of which the individual remains unaware are taken to be nonexistent. Moreover, this approach does not allow to compare utility between individuals or to consider how one person's utility may be affected by that of others.

Sen further points out that in situations of adversity which cannot be individually changed, people tend to 'concentrate their desire on those limited things that they *can* possibly achieve'. Even when third parties would regard them as thoroughly deprived, individuals may be used to accepting their hardship 'with non-grumbling resignation' (Sen 1992: 55). Consciously or unconsciously, such individuals decline to recognize their needs. Women, as Sen further remarks, tend to identify the utility of their children or husband with their own. This is one example of how an individual's utility can be affected by the utility of others. 'The misleading nature of utility metrics', as Sen sums up his critique, 'may be particularly important in the context of stable differentiation of class, gender, caste or community' (Sen 1992: 7).

Relations of production of goods and services

Four types of relations governing the production of goods and services

The relations governing the production of goods and services also determine the ways in which incomes are earned (or not earned). Relations of production can be distinguished into four types, as shown in Table 2.1, based on whether or not commoditized labour power (wage labour) is used in the production process, and whether or not the goods and services that constitute the output of that production are commoditized. Namely, (1) production of commodities using wage labour (including the work performed by paid employees of not-for-profit organizations in addition to those of for-profit enterprises); (2) production of non-commodities using wage labour (such as public services provided by civil servants, advocacy work by paid employees of environmental NGOs, etc.); (3) production of commodities using non-wage labour (in the case of self-employment, workers' collectives, plantation slavery, etc.); and (4) production of non-commodities using non-wage labour (such as housework performed by family members or domestic slaves, labour for household consumption in self-employed households and volunteer activities).

This framework can be used to shed light on the position and function of not-for-profit organizations as well. NPOs, though operating on a not-for-profit basis, may employ wage labour to produce and market commoditized goods and services (social enterprises). In other cases, commodities may be directly produced by an NPO's self-financed and self-managed constituent members (workers' collectives). Paid staff may also be employed to produce services for the collective good (in the case of advocacy organizations such as environmental NGOs, for example). Finally, there are the team and volunteer activities of co-ops and the like. In other words, NPOs may fall into any of the four quadrants defining relations of production as defined above. NPOs are sometimes seen as nothing more than stopgap measures or supplements to capitalism with poor growth prospects, but if relations of production of goods and services are considered as schematized in Table 2.1, they will be seen to occupy a core position. This matches the European understanding in which the 'fundamentally open, mixed, pluralistic and *intermediary nature* of the third sector' has been emphasized, as opposed to setting it 'apart from state and market as a kind of "independent" sector' (Evers and Laville 2004: 36).

In mainstream economics as well as in common parlance, only the relations shown in quadrants (1) and (3) are properly considered 'production', with for-profit companies falling under (1) forming the foundation. In the advanced industrial countries, quadrant (1) undoubtedly dominates. The economies of developing countries, by contrast, are heavily weighted toward the agricultural, fisheries and forestry sectors and small-scale industry through self-employment falling under quadrant (3). Quadrant (2), as will be discussed in more detail in Chapter 4, also includes the government sector, whose size (measured by indicators such as the share of national income that goes to taxes and social insurance contributions) varies widely even among the developed countries, with the United States and Japan

Table 2.1 Classification of relations of production of goods and services according to commoditization

		Labour used	
		Commoditized (wage labour)	Non-commoditized (self-employed, family workers, slaves, domestic work)
Goods and services produced	Commoditized	(1) Firms for profit, market-oriented production by NPO employees	Family businesses, members of workers' collectives, market-oriented production by slaves (3)
	Non-commoditized	Public sector, public services of NPO employees (2)	Domestic work (family members, domestic slaves) domestic consumption by family businesses, volunteer activities (4)

occupying the low and the Northern European countries the high ends. Quadrant (4), if estimates of the monetary value of household labour for child care and nursing care services are made the basis of calculation, amounts to only around 20 per cent of GDP in Japan, but occupies between 50 per cent and 60 per cent in Germany and Canada (Keizai-kikaku-chō 1997: 3 (7); Keizai-kikaku-chō 1998).

The livelihood security system of a given society can thus be characterized on the basis of the following markers: (1) Quantitative relationships that exist among the four relations of production regulating flows of income from the production of goods and services (such as the share of GDP constituted by government spending or the scale of the self-employment sector); (2) Qualitative relationships among the four relations of production (such as ways in which payment of a family wage by companies to full-time male workers affects gender role division within households, or ways in which public works and industrial regulation affect the agricultural sector and self-employed businesses); (3) Working conditions and qualitative characteristics of the goods and services produced within each relation of production (such as biases in the employment policies of private sector companies, progressivity of government expenditures and revenues, the extent of public services to support families and so on); and (4) Quantitative and qualitative characteristics of NPOs falling into each of the four quadrants, and the ways in which the respective relations of production are, quantitatively and qualitatively, influenced by them.

The indeterminacy of distribution and the concept of welfare

The distribution of goods and services produced, and the distribution of income that constitutes the purchasing power to procure them, varies according to 'status' of participation in these four types of relations of production, and even with equivalent status according to gender, age, existence (type and degree of) disability, ethnicity and other personal 'attributes'. Possible statuses of participation in production include hired worker, business owner, family member working in a family business, domestic worker, slave owner, slave and so on. With respect to distribution, it is necessary to take into account landowners and investors as well. Land and money (investment capital) constitute, along with labour, the primary factors of production. The landowners or investors, who are the owners of these factors, provide them to the producer unit, receiving rent or interest/dividends in return. Status and attributes are emphasized here in contrast to the assumptions and emphases of mainstream economics, since distribution is not proportional to the actual contribution to production.

It may seem peculiar to include 'slave' as a 'status' in this framework. However, slavery is not confined to the ancient world or the serfdom that continued into the early modern era. Even today phenomena such as human trafficking of sex workers and plantation workers in debt bondage exist on a scale too large to ignore. Such people are not able to freely participate in the labour market as owners of their own labour power, which is what sets them apart from wage labourers.

Even those wage labourers who should be able to 'freely' trade their labour, often receive reduced wages solely on account of attributes such as female gender or foreign nationality, even when their qualifications, such as educational background and experience, are equal and they input (contribute) the exact same amount of labour power (wage discrimination against women or foreign workers). In addition, domestic labour is often performed by women irrespective of their roles outside the home (gender role differentiation). Unlike goods, which can be accumulated, it lies in the nature of a personal service that its provider cannot simultaneously be on its receiving end. Women who are primarily responsible for providing services within the home get to enjoy only a very small part of such services themselves.

Moreover, goods and services, or the income to purchase them, are not necessarily distributed in remuneration for (direct or indirect) participation in production. In other words, they are not always 'earned' through contributions to production. It is not unusual for goods and services or income to be directly allocated in response to given needs. Commonplace examples include family members giving each other support in cash or in kind, income transfers by means of taxation, public services in the form of social insurance, and the provision of nursing care services by public agencies or family members. Income that is directly distributed to meet needs (e.g. cash benefits for low-income households or individuals) and goods and services provided for free are typically labelled 'welfare'. The livelihood security systems approach takes into consideration the production and distribution of all goods and services, and the flows of income that accompany them.

Production within the household: division of labour, conflict and cooperation

Domestic labour producing household services, in quadrant (4), is a relation of production not treated as production by conventional economics at all, but regarded as 'consumption' instead. Even the heavy labour involved in drawing water and gathering firewood for household use that absorbs a large share of household activity in the developing world is considered 'consumption'. In societies with fully developed money economies, there are many personal services that are produced and supplied free as needed as well, because they would be too expensive to procure in the open market, if available, or defy standardization. Child care, nursing care and tending to emotional needs would be typical examples. Unless a good or service is sold on the market as a commodity to meet a market demand, no production is deemed to have taken place in the view of mainstream economics, which sees things from the viewpoint of capital and is concerned with markets rather than people. Since the 1960s, the idea of 'household production' encompassing housework, child-rearing and nursing care has become established in mainstream economics as well in the form of Gary Becker's 'new household economics' (Becker 1965; Becker and Ghez 1975). This theory explains differentiated gender roles within the family, such that the husband earns the income for the household budget and the wife is primarily responsible for housework and child-rearing, 'rationally' in terms of a man's and woman's preferences (what they perceive as having higher utility) and relative advantage (what they are better at doing), as well as amount and combination of available resources, including acquired skills. Its basic assumptions are that households are selfish in seeking to maximize utility vis-à-vis the external world, and that the preferences of individual family member can be subsumed within a joint utility function. The head of the household is assumed to consolidate the interests and preferences of all household members into a joint utility function by accounting for them. This presupposes the existence of an altruistic relationship between household head and household members.

Since the late 1980s, the 'new household economics' has been subjected to critique by feminist economics (Folbre 1986; Dwyer and Bruce 1988; Sen 1990; Elson 1994). The new household economics envisions the family or the household as a world pervaded by altruism. The possibility that there could be conflicting preferences between members of a household generating clashes of interest, or that inequality could prevail preventing some members from enjoying utility maximization, is not considered at all. Amartya Sen, by contrast, insists that relationships between family members should be understood in terms of 'cooperative conflict' since 'the members of the household face two types of problems simultaneously, one involving *cooperation* (adding to total availabilities) and the other *conflict* (dividing the total availabilities among the members of the household' (Sen 1990: 129).

Domestic labour is today acknowledged as 'work' even by official documents such as the Ministry of Internal Affairs and Communications' *Survey on Time Use and Leisure Activities*. At the macro level, feminist economics and related analyses of 'gender and development' have argued for a 'reproductive' sector reproducing human life and society set against the 'market/productive sector', or contrasted the 'money economy' with a 'caring economy'. It has further been emphasized that the economy of public services and the economy of care/reproduction should be put on a par with the economy of private commodities (Muramatsu 2005).

The four-way classification adopted in this volume not only avoids the dichotomy between production and consumption that plagues mainstream economics, but also the dichotomy between production and reproduction adopted by feminist analyses of labour and the economy, as well as the dichotomy between paid and unpaid labour. The dichotomy between production and reproduction is not adopted on the grounds that there ultimately is no difference between domestic labour and other productive labour in terms of resources being procured and transformed into goods and services. Likewise, the dichotomy between paid and unpaid labour is avoided on the grounds that, even without resorting to the concept of 'exploitation' in Marxian economics, no small fraction of wage labour is undertaken at wages so low and working conditions so poor that it virtually amounts to unpaid labour.

Independence/dependence and the limits of labour power commoditization

Having the goods and services one needs, or the purchasing power required to procure them, supplied by someone else is typically considered 'dependence'. However, human beings are not able to be truly self-sufficient in the sense of autonomously supplying each and every good or service they need to begin with. In many cases, even healthy individuals with decent incomes have needs (which they may not actually recognize as such) met by a third party. And even where there is effective demand, if there is no one to meet it by producing goods or services for sale, money becomes nothing more than grubby bits of metal and paper. In other words, there is a gap between what individuals demand, the goods and services they need, and the goods and services they can actually obtain for use via channels such as self-provision, purchase, exchange, gift and so on. This is not solely applicable to the underprivileged, but a universal condition. The livelihood security system, in other words, does not only exist for the sake of a segment of society composed of the deprived or disadvantaged. It is universally required.

The nature and magnitude of this gap between needs and provision is of course linked to gender, life stage, health status, employability on the labour market, market prospects of goods produced, ownership of real property and capital (or purchasing power derived therefrom) and so on. Nevertheless, it is not the case that people whose ability to produce goods and services is deficient, or who suffer from low incomes, do not produce any services at all. Take, for example, infants and elderly persons requiring nursing care: their cries or groans transmit feelings of comfort and discomfort to their caregivers, thereby producing a change in their condition. The production of a change in the caregiver's condition can hardly be called 'production of a service'. However, even in this case the recipients of care are providing the care-giver with vital information about their needs to alleviate a shared situation. As long as persons care about each other, care-giving constitutes a joint undertaking. In a society (even more so in a society with role differentiation), every person is dependent upon others. Independence and dependence are ultimately relative terms.

No matter how highly developed markets become, the gap described above can never be completely bridged. This is because markets respond to demand, not needs. Moreover, as Masaru Kaneko has emphasized, due to the existence of fundamental limits on the commoditization of the primary factors of production, markets themselves require various kinds of social safety nets to function (Kaneko 1997;

Kaneko 1999).[1] The limits on the commoditization of labour are especially rigid. For most commodities, the seller will cease to supply or make a good if its price falls below its cost of production due to oversupply. Fresh foods and hotel rooms are examples of so-called perishable goods, which pose difficulties in adjusting supply to demand in the short run, and thus tend to be sold off at fire-sale prices. Labour, in this sense, might be called the most perishable good of all.

Reproduction of labour power and social policy

(Re-)production of labour power encompasses both the short-term dimension of sustaining the mental and physical fitness of individuals to live and work, and the medium- and long-term dimension of giving birth to, rearing and educating the next generation. Even in the absence of income due to unemployment, sickness or injury, or setbacks in the operation of a family business, so long as human beings are alive they continue reproducing their labour power through the consumption of food, clothing, shelter and so on. To do so, and to raise the next generation, they require goods and services. Beyond basic necessities, investment in training and education to retain and refresh skills and knowledge is needed. Human beings also require opportunity to socially interact with others, participate in community activities, and make their voices politically heard. In the event of sickness or injury they depend on health and medical services. All such expenditures on basic livelihood, including those related to raising the next generation, constitute (re-)production costs of labour power.

What sets wage labourers apart from small producers (the self-employed, members of workers' cooperatives, etc.) is that wage labourers are separated from the means of production (i.e. the means of sustaining a livelihood) such as land, tools, workplaces and so on. Small producers own their means of production and slaves are themselves means of production under the ownership of others. Wage labourers, on the other hand, must live off selling their labour power. Prices (wages) paid for labour are not necessarily commensurate with actual contribution to production (productivity). They rather tend to be controlled by personal attributes such as gender, age, ethnicity, etc.

Even if the price of their labour (wages) falls below its (re-)production costs (basic living expenses), workers cannot cease to be alive and thus stop (re-)producing their labour power (as opposed to small producers, who can stop producing their products). Historically, workers have joined together into labour unions to bargain over working conditions and forestall distress sale of labour power to secure labour prices that at least cover the cost of living. Unless the living costs not covered by wages are provided for in some form, the labour power of the working-age population will be enfeebled. And unless the expenditures to educate the next generation are provided for, the labour power of the next generation will deteriorate. In the big picture, the reproduction of total wage labour power through wage routes as well as non-wage routes (such as public assistance in the form of charity and poor laws) is of concern to employers and capital interests (just as sustaining the labour power of slaves is of direct concern to the slave owner).

What about livelihood security for the elderly or infirm, for whose labour power there are no conceivable buyers? In a society where labour power is regarded as disposable, and those whose labour power is accorded no value are left to die by the roadside, what legitimacy would there be to prohibitions on robbing or begging? Under such conditions, protection of property rights would require exorbitant expenditures. Yet protection of property rights, it goes without saying, is indispensable to the functioning of a market economy.

Thus, even setting asides any expectation that the evolution of labour relations would be accompanied by the establishment of social rights such as the right to have one's life sustained, social policy measures in the form of regulations and benefit payments came to be adopted as one essential component of livelihood security provision, including labour standards laws setting minimum wages for workers and restricting maximum working hours, labour relations policies recognizing labour unions and instituting collective regulation of labour conditions, public job training and certification programmes, public labour exchange services, income transfers through social security and taxation, and public welfare services. In other words, markets do not insist on the abolition of all regulation and social policy by all means, as the limits to commoditization of labour power can lead to paralysis of the market itself, if social policy offers no 'safety nets'.

Of course, when the working masses possess political rights, the securing of fundamental labour and social rights may also exceed the scope of what is in the interests of capital. Capital, on the other hand, may become more mobile as a result of deregulation and flee from countries where 'excessive' social rights are guaranteed. In this respect, the mobility of capital places limits on social policy. In fact, as touched upon already in Chapter 1, economic globalization, with financial liberalization at its core, has severely constrained sovereign states in the exercise of an independent economic and social policy. It is thus widely held responsible for the welfare state's fall into dysfunction. As we will see in the next section, it has come to be taken for granted that national economies are exposed to globally propagating fluctuations, driven by a boom-and-bust cycle of economic crisis and accompanied by conspicuous manifestations of social exclusion in multiple forms.

Economic globalization and social exclusion

The age of economic crisis

Global imbalances and the bubble economy – background to the crisis

Some say that economic crises are as old as capitalism. But analysis of a database covering the 120 year period from 1880 onward has revealed that crises have become twice as frequent since 1973 (Bordo, Eichengreen, Klingebiel and Martinez-Peria 2001).

The year 1973, of course, marked the collapse of the Bretton Wood system that had regulated international currency movements in the post-war period, and the advent of floating exchange rates. Before 1973, under the gold standard and the

Bretton Woods system, economies had been essentially self-regulating via the mechanism of the amount of gold in national treasuries, making it impossible for imbalances to continue for a prolonged time or to expand indefinitely. In contrast, under the floating exchange rate system, trade imbalances soared astronomically, fuelled primarily by the US current account deficit. The age of global imbalances had arrived.

The prime mover of the cycle of economic bubbles and crises that ripple across the globe from country to country is the US current account deficit (Duncan 2003). Since 1973, when trade imbalances ceased to be self-correcting, and particularly since the 1980s, the world has experienced an age of economic crises. With the collapse of the planned economies of the Soviet Union and Eastern Europe and the transition to market economies in other socialist nations like China and Vietnam, crises became even more global from the early 1990s onward. In the latter half of the 1990s, the US current account deficit rose sharply, and in the 2000s its ascent continued to accelerate, reaching $800 billion by 2006 (diminishing slightly in 2007). This figure dwarfs the entire GDP of countries like South Korea and the Netherlands.

Only the US was in a position to continue accumulating such a massive deficit, thanks to the US dollar's status as the world's de facto reserve currency. This status enabled the US to pay for its imports simply by printing more dollars. Countries with surpluses often used their dollars to purchase US Treasury bonds and other dollar-denominated securities, thereby recycling the dollars flowing out to pay for exports back into the US economy. This dollar recycling bridged the US current account deficit while inflating the securities markets. Interest rates on consumer finance, notably home loans, were pushed to historically low levels. Consumption grew faster than personal income, and personal debt grew faster than consumption (Duncan 2003: 77–9). In 2005, the US savings rate turned negative for the first time in 72 years (Doihara 2006).

In countries with current account surpluses, money supply, which consists of cash and bank deposits, inexorably increased. In the case of Japan, the late 1980s was a period of conspicuous surplus accumulation. A massive boom in property investment triggered skyrocketing asset price inflation, bringing about the so-called 'bubble economy'. Following the burst of the bubble in the 1990s, disinflation (a slowing of the rate of price increases) was followed by outright deflation (a falling price level). The explosive appreciation of the yen ushered in by the 1985 Plaza Accord, on the other hand, induced off-shoring of Japanese manufacturing to the Asian NICs. Along with a surge in other investment, the resulting rapid growth in foreign currency reserves produced a bubble economy there. According to Joseph Stiglitz, who served for three years concurrently as Chief Economist and Senior Vice President of the World Bank starting in 1997, a major factor in the East Asian bubble economy and its bursting was liberalization of financial markets that were still immature (Stiglitz 2002: 99).

South Korea's financial liberalization measures, for example, began in 1985 and were accelerated in the 1990s to win admission to the OECD. In Thailand, the first wave of liberalization took place in 1990–2, and the second in 1993–5.

This triggered rapid growth in bank deposits from offshore investors lured by high interest rates (volatile and foot-loose hot money flows). But when these NICs were struck by the Asian currency crisis, it became clear that financial liberalization must be carried out in order: regulation that enhances supervision of the domestic financial system must be put in place to stabilize it before the foreign investment regime is liberalized (Iwami 2007: 98–9).

According to Stiglitz, over-hasty liberalization was prompted by the interests of the US financial sector (Stiglitz 2002: 102–4). The backdrop to the promotion of liberalization was the so-called Washington Consensus formulated in the 1980s between the IMF, the US Department of the Treasury and the World Bank. The IMF, which was established to serve as the institutional lynchpin of the Bretton Woods system, had in its early years aimed at cooperation between member nations to sustain aggregate demand, based on the understanding that markets frequently fail to function effectively. However, in the era of UK Prime Minister Margaret Thatcher and US President Ronald Reagan, not only the IMF but also the World Bank switched to so-called market fundamentalism, adopting the three policy pillars of the Washington Consensus: fiscal austerity, privatization and market liberalization (Stiglitz 2002: 11–13, 16, 53).

Trickle-down economics or jobless/joyless recovery?

The Washington Consensus flew the banner of 'trickle-down economics', the belief that the benefits of economic growth trickle down to impoverished social strata. Accordingly, 'pro-poor' developmental strategies focused on ameliorating the state of the impoverished were eschewed. Pro-poor strategies include such policies as rural land reform, expanding educational opportunities, generation of employment opportunities and regulation of the financial sector. It is now widely acknowledged that the mooted benefits of economic growth did not in fact trickle down to the poor. Inequality in global income distribution widened from the 1980s onward (Wade 2002).

Spurred on by the massive wage difference between the developing and the developed countries, the US manufacturing base, more than that of any other country, was rapidly off-shored, facilitated by advances in information and communication technologies that slashed telecommunications costs. Goods manufactured under these auspices flooded into the US market as cheap imports, while the world's lightest taxation of fuel spurred extravagant gasoline consumption fed by massive imports of petroleum. The US household sector had traditionally generated surplus capital, but by 1999 it flipped over to become a net drain on capital as bank loans soared. The household sector's savings rate fell, which is another way of saying that households over-consumed, and thus became a major factor in the ballooning US current account deficit of the 2000s (Naikakufu 2008b).

The Washington Consensus at the very least played a part in bringing about the economic crisis by adopting a development strategy, based on trickle-down economics, that declined to set as a goal the shrinking of global income disparities and promoted liberalization of immature capital markets instead. The response of

The livelihood security systems approach 39

the parties to the Washington Consensus to the crisis further exacerbated the situation. The IMF dealt with crisis-struck countries not by addressing the occasion for or background to the crisis, but by imposing so-called 'conditionality' for bailout packages, entailing interest rate hikes, fiscal austerity and 'structural reforms'. These so-called structural adjustment programs (SAP) not only savaged employment and corporate balance sheets, but countries' social safety nets.

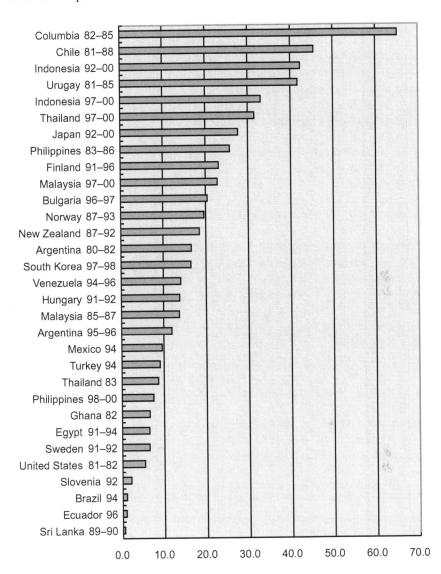

Figure 2.1 Estimated length of crisis (recovery time) and gross output loss (in per cent of GDP)

Source: Honohan and Klingebiel 2000: Table A 4.

The duration and magnitude of the crisis suffered by the Japanese economy after 1992 is shown by Figure 2.1. The size of Japan's economy is by orders of magnitude larger than that of countries like Colombia or Indonesia, where losses reached a huge fraction of GDP, and its losses from the crisis were correspondingly vast. Despite the repeated calls for financial reconstruction and structural reform in these years, economic revival proved elusive. Even to the degree recovery did occur, benefits failed to trickle down.

Japan's economy is said to have been recovering since the beginning of 2002, but according to the *2004 METI White Paper on International Economy and Trade*, even though corporate operating profits expanded, workers' wages failed to rise, and there was a pronounced disarticulation between the macro-economic climate and employment trends (METI 2004). Moreover, the Cabinet Office's *2007 Annual Report on the Japanese Economy and Public Finance*, issued in early August 2007, reported that profitability was up and cash flow strong in the corporate sector, but there was a gap in earnings between large corporations and small and medium-sized enterprises (SMEs). Dividends to shareholders and executive compensation rose, but employee salaries were flat. The stagnant income of the household sector kept consumer spending anaemic. The number of employed people increased, but aggregate cash wages, which had remained at the same level in 2006, dipped in the first half of 2007, as wages remained stuck (Naikakufu 2007: Chapter 1).

Until 2004, Japan boasted the world's largest current account surplus. Then a spike in oil prices brought Middle Eastern countries to the head of the table, in turn to be succeeded by China in 2006. Meanwhile, Japan's current account surplus continued to increase (Naikakufu, Seisaku tōkatsukan shitsu 2008b). Japan is an exception among the developed industrial countries in having excess savings. Under conditions of export-driven economic growth, in which investment plateaued while the savings rate slightly rose, excess savings continued to accumulate (Naikakufu, Seisaku tōkatsukan shitsu 2008a).

The trend toward macro-economic growth without growth in worker income surfaced at first in the United States, and has been called 'jobless/joyless recovery'. Financial globalization appears to have brought forth an economy in which a rebound in growth fails to lift employment and wages at the same time. If that is indeed the case, it is chipping away at the very roots of the livelihood security system. Concomitant to these developments, social exclusion has become a global concern.

Social exclusion/inclusion and livelihood security systems

Social exclusion and inclusion in the EU

According to Takuji Tanaka, the notion of social exclusion was first introduced in France in the mid-1970s. Initially, this term was applied to 'socially maladjusted' individuals who did not fit the framework of the welfare state. The framework of the French welfare state was predicated on workers supporting their families by pursuing a vocation under long-term employment and participating in social insurance schemes managed jointly by workers and employers. In other words, it was based on the ideal of occupational solidarity between male breadwinners (Tanaka 2005).

The French social insurance system had been formed through incorporation of pre-existing occupational mutual aid associations and social work projects into a government-maintained system. This led to the existence of multiple parallel, occupational funds for both pension and health insurance, known as *caisses*. Each *caisse* was managed by a board of directors composed of stakeholders including insurants and employers (Tabata 1989). However, from the 1980s onward it became evident – due to factors such as increasing dysfunction of the French school system, lack of job training opportunities, structural unemployment, the spread of precarious or non-regular employment and increasing family instability – that mere extension of social insurance schemes would not suffice to guarantee inclusion in the social security system. The concept of exclusion thus evolved into a concept referring not only to problems faced by specific groups, but to the spread of precarious conditions through industrial society as a whole (Tanaka 2005).

The preamble of the 1989 European Social Charter brought the concept of social exclusion to more widespread attention by explicitly including this term in its text. The Treaty of Amsterdam in 1997 for the first time listed the fight against social exclusion among the main objectives of the EU (Bhalla and Lapeyre 1999, 2004: 6–7). In June 2000, to support the EU and its member states in this fight, the European Council established an advisory body called the Social Protection Committee. According to the material about this body on the EU website, the fight against poverty and social exclusion is assigned top priority alongside safe and sustainable pensions.[2] And in December 2000, the Nice meeting of the European Council adopted the following common 'Objectives in the Fight Against Poverty and Social Exclusion': (1) 'to facilitate participation in employment and access by all to the resources, rights, goods and services'; (2) 'to prevent the risk of exclusion'; (3) 'to help the most vulnerable'; and (4) 'to mobilize all relevant bodies' (European Council 2000).

The Social Protection Committee's *Report on Indicators in the Field of Poverty and Social Exclusion* of October 2001, compiled 18 'commonly agreed indicators' to allow the EU member states and Commission to 'monitor progress in the fight against social exclusion', or towards achievement of social inclusion, in the four dimensions of monetary poverty (low income and income distribution), employment, education and health (Social Protection Committee 2001). In 2006 and 2008 the indicators were improved and expanded.[3] In this fashion, the EU adopted a multidimensional approach to social exclusion along with a dynamic approach emphasizing process over results at any given point in time. For example, the SPC indicators pertaining to low income include not only the percentage of the population living in households with low income and income distribution, but also register the persistence of low income. In concrete terms, households that in a given year and the three preceding years fall below the poverty line (60 per cent of the median per capita income) for at least two of those years are counted. For unemployment as well, it is persistence (long-term unemployment), and for education the percentage of young adults (ages 18–24) who are classified as NEETs (not in employment, education or training), that is held to be crucial (Social Protection Committee 2001).

Actors in the fight against exclusion include not only the EU and the governments of its member states, but institutions of the social economy and social partners are also emphasized. For example, under the first of the common objectives cited above, 'facilitating participation in employment', access is promoted to what is described as 'stable and quality employment', by 'putting in place, for those in the most vulnerable groups in society, pathways towards employment and by mobilizing training policies to that end, by developing policies to promote the reconciliation of work and family life, including the issue of child- and dependent care' and 'by using the opportunities for integration and employment provided by the social economy' (European Council 2000). A need to respond to the 'new social risks' touched upon in Chapter 1 is thus clearly acknowledged. The fourth of the common objectives, 'to mobilize all relevant bodies', begins by citing the need to 'promote, according to national practice, the participation and self-expression of people suffering exclusion' and stipulates to 'promote dialogue and partnership between all relevant bodies, public and private' (European Council 2000).

Community welfare and social inclusion in Japan

The term 'social inclusion' became part of the vocabulary of the Japanese government in connection with the pursuit of basic structural reform of social welfare, and in particular the idea of community welfare. However, in Japan this concept was more narrowly circumscribed than in Europe.

In July 2000, for example, the Investigative Committee for the Shape of Social Welfare for the Socially Vulnerable established in the Social Welfare and War Victims' Relief Bureau of the Ministry of Health, Labour and Welfare included the 'idea of social inclusion' on its agenda (Shakaiteki na engo o yōsuru hitobito ni taisuru shakai fukushi no arikata ni kansuru kentōkai 2000). Consistent with the aim of basic structural reform of social welfare, the Social Welfare Act and other legislation were amended in June 2000 to implement a switch from a placement to a use-based/contractual system. The way the placement system had worked was that administrative agencies of prefectural or municipal governments would determine requirements within their sphere of authority and decide the types of services and institutions to be provided on that basis. Prefectural or municipal governments had handled 'placement' by granting admission to welfare facilities such as child care facilities and care homes for seniors or enrolment in associated services. Once the Social Welfare Act had been revised, the committee turned its attention to 'the segment of society that falls through the cracks of the social welfare system' (Explanation of the committee agenda by Director-General Shigeru Sumitani of the Social Welfare and War Victims' Relief Bureau, Minutes of the 1st Meeting of the Investigative Committee for the Shape of Social Welfare for the Socially Vulnerable).[4] According to Sumitani, this committee report marks the first use of the term 'social inclusion' in an official document by the Japanese government (Sumitani, Ōyama and Hosouchi 2004: 13).

These basic structural reforms of social welfare supposed local governments to independently formulate their own community welfare plans. Local governments received notification regarding this policy from the Ministry of Health, Labour and Welfare in April 2002. The notification instructed local governments to refer to a document issued in January 2002 by the Welfare Working Group of the Ministry of Health, Labour and Welfare's Social Security Council entitled 'Guidelines for the Drafting of Municipal Community Welfare and Prefectural Welfare Assistance Plans (An Appeal to Every Local Citizen)'. This report named as one of its principles for promoting community welfare, 'building a cohesive society (*tomo ni ikiru shakai-zukuri* 共に生きる社会づくり) (social inclusion)' (Kōsei-rōdō-shō website 'Chiiki fukushi keikaku'[5]).

In considering the meaning of social exclusion, the report of the Investigative Committee for the Shape of Social Welfare for the Socially Vulnerable goes no further than presenting as examples of 'social exclusion and social friction' such matters as traffic deaths, the return of Japanese orphans left behind in China in the aftermath of World War II, and exclusion and friction involving foreign residents in Japan. In the January 2002 report of the Welfare Working Group of the Social Security Council, the categories of people targeted for 'integration' were 'those suffering poverty and unemployment, those with disabilities, the homeless, etc.' This represents a broader use of the concept than that found in the Investigative Committee report, but it unquestionably remains more narrowly defined than the EU one. Interestingly, the Welfare Working Group report also drew attention to such 'means of social inclusion' as community businesses, 'social entrepreneurship' and local currencies in listing its basic objectives in promoting community welfare.

In the years around the turn of the millennium, poverty and social exclusion were more threatening problems for Japan than for Europe. An OECD report of March 2005, for example, ranked Japan third after Mexico and the US among 27 member countries by its composite measure of relative poverty among the entire population. The composite measure of relative poverty is the 'poverty rate' multiplied by the 'poverty gap'. The poverty rate is the percentage of the population falling below a poverty threshold (the poverty line) defined as 50 per cent of median equivalized disposable income. The extent to which the average income of the poor falls below the poverty line, on the other hand, measured as a proportion of the income at the poverty line, is the poverty gap. The composite measure of relative poverty thus measures the size of the income transfer needed to raise all those in poverty up to the poverty line as a proportion of total disposable income (OECD 2005b: 23).

When income inequality is measured by the Gini coefficient, Japan ranks 10th among 27 countries according to degree of inequality as of 2000. This shows that inequality widened during the 1990s. Not only the Northern European countries, but also the major Western European countries like Germany and France had a lower Gini coefficient than Japan, and were in that sense more equal societies (OECD 2005b: 23, 10). As we will see in Chapter 4, since the OECD report of 2005 a series of comparative studies have appeared analyzing income inequality and poverty in Japan, and also proposing policy options to address them.

Exclusion and extra-legality in the labour market

Poverty and social exclusion are, of course, not problems confined to the industrialized world. In their foreword to the Japanese edition (2005) of *Poverty and Exclusion in a Global World* (first published in 1999 with a second edition in 2004), A.S. Bhalla and Frédéric Lapeyre state that 'the phenomena of poverty and unemployment have become phenomena common to developed and developing countries alike for perhaps the first time since the 1930s' (Bhalla and Lapeyre 2005: iv).

Their point, strictly speaking, is not that the ways in which social exclusion manifests itself in the developed and developing countries would be the same. Bhalla and Lapeyre call attention to how the concept of social exclusion/inclusion has not only a distributional (economic) dimension concerning poverty, deprivation and income inequality, but also a relational (social) dimension comprising social isolation, apathy, crime and violence, and a political dimension concerning the denial of certain civil or political rights and active citizenship. They go on to point out that in societies where the degree of economic development measured by GDP per capita is low, the distributional dimension weighs more heavily than the relational one (Bhalla and Lapeyre 1999, 2004: 16–26).

In Continental Europe, social exclusion most prominently takes the form of structural unemployment. In the developing countries, on the other hand, sufferance of social exclusion by workers who are inside labour markets is not negligible either. A situation in which job opportunities are scarce can occur in any society, but only in a handful of developed welfare states are the conditions in place for a person to persist in a state of unemployment through drawing unemployment insurance benefits or public assistance. In labour markets where unemployment is kept from manifesting itself as complete joblessness, there will be a 'precarious segment' of workers, like those engaged in involuntary part-time work. Precarious job holders suffer short terms of employment, poor working conditions and partial or full exclusion from access to social security. At the same time, so-called discouraged workers (who are no longer counted as unemployed since they have exited the labour market either because they consider further job search futile or because they have been encouraged or forced to opt for early retirement) are too numerous to be overlooked (Bhalla and Lapeyre 1999, 2004: 59–60). This follows the logic of the evolution of the concept in France and coincides with Sen's concept of 'unfavorable inclusion' (Sen 2000).

Bhalla and Lapeyre thus effectively revise the EU concept of social exclusion to discuss informal and precarious employment in the developing world as a 'phenomenon which forms part of a broader notion of informality and extra-legality'. However, they do not elaborate on the details of extra-legality other than touch on 'the absence of formal property rights' (Bhalla and Lapeyre 1999, 2004: 171). And their gender perspective is weak overall.

In Japan, exclusion within labour markets is significant as well. This exclusion is all too often accompanied by extra-legality, such as illegal use of temporary workers, sub-minimum wages, unpaid overtime and evasion of social insurance obligations. Bhalla and Lapeyre point out that extra-legality has become the norm rather than the exception in most developing countries. There is no escaping the fact that social exclusion in the form of extra-legality is also spreading in Japan. My contention, as argued in more detail in Chapter 5, is that Japan's social security system has not only fallen into dysfunction, but has reached a state where it is actually functioning in reverse.

The functioning of livelihood security systems

How does this book conceive of the processes by which a livelihood security system and its subsystems *function*? The totality of the livelihood security system and its subsystems consist of policy measures that government or non-government actors put into effect directed toward livelihood security as a goal, as well as policies that generate livelihood security as a byproduct while pursuing other direct goals (such as profit maximization of an enterprise, for example). Policy processes or cycles of this kind are typically described as 'plan-do-see' (or 'plan-do-check-act'). Figure 2.2 models this cycle schematically.

The critiques of Esping-Andersen's typology mentioned in Chapter 1 included Deborah Mitchell's *Income Transfers in Ten Welfare States*. This pioneering research on comparative analysis of income transfer systems, such as taxation and social security, sought to shed light not only on the operation of income transfer systems in different welfare states, but centrally paid attention to their 'outcomes' as well, bringing the model of 'production of welfare' initially proposed by Hill

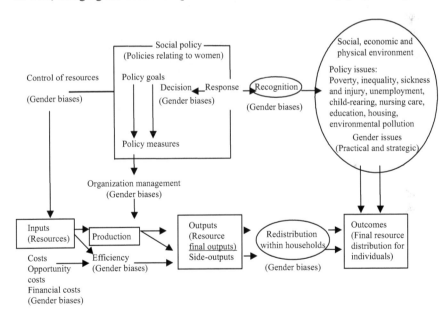

Figure 2.2 Comprehensive process model of gendering social policy
Source: Ōsawa (1996)

and Bramley to bear. Figure 2.2 is a revised version of her process model of 'welfare production'. In the welfare production model, a distinction is made between outputs and outcomes: *outputs* represent intermediate results whereas *outcomes* are 'welfare final outputs' (Mitchell 1993: 9–10, Figure 1.1). This conceptual distinction lacks in clarity. The distinction applied by Mitchell in her actual analysis, however, is clearer.

Based on her approach, Figure 2.2 has made the following amendments: (1) In the policy determination process, it minimally distinguishes the setting of *policy objectives* and the choosing of *policy measures* as separate factors. On this basis; (2) it differentiates *output* (product/result) as the degree to which policy measures are implemented, from *outcome* as the degree to which policy objectives are achieved; (3) Outputs that were not initially intended as policy objectives are indicated as 'side-outputs'; (4) Moreover, while Mitchell's analysis was based on the household as unit for data quality reasons, what matters are outcomes at the individual level. Figure 2.2 therefore indicates a process of resource redistribution within households, which interposes between outputs and outcomes; and (5) The gender biases that pervade the policy process in all of its aspects are entered into the picture.

The starting point in the process schematized by Figure 2.2 is recognition by governments and other policy actors of various livelihood security needs as policy issues (process initiation). Policy actors set clear objectives for fulfilment of these recognized needs and decide on adequate policy measures in light of them, together with the kinds and amounts of policy resources (such as budgets, personnel and authority) required to carry them through. This is the 'plan' phase. As noted previously, it must be kept in mind that needs are not limited to those recognized and voiced by those concerned. Even when needs are voiced, it is by no means uncommon for them to either be neglected as a policy issue, or to be inadequately addressed by policy objectives and measures chosen. What is more, gender bias lurks right through the policy cycle, beginning with the needs recognition stage. Thus, lack of employment opportunities for men, for example, may be held of grave concern while unemployment issues pertaining to women are brushed off.

In the 'see' or 'check' phase of the policy cycle, metrics such as efficiency, effectiveness and sustainability are employed. Effectiveness is measured by the degree to which policy outcomes conform to established objectives, and efficiency by the proportionality between policy resources inputted and outcomes achieved. However, if the objectives and measures chosen were inappropriate to begin with, effectiveness and efficiency are difficult to evaluate.

In order for the 'do' phase to be successful, the policy resources (budgets, personnel, authority, etc.) required by the selected objectives and measures must be inputted first. On the policy implementation side, the planning of policy actors must account for the behaviour of actors in the spheres of family life, the workplace, local communities and so on. The policy output must result in the intended objective, while unintended outputs (ripple effects and externalities) must be kept in check. This is the 'do' phase. In the 'act' phase improvements are made based on the findings of the 'check' phase.

If outcomes that contribute to the initial objectives are achieved without squandering or illegitimate diversion of resources at the point where outputs are realized (to be verified in the 'see' or 'check' phase), the process can be described as 'functioning'. If, on the other hand, due to shortcomings in various aspects of the process policy outcomes are poor compared to the envisioned objectives, the process is 'dysfunctioning'. But cases where unintended outputs lead to negative outcomes must also not be overlooked. When a state of affairs supposed to be ameliorated by social policy is exacerbated by it instead, the term 'reverse functioning' is more appropriate.

The notion of extra-legality laid out above can be expressed in terms of the policy cycle as follows: laws and regulations that policy actors have adopted and endeavour to implement are met by behaviours from actors in spheres such as the family, workplace or community, that not only fail to fall within the parameters set by the plan, but intentionally evade or violate existing laws and regulations.

In fact, just as measures towards achievement of more encompassing objectives are frequently at the same time policy objectives of more specific programmes or projects, policy objectives and measures combine into a policy system where higher-level objectives are linked to measures (lower-level objectives) and on to multiple additional layers of subordinate measures. It is also not unusual for the same programmes and projects to serve as measures for multiple contiguous yet distinct policy objectives. In some cases multiple programmes have synergy. But in others they may compete and their outcomes be at cross-purposes to each other. Furthermore, objectives and measures associated with a policy A that seem to have no relevance to a certain type of need B may yet promote or obstruct the fulfilment of the latter. In other words, consistency within a policy system and consistency among policies must be seen as a question of the function and dysfunction of the system as a whole. In recent literature on development economics, such consistency has been termed Policy Coherence for Development (PCD) and become established as a central concept (Kawai and Fukusaku 2006).

Structural components of Japan's rigid male breadwinner model

Let us now review the structural components of Japan's livelihood security system circa the 1980s based on the analytical framework laid out above. During this decade reforms were carried out in various social policy areas following the slogan of 'a Japanese-style welfare society'. Emblematic of these changes were the implementation of the Class 3 insurants scheme and the alteration of the surviving spouse pension system, which had undergone repeated changes already since the 1950s.

Labour market segmentation and divided social insurance schemes

Let us begin by considering the so-called 'Japanese-style employment practices' such as lifetime employment and seniority wages, pertaining to the relations of productions covered in quadrant (1) of Table 2.1. As we do so, the flip-side of these practices must be kept in mind. So-called lifetime employment and seniority wages apply only to male regular workers of large corporations and government agencies, but not to employees of SMEs or casual labourers. Moreover, even at large companies female employees are given only peripheral duties and paid low wages under the seniority system while young, and are expected to exit the workforce (upon getting married or having children) thereafter. The Japanese labour market has thus been segmented by gender and firm size. Gender-based disparities in employment protection and wage levels have been especially pronounced, with a concomitantly large gender gap in employment performance.

The gender bias in employment protection was most tellingly revealed in the wake of the first oil shock in 1973. At that time, sharp economic recession led to sharp job cutbacks. The size of Japan's female labour force dropped by 600,000 between 1974 and 1975, while the labour force participation rate of women fell by 2.5 per cent to a record low of 45.7 per cent. The male labour force, however, grew by 570,000 during the same time span, while the labour participation rate of men dropped by only 0.7 per cent. In contrast, the OECD calculated that in Europe and the US, women did not exit the work force at any greater rate than men (OECD 1976).

Second, the segmentation of Japan's social insurance system mirrors the segmentation of its labour market, which exhibits an uneven, vertically divided structure. 'Uneven' refers to the fact that benefit and contribution conditions vary from scheme to scheme, such that regular employees of large corporations bear lighter burdens while enjoying more robust benefits. It may be helpful to note here that one indicator used by Esping-Andersen for the conservative welfare regime was *corporatism*, identified by the degree to which social insurance (pensions in particular) is differentiated and segmented into distinct occupational- and status-based programmes.

Japan's social security system draws a first line of distinction between schemes for employees and schemes for those who are not, such as the self-employed and the non-employed. Social insurance coverage for employees consists of: (1) Workers' compensation insurance, which applies to all businesses that employ or hire workers and to all who receive pay from these businesses (thus excluding co-resident family members and domestic workers, but including contract workers provided they are required to work certain hours under the immediate direction of the business). Premiums are paid solely by the employer; (2) Employment insurance, which applies to businesses that employ workers and all workers so employed. This includes part-time workers who are expected to remain in the job for more than a year and have fixed working hours exceeding 20 hours per week; and (3) Employees' Health Insurance (EHI) and Employees' Pension Insurance (EPI) are both applicable to incorporated businesses that have one or more employees, and all sole proprietors with more than five employees, as well as workers employed by these businesses. It also applies to part time workers whose set working hours are three-quarters or more of a full-time worker.

However, the health insurance system is not uniform even with respect to employees. Employees of SMEs are under government-managed health insurance[6] while those of large companies have coverage managed by health insurance societies. (Civil servants and teachers are covered by mutual aid associations.) Under Employees' Pension Insurance (EPI), large companies and federations of companies may have their own Employees' Pension Funds (EPF), which maintain separate, independent balance sheets. Those insured by health insurance societies or Employees' Pension Funds are full-time employees of large companies, most of them men. Since the pension reform of 1985, insurants under the Employees' Pension Insurance scheme and of mutual aid associations have been classified as Class 2 insured persons under the National Pension (Basic Pension) Plan. Part-time workers whose set working hours amount to three-quarters or more of full time are covered by Employees' Health Insurance and EPI (in accordance with the so-called 'three-quarters standard'). Workers whose annual income exceeds 1.3 million yen, even if they do not meet the three-quarters standard, are classified as Class 1 insured persons under the National Pension Plan and must pay flat-rate contributions.

Self-employed people (business owners and their family workers), the non-employed and others are enrolled in National Health Insurance (NHI) with municipalities acting as the insurer for resident citizens. They are enrolled in the National Pension Plan and classified, since the 1985 pension reform, as Class 1 insured persons. However, dependent family members of insurants under Employees' Health Insurance receive EHI benefits, while dependent spouses of Class 2 insurants under the National Pension Plan are classified as Class 3 insured persons. To qualify as a dependent, the spouse's annual income must not exceed 1.3 million yen. The scheme of Class 3 insurants was introduced with the pension reform of 1985. Class 3 insurants receive the Basic Pension without having to make social insurance contributions, meaning that their share of contributions is jointly borne by all employees (Class 2 insurants), including those in single-member and dual-earner households. Ninety-nine per cent of Class 3 insurants are women.

It should be noted that the reforms of the 1980s, such as the establishment of the Health and Medical Service System for the Aged (1982) and the introduction of the Basic Pension scheme, also effected fiscal cross-subsidies between segmented social insurance schemes. But be that as it may, Japan's present predicament amply illustrates how far these reforms have veered from the path towards universalistic uniformity.

A pension system oriented toward male breadwinners

Third, the public pension system as one component of the social insurance system is systematically oriented toward male breadwinners. Since the 1985 reform, insurants have been segmented into Classes 1 through 3, with Class 2 serving as the standard. Those who are forced to drop out of Class 2 include workers who leave their jobs and those whose work hours have been reduced to below the three-quarter time cut-off. They must enrol themselves under Class 1, report as a dependent spouse under Class 3 or lose pension coverage entirely. In contrast, those eligible for Class 2 need not take any action as their employer files for them at the social insurance office local to their workplace. That is what makes Class 2 the standard.

Within Class 2, a couple that perfectly conforms to the male breadwinner model (with the husband continuously employed and enrolled in EPI for 40 years and the wife having zero years of EPI contribution history), will receive a 'model pension'. In such a case, the wife, as a dependent spouse of her husband, spent 40 years as a Class 3 insurant, never having had to pay contributions and yet receiving a full Basic Pension. The so-called pension benefit level, which was established for this model pension, is since the 1985 pension reform defined as the ratio of pension benefits, including the Basic Pension, to nominal household wage income. As we will see in Chapter 4 also in comparison to other countries, the benefit levels of dual-earner as well as single-member households fall below that of the 'model pension'.

As to Class 3 insurants, before the 1985 pension reform, the pension entitlement amount in EPI and mutual aid association pensions for a married couple belonged solely to the insurant (i.e. the husband). A dependent wife not in employment lacked a pension of her own unless she elected to enrol in the National Pension Plan. In the 1985 reform, every citizen of Japan became obligated on an individual basis to be enrolled in the newly introduced Basic Pension. For dependent wives of Class 2 insurants, the Basic Pension was listed in the wife's name (earning it the nickname of 'housewives' pension'). The 1985 pension reform thus did not only contribute to a strengthening of the male breadwinner model.

Still, the reform fell far short of making individuals the benefit-receiving unit. Wives of employees were classified as Class 3 insurants provided they were full-time housewives or worked only part time with an annual income falling below a set threshold. They were not required to pay premiums for the Basic Pension, but if a husband lost his status as an employee due to quitting the workforce or starting his own company, for example, his wife, despite having no substantial income of her own, would lose her Class 3 status and henceforth be required to pay premiums. In other words, a wife's treatment by the pension system was contingent on her husband's status. Also, the amount of the Basic Pension benefit, even with a full 40 years of enrolment, was not enough for an adequate standard of living. With fewer years of enrolment, the entitlement amount was even less, and 25 years was the minimum to draw any pension at all. The so-called 'housewives' pension' thus clearly did not constitute a move towards a work/life balance model. Rather, by designing the scheme such that a dependent housewife does not have to make pension contributions, it created an incentive for her, even if she did work, to keep her income below the threshold still allowing her to retain her status as a dependent. In short, it promoted part-time, low-wage work by married women.

The conditions for receiving surviving spouse pensions, on the other hand, stipulated non-uniformity in treatment of men and women in express terms. A survivors' Basic Pension can be drawn only by a *wife* (not a *spouse*) who is caring for the husband's children under the age of 18, or by the children themselves.[7] Those eligible for the surviving spouse EPI pension, in addition to those eligible for the survivors' Basic Pension, are (1) a wife with no minor children, (2) a husband, parent or grandparent age 55 or older or (3) a grandchild below the age of 18. But a 'wife' enjoys the highest priority and no age restrictions are set on her eligibility. In summary, the scheme assumes that the husband is a male breadwinner, his wife is his dependent, and that even if there are no minor children, she has low earning potential throughout her life. In few other countries can examples of this kind of differential treatment of men and women be found.

Between 1954 and 1965, a wife without minor children who was below the age of 40 at the time of her husband's death was not recognized as his survivor, and even those above age 40 had their benefits suspended until age 55 (Shakai hoshō shingikai nenkin bukai, 22nd Meeting, Material 1–2). The Director-General of the Ministry of Health and Welfare's Health Insurance Bureau told the Diet in 1954 that 'we expect those who can work, to work' (Tamiya 2003). In the early years of the rapid economic growth era, from the late 1950s through the early 1960s, when the gender gap for job opportunities and wages was much greater than it is today, the Japanese government's stance was that a bereaved wife without children should work rather than draw benefits.

This all changed in 1965, when the age restrictions on a wife's eligibility for survivor benefits were abolished, and the suspension of benefits until age 55 was eliminated. In the pension reforms of 1980, the government proposed a bill to exclude childless wives under age 40 from survivor benefits, but this provision was excised by the Diet. In the 1985 reforms, the Council recommended restricting the scope of survivor benefit eligibility (Tamiya 2003), but in the event, a 'supplemental benefit for widows of middle age and older' to be paid after age 40 to wives who met certain criteria, such as having been aged 35 or older at the time of her husband's death, was introduced. Those having short periods of enrolment as insurants were 'topped up' to benefit levels corresponding to 300 enrolment months (Shakai hoshō shingikai nenkin bukai, 22nd Meeting, Material 1–2). Between 1965, at the midpoint of the rapid growth era, and 1985, cumulative pension reforms increasingly accentuated the degree to which women, simply on account of having been bereaved of their husbands, were considered 'impotent' or 'unable to earn', even if they were still young and childless.

Entrenched subsidiarity

Fourth, the Livelihood Protection Scheme (public assistance) as the 'last resort' of a citizen's livelihood requires a closer look. As we saw in Chapter 1, Esping-Andersen listed the principle of subsidiarity among the defining features of a conservative welfare state. Among Japan's various systems, the Livelihood Protection Scheme is most clearly based on the principle of subsidiarity. Esping-Andersen uses the term 'subsidiarity' to refer to the principle that individuals' needs should be met first by their families, and that only if the family has no capacity to do so should the state intervene. The conservative ideal of the family strongly emphasizes the woman's role as wife and mother (Esping-Andersen 1990: 26–9). Japan's Livelihood Protection Law stipulates the principle that concerned individuals must first fully utilize their own assets, earning power and 'everything' else at their disposal, and second, draw on all available care and assistance from persons obligated by law to give it (i.e. relatives within three degrees of relational proximity), before its protections can be invoked.

Moreover, in the area of public assistance and social welfare, the 1980s saw Japan institute various reforms that strengthened family responsibility and private assistance, while tightening income restrictions on eligibility for government benefits. For example, from 1981 onward income restrictions for eligibility to receive child allowances were reinforced, and greater selectivity on livelihood protection, in the name of 'making it more appropriate', began to be imposed. In 1985, income restrictions were tightened even on child-rearing allowances intended mostly to serve lone mother households. Greater selectivity in livelihood security meant stricter review of eligibility when applying for assistance, which also impacted mainly lone mother households. This was prompted by the fact that the proportion of lone mother households receiving public assistance rose between the late 1970s and 1983, whereas it fell for all other types of households. At the same time, the Ministry of Health and Welfare's 'direction and oversight' of public assistance administration by prefectural and municipal authorities tightened its policy toward divorced lone mother households year by year. The rationale for this was to induce mothers to pursue alimony and child support from their former husbands and maximize their own earning potential. Moreover, there was a tendency to make exertions in this direction a prerequisite for even processing an application for assistance, as opposed to judging eligibility on the basis of an application submitted. Here was an example of subsidiarity pursued with zeal beyond the letter of the law (Ōsawa 1993: Chapter 4; Ōsawa 1999).

As will be detailed in subsequent chapters, under the Japanese-style welfare society policies of the 1980s, the slogan 'a firm foundation for families' was brandished about, but increased selectivity of public assistance and revisions to child-rearing allowances failed at the very least to provide a firm foundation for families that are lone mother households. It seems that the livelihoods of women when detached from the role of wife, even if they continue to undertake the role of mother, were deemed not to merit support in shoring up foundations of family livelihood. This official reinforcement of subsidiarity can only be pronounced a blatant bolstering of the male breadwinner model.

Fifth, let us consider government expenditures on welfare policy. Looking at the proportion of GDP spent on 'public social expenditure' according to the OECD definition, Japan in 1980 was fourth from the bottom at 10.6 per cent, with Turkey, Portugal and Greece trailing. The group of countries below OECD average 16.0 per cent included also Spain, Canada, Switzerland, the US and Australia.[8] On the revenue side, tax and social security burdens were low. In 1980, the proportion of GDP of these combined burdens (referred to as the 'national burden ratio' by the Japanese Ministry of Finance) was 25.4 per cent. Not only was this far below the figures in the 35–47 per cent range returned by the nations of Northern and Western Europe, it was even lower than the US figure of around 26 per cent (OECD 2007: 74).

Turning to the design of Japan's income tax system, the unit of taxation is the individual, but tax exemptions for dependent spouses and children or co-resident elderly and disabled relatives make it heavily influenced by family structure. When it comes to the tax and social insurance contribution burden, personal exemptions play as large a role as the formal unit. In the 1980s, a set of reforms was carried out under the slogan 'a firm foundation for families' in taxation as well. The statutory share in inheritance of a spouse was increased from one third to one-half in 1980 and the spousal deduction of income tax repeatedly raised in 1984, 1987, 1988 and 1989. A special spousal deduction and a special spousal exemption from gift tax were added in 1987 and 1985 respectively. Spouses already were the subject of a deduction enacted in 1961. With the addition of the spousal special deduction in 1987, the treatment of spouses has reached a point that can only be described as excessively favourable to male breadwinners. Setting the system aside, this also raises the question of the incidence of taxation on household budgets. In Chapter 4 we will review recent developments in this regard.

Sixth, let us take a look at how Japan's family-related policies and household budgets compare internationally. Walter Korpi conducted an international comparison of income transfers and services benefits in the latter part of the 1980s, and placed Japan in the group of countries where the lowest values for family formation and child-rearing, both for general and dual-earner households, are found (Korpi 2003: 147; Tokoro 2003).[9] Although tax deductions in Japan are significant in income transfers, child allowances are an order of magnitude smaller (Tsumura 2000; Kita 2004). Not only dual-earner households, but also those where only the husband works while the wife takes care of the children (0–2 years), receive little support.

How are these characteristics reflected in household budgets? Uzuhashi conducted a comparative analysis of the US, the UK, New Zealand, West Germany (distinguishing blue collar and white collar workers), Israel, South Korea and Taiwan for the years 1983–4. The results show that in Japan's employee households the share of household income earned by the male head of household in wages and salary was exceptionally high. In South Korea and Taiwan, gifts and remittances of money between households played an important role. The prominence of the male breadwinner is therefore not as pronounced as it is in Japan (Uzuhashi 1997: 44–50). Takuo Irokawa also conducted a comparative analysis of the US, Germany, Japan and South Korea in 1993, in which Japan's male breadwinner orientation again stands out. Germany and South Korea were notable for their diversity of income streams, social security benefits being prominent in Germany and 'other sources of income' in South Korea (Irokawa 2003).

In summary, the Japanese-style welfare society policies of the 1980s strengthened the grip of the male breadwinner model. In 1985, Japan adopted the Equal Employment Opportunity Law and ratified the Convention on the Elimination of All Forms of Discrimination Against Women (CEDAW), but the major vector of social policy continued to emphasize the family as opposed to the state, and particularly the role of women as agents of welfare provision, thus perpetuating the established structure that advantaged the employees and management of large corporations. On the other hand, if women assumed the tasks of housework, child-rearing, attending to the needs of their husbands and nursing care, while limiting their own employment to part-time work merely supplementing household income, they received welfare in the form of special treatment under the tax and pension

Table 2.2 Classification of relations of production of goods and services according to commoditization, the case of Japan

		Labour used	
		Commoditized (wage labour)	Non-commoditized (self-employed, family workers, slaves, domestic work)
Goods and services produced	Commoditized	(1) Firms for profit, market-oriented production by NPO employees **Male breadwinner orientation**	Family businesses, (3) members of workers' collectives, market-oriented production by slaves **Gender gap**
	Non-commoditized	Public sector, public services of NPO employees **Construction government, male breadwinner oriented welfare government** (2)	Domestic work (family members, domestic slaves) domestic consumption by family businesses, volunteer activities **Gender gap** (4)

schemes. As a result, since the 1990s Japan's livelihood security system has been even more rigidly locked in to the male breadwinner model than that of any other country (Ōsawa 2002: 106–10).

To anticipate somewhat, if Table 2.1 is brought to an analysis of Japan's livelihood security system, the result will be as shown in Table 2.2. The picture is that of a corporate-centred society, in which for-profit companies with employment practices oriented towards male breadwinners dominate and the government sector is orders of magnitude smaller than in comparable countries. At the same time, self-employed businesses as well as agriculture, fisheries and forestry continue to shrink, while the scale of the NPO sector is small. Household budgets are heavily dependent on the income of a male breadwinner, and unpaid labour such as child-rearing, nursing care, volunteer activities and the like – despite their relatively small scale in terms of aggregate time spent compared with time spent in paid work – poses a heavy burden on women, as these activities are almost exclusively shouldered by women.

3 The 1990s – Japan's lost decade

Locating Japan along the 'three routes' of welfare state transition

The typology of welfare states developed by Gøsta Esping-Andersen in *The Three Worlds of Welfare Capitalism* was based on cross-national comparisons circa 1980. But how did the countries studied by him adapt to 'post-industrialization' from the 1980s to the 1990s? In his introductory chapter to the edited volume *Welfare States in Transition: National Adaptations in Global Economies* of 1996, Esping-Andersen proposed to distinguish 'three routes' along which the countries belonging to each type continued to diverge in line with basic strategies followed.

The 'Scandinavian route', taken by the Nordic countries, consisted in a strategy of 'social investment' supporting employment of both men and women through family policy and vocational training. The 'neo-liberal route', followed by the Anglo-Saxon countries, pursued deregulation and increased selectivity of social policy. The 'conservative' nations of Continental Europe, finally, moved along a 'labour reduction' route resulting in a strengthened insider-outsider divide in the labour market and a decline in the overall employment rate (Esping-Andersen 1996: 10–20). 'Labour reduction', as I will detail further below, does not adequately characterize the situation of middle-aged and older male employees in Japan. The case of Japan, therefore, does not sit well with Esping-Andersen's 'three routes' of post-industrialization either.

According to Esping-Andersen, the 'route' that is most obviously faced with an impasse in coping with post-industrialization is the strategy of 'labour reduction' adopted by the 'familialist' Continental European nations representing the 'male breadwinner model' (Esping-Andersen 1996: 24).[1] This impasse has come about because a post-industrial economy and society confront labour markets and families with increased flexibility needs. From the vantage point of employers, what counts are wage flexibility (wage setting based on productivity and profitability), functional flexibility (greater adaptability to new technologies) and employment flexibility (ability to hire and fire as needed). From the perspective of the family and the individual, on the other hand, flexibility means the degree to which spouses can pursue careers while simultaneously fulfilling family obligations, in addition to a rising probability of family dissolution, as in the case of divorce, and of mid-career changes such as job loss, reschooling or change of occupation (Esping-Andersen 1996: 80).

The response of the male breadwinner model to post-industrialization has been to secure employment for men in their working prime by constricting job opportunities for young people and women and promoting early exit of middle-aged and older workers from the labour market. In short, this model has actually inhibited flexibility of the labour market while promoting labour reduction. Families have been forced to remain as dependent as ever on the income of a male breadwinner. As a result, the tax and social insurance contribution base has been constrained, raising the burden of tax and social insurance contribution per active worker in turn. Meanwhile, corporations seeking to escape the burden of the employer's share of social insurance contributions have increasingly avoided hiring additional full-time workers, thus spurring labour reduction further. Esping-Andersen describes this regime as a 'self-reinforcing negative spiral' with 'an inbuilt tendency to eat the very hand that feeds it'. Another side effect is extreme depression of the birth rate (Esping-Andersen 1996: 68, 78–80, 83).

In other words, in countries following the labour reduction route, young people and women are subject to exclusion both within and without the labour market, an outcome driven to a conspicuous extent by employers' desire to escape the burden of social insurance contributions.[2] Simultaneously, there has been a tendency to defer action on the 'new social risks', such as needs related to work-family balance and child-rearing or nursing care obligations, thus exacerbating fertility decline even further.

The Netherlands provides an instructive reference case for this kind of impasse. In the 1970s, the Dutch social security regime adhered to a typical male breadwinner model. But in 1982 a deal was reached between the government and labour and employer interest groups with the 'Accord of Wassenaar'. In its wake, the employment and welfare regime was restructured to create the 'Dutch model' in which husband and wife either both work part-time (the so-called 'fifty-fifty breadwinners' arrangement), or alternatively work the equivalent of one and a half full-time jobs between the two of them (a '1.5 breadwinners' arrangement) (Mizushima 2002; Mizushima 2006). Japan by contrast, as we saw in the previous chapter, took the opposite course: the 'Japanese-style welfare system' policies of the 1980s reinforced the male breadwinner model. But how did Japan fare during the 1990s?

To restate the fundamental outlook of this book: since the 1990s, despite monumental structural changes in the economy and society headlined by globalization and rapid demographic change toward an aging, low-fertility society, Japan's livelihood security system was not restructured, but continued to operate in its existing configuration. It thus had the opposite of its intended effect: it actually diminished the Japanese public's sense of security in their livelihood.

This is not to say that there were no efforts at reform in the 1990s. Politicians continually and vociferously called for 'reform'. When the Koizumi government entered office in April 2001, the need for restructuring the system founded on the male breadwinner model was echoed in the basic policy line of the cabinet, under such rallying phrases as 'structural reform for quality of life' and 'realization of a gender-equal society'.

As Section 2 of this chapter will show, the prevailing model of corporate practices and the features of Japan's corporate-centred society had already come under scrutiny during the early 1990s, well prior to the advent of the Koizumi government. Yet any awareness of the need to revisit the prevailing model of the family remained lacking. This oversight was exemplified by the Miyazawa cabinet's *Five-Year Plan for Building a Lifestyle Superpower*, which failed to recognize the need for reforms that would remodel Japan's livelihood security system. Even so, the problems entailed by a livelihood security regime based on the male breadwinner model were gradually brought to the fore, and by the mid-1990s a government advisory body worked out a proposal for 'forming a society with no gender-related prejudice', that became a plank in the 'Six Major Reforms' pursued by the Hashimoto cabinet.

Meanwhile, as we will see in Section 3 of this chapter, change was an undeniable reality for corporations and families. In the realm of corporate employment practices, we will trace major shifts towards performance-based compensation and promotion (*seikashugi* 成果主義) and non-regularization of the workforce (*hiseikika* 非正規化), i.e. more extensive use of part-time, temporary and other contingent workers as opposed to permanent, regular employees), and chart shifts in the burden of livelihood security expenditures based on changes in labour costs. With respect to families, on the other hand, we will consider changes in Japan's divorce system, consumer spending, and beliefs and behaviour related to the practices of family formation, that is, marriage and childbearing. The picture that will emerge is one of Japanese corporations shedding their role in livelihood security while individuals shy away from having children or even getting married out of trepidation at the excessive responsibilities that the institution of the family is expected to bear.

Clinging to the male breadwinner model: from *The Five-Year Plan for Building a Lifestyle Superpower* to Hashimoto's 'Six Major Reforms'

The Five-Year Plan for Building a Lifestyle Superpower *and the* Twenty-First Century Welfare Vision

Reconsideration of the corporate-centred society and inadequate policy responses

The administration of Kiichi Miyazawa took power on 5 November 1991. It turned out to be the last single-party LDP cabinet of the 20th century. In June 1992 the Miyazawa cabinet adopted an economic plan titled 'The Five-Year Plan for Building a Lifestyle Superpower: A Scenario for Japan's Coexistence with the Global Community'. The preface of this document stated the case for a shift away from 'giving priority to efficiency', towards 'paying greater attention to social justice' and 'creating a society that provides each individual with sufficient freedom and opportunity to fully express himself or herself'. In addition, various measures were proposed based on policy concepts such as 'respect for individuals', 'enrichment of the lives of ordinary people' and 'economic growth based on domestic demand' (Keizai-kikaku-chō 1992).

The use of key phrases such as 'respect for individuals' and 'enrichment of the lives of ordinary people' reflects a critique of Japanese society's 'corporate-centeredness'; i.e. an excessive orientation towards the needs of organizations, particularly large corporations, that tends to make Japan a society of 'company men'. These phrases were adopted at the start of the 1990s to symbolize reform.

By the time the Miyazawa cabinet's *Five-Year Plan* was rolled out in 1992, it had already become clear in the previous year that the bubble economy had burst. In August 1990, the First Gulf War was triggered by Iraq's invasion of Kuwait. This event heightened worries about the prospects of the Japanese economy, causing, on 1 October, the average stock price on the Tokyo Stock Exchange to fall below 20,000 yen. Moreover, in June 1991 a securities scandal came to light that involved major brokerages, including Nomura Securities and Nikkō Securities, compensating big customers for losses.

Amid this turmoil, in late 1991, a subcommittee of the National Lifestyle Council (*Kokumin seikatsu shingikai* 国民生活審議会) released an interim report entitled 'Toward a Society that Prioritizes Individual Life'. This document expressed surprisingly bold and sweeping criticisms of the corporate-centred society, considering that it originated from an advisory council for a government agency (the Economic Planning Agency). Its proposals included the following: companies should abolish sales and production quotas, increase overtime premium rates to reduce hours worked and scale back construction of company-provided housing that fosters a 'company man' mentality (Keizai-kikaku-chō 1991). Incidentally, the report also listed several aspects of what was meant by a 'company man' mentality, including 'a one-dimensional outlook that identifies success solely with rising up the ladder within the organization', unburdened by concern for law and ethics and with small regard for international problems and domestic social issues; long working hours and far-reaching commitment to the corporation causing 'organizational resource misallocation and inefficiency' and a 'warped family life', as exemplified by the detachment of the husband/father from the home; and far-reaching dependence on the company in every area of life, including housing and education (Keizai-kikaku-chō 1991).

Despite its evident awareness of the problems associated with Japan's corporate-centred society, in terms of concrete policy measures the *Five-Year Plan for Building a Lifestyle Superpower* offered grossly inadequate initiatives to reform the Japanese social model. Japan's livelihood security system is based on a male breadwinner model that depends heavily on corporations and the family. This is the flip-side of a corporate-centred society fostering a 'company man' mentality. There is no way to remedy corporate-centeredness without changing the model on which the livelihood security system is based. But no recognition of this key point is found in the *Five-Year Plan*. The Japanese male breadwinner model demands that the male head of household secure the income needed for household expenditures by maximizing his involvement in the market/company. Responsibility for the welfare and care of the family, on the other hand, must be fully borne by the woman. Under this social model, a minting of 'company men' is inescapable.

What concrete policies for livelihood security did the *Five-Year Plan* actually include? Its policy measures section opens with a chapter called 'Respect for Individuals'. The fourth section of that chapter, 'Ensuring a Safe and Reliable Life', proposes four policy measures. The first is to promote health and welfare facilities for the elderly while 'making the fees for accommodation in these institutions more reasonable and better balanced relative to the costs of supporting the aged in their own homes'. The second addresses public pensions, proposing 'to equalize the burdens borne by different generations' by raising premium rates and the benefit eligibility age by stages. The third measure aims to 'support self-help efforts' through encouraging more widespread adoption of corporate pensions and individual pension schemes. The fourth, finally, stipulates 'promotion of measures to achieve moderation of medical costs' and 'encouraging lifelong health and wellness'.

These initiatives in no way amount to an effort to break away from the male breadwinner model. The second and third policy measures would degrade conditions of public pensions on both the contribution and benefit sides, relatively reduce the scope of their protections, and expand the role of corporate pensions. Such narrowing of the guarantees offered by public pensions, unless coordinated with policies to eliminate gender differentials in 'employment performance' (i.e. in patterns of unemployment risk and income maintenance), would seriously threaten to expand the gender gap in income security for the aged. The *Five-Year Plan* did not evince awareness of the need to eliminate the gender gap in employment performance.

As for the first and fourth policies, they are fundamentally an extension of 1980s 'Japanese-style welfare society' policies, summed up in the mantra, 'from facilities to own homes, from free to charged services, from public responsibility to private initiative'. Moreover, the first policy means that to achieve a 'balance', since room, board and utilities expenses incurred in the course of receiving medical or nursing care at home (which later came to be called 'hotel costs') are borne by the individual (or his or her family), those receiving care in hospitals or senior care facilities would also be obligated to bear these costs themselves (Kōseishō 1985: Part 1, Ch. 2, Sec. 4, Item 2–2). With the revision of the Long-Term Care Insurance Law in 2005 and the passage of health-care reform legislation in 2006, this policy was in fact implemented. Adopting the above-mentioned policies to 'balance' and 'achieve moderation of costs' of medical care provision (in the absence of policies to also eliminate the gender gap in employment performance and significantly ease responsibilities for welfare and nursing care within the family) inevitably invites a drastic widening of the gender gap in welfare.

The *Five-Year Plan* actually expected that the Japanese family model would remain static as opposed to undergoing change, and 'properly maintain' functions such as providing a domestic retreat for its members, rearing and educating children, and caring for the ill and elderly (Keizai-kikaku-chō 1992: 15).

The social security vision of the early 1990s

In the first half of the 1990s, a series of future visions for social security and welfare were rolled out. One crucial event that took place during this period was the formation of a coalition government of eight non-LDP parties under Morihiro Hosokawa on 9 August 1993, bringing about the end of the so-called '1955 system' of LDP dominance. The Hosokawa administration focused its efforts on political reform: in particular the introduction of an electoral system for the Lower House combining single-member electoral districts (SMD) with proportional representation (PR). However, following the failure of his proposal for introducing a 'national welfare tax', Prime Minister Hosokawa resigned on 28 April 1994. He was succeeded by a minority government, due to the withdrawal of the JSP (later called the SDP) from the coalition, under Tsutomu Hata. This cabinet lasted until 30 June. A coalition of the LDP, JSP and New Party Sakigake under JSP leader Tomiichi Murayama as prime minister returned the LDP to power after less than a year. The non-LDP governments simply had too short a lifespan to enact a paradigm shift in social policy.

Nonetheless, it is noteworthy that the *Second Report of the Committee on the Future Image of Social Security* issued by the Prime Minister's Advisory Council on the Social Security System (*Shakai hoshō seido shingikai* 社会保障制度審議会; Chair: Mikio Sumiya) in early September 1994 explicitly stated that 'social institutions such as social security and the tax system ... that are premised on the configuration of the family that used to be standard, with the wife remaining in the home supported by the husband', were to be overhauled. It called for 'the existing social security system erected primarily with the male regular worker in mind' to be reconfigured, and for 'the benefit-receiving unit to be switched from the household to the individual wherever possible' (Shakai hoshō seido shingikai 1994: 6). As concrete examples for the switch to individuals as beneficiaries, the report called for a review of the survivor's pension scheme and raised the issue of splitting pension entitlement between spouses. Here we have the earliest example of a government advisory council advocating that Japan break away from the male breadwinner model.

But these statements by the Advisory Council on the Social Security System were not taken up by the consultative bodies of the Ministry of Health and Welfare. In late March 1994 the Ministry's Council on Welfare Vision for an Aged Society (*Kōrei shakai fukushi bijon kondankai* 高齢社会福祉ビジョン懇談会) issued a report entitled *21st Century Welfare Vision: Toward an Aged Society with Fewer Children*. Although it was formulated under the Hosokawa government, this report exhibited no sense of concern about the structure of social insurance in Japan. (Kōseishō 1994).

The *21st Century Welfare Vision* identified the need to restructure the social security system with an emphasis on welfare, defined as social services supporting nursing care and child-rearing. This emphasis on welfare was indicated, first of all, by the proposals for a 'New Gold Plan' and 'Angel Plan'. The New Gold Plan was supposed to effect a 'bold raise' in the benchmarks established by the original Gold Plan, which was the nickname for the 'Ten-Year Strategy for Health Care and

Welfare for the Elderly' of 1989. The New Gold Plan was adopted in December 1994 with the agreement of the three cabinet Ministers of Finance, Health and Welfare, and Home Affairs.

The Angel Plan, on the other hand, was conceived as a comprehensive plan for the 'social support of child-rearing'. Anticipating that the labour force participation rate for women in their years for childbearing and -rearing would rise to the 70 per cent range by the early 21st century (in 1994 it was in the 50 per cent range), the plan promised access to childcare services and crèches from infancy through the lower years of elementary school. In particular, it promised to beef up extended care covering the hours before and after the workday, and to provide more childcare facilities located along commuting routes and at workplace sites. This plan was agreed to by the Ministries of Education, Health and Welfare, Labour, and Construction, in December 1994.

Meanwhile, Japan's 1994 pension reform lifted the minimum age of pension benefit eligibility from 60 to 65 (to be gradually implemented by 2030). The standard for pension indexation was changed from nominal wages to net wages, i.e. wages after deduction of income tax and social security contributions. In the area of health insurance, the relevant laws were amended to promote in-home medical care. Taking its cue from these reforms, *21st Century Welfare Vision* proposed to shift the component of nursing care that had been covered by Health Insurance Schemes onto individuals and into the domain of welfare services with the introduction of 'long-term care insurance' as a new cost-sharing system. The overall concept of the *21st Century Welfare Vision* was to emphasize welfare services, controlling expenditures of pension and health care under the existing regimes, and at the same time expanding services for nursing care and child-rearing, as described above. Despite the expansion of nursing care services, the push for in-home medical care signalled that no real attempt was being made at 'de-familialization' in the sense of substantially reducing family obligations for providing child-rearing and nursing care for the aged and ill.

This is clear when we consider projected social security expenditures. The *21st Century Welfare Vision* forecast that social security benefits, which made up 16.3 per cent of national income in 1993, would reach the range of 28 per cent by 2025. (In 2025, senior citizens were projected to make up 26 per cent of the total population, up from 13 per cent in FY1992.) What standard of social security does this imply? In Part 2 of the *21st Century Welfare Vision*, figures are given which show that social security benefits in the former West Germany were equivalent to 28 per cent of national income as of 1989, when the aged composed 15.4 per cent of the West German population (Kōseishō 1993: 37, 145). In 2025, with the aged in the Japanese population making up a share 10 per cent greater than in the West German population in 1989, Japan would 'boldly' aim for social security benefits amounting to the same 28 per cent of national income. One cannot avoid being deeply concerned about the quality of life that this level of public expenditure would secure for anyone unable to afford private-sector welfare services.

In short, the policy path laid out by the *21st Century Welfare Vision* continued to conform to the male breadwinner model. If the Ministry of Health and Welfare's

Council on Welfare Vision for an Aged Society had adopted the recommendations arising from the analysis in the *Second Report of the Committee on the Future Image of Social Security*, it would have seized this opportunity to make a break with the male breadwinner model. But the chance was missed.

Hashimoto's Six Major Reforms and the Vision of Gender Equality

The Vision of Gender Equality *as the key to structural reform*

Ryūtaro Hashimoto served as Prime Minister from 11 January 1996 to 30 July 1998, and embarked on the so-called 'Six Major Reforms' consisting of administrative reform, structural reforms of the fiscal, economic and social security systems, financial system reform and educational reform. In addition, Hashimoto proclaimed that 'the realization of a gender-equal society' was a 'key' and a 'pillar' of such structural reforms in Japan. By the time of the mid-1990s, the Japanese government under Hashimoto was thus cognizant of the need for reforming the male breadwinner model of the corporation and the family, and the policy regimes predicated upon it. The question then is to what extent was this awareness translated into meaningful policy objectives and enacted in the form of policy measures consistent with them?

First of all, we must consider what Hashimoto meant in designating the 'realization of a gender-equal society' as a 'key' and 'pillar' of structural reforms. In July 1996, the Council for Gender Equality, chaired by Yōko Nuita, submitted to Prime Minister Hashimoto its 'Vision of Gender Equality'. This document offered a 'view sensitive to gender as a social and cultural construct', and placed at the top of its policy recommendations a group of measures bearing the heading 'Forming a Society with No Gender-related Prejudice'. Concerning that policy objective, the *Vision of Gender Equality* states that

> 'it is necessary not only to correct, from a perspective of gender equality, the systems and customs that have been premised on fixed role divisions between women and men, but also to replace the household with the individual as the conceptual unit embedded in various practices and systems, and on this basis establish a social framework that will operate neutrally with respect to whatever living arrangements the individual chooses'

In other words, it advocated the abolition of the male breadwinner model.

The concrete measures proposed by the *Vision of Gender Equality* were as follows: (1) to amend the Civil Code as soon as possible to allow married couples the option of retaining separate family names; (2) to identify and bring into alignment with a gender-equal society various areas of gender inequality, such as treatment of spouses under the tax code, treatment of dependent spouses of employees under the National Pension Scheme (so-called 'Class 3 insured' persons), survivors' pensions and splitting of pension rights between husband and wife, dependent spouses under the Employees Health Insurance scheme, spousal allowances paid by companies for employees, and others; and (3) to revise any customary practices that may contribute to gender prejudices (Council for Gender Equality 1996[3]).

Part 1 of the *Vision of Gender Equality* states: 'If traditional concepts of work, family and the community are left as they are, despite the socioeconomic changes taking place, things will get worse than they currently are and might even lead to massive social costs' (Council for Gender Equality 1996).[4] In other words, it was delivering a warning that if Japan persists in its male breadwinner model-based regime, the country's economy and society will plunge into dire straits.

In September 1995, the UN held its Fourth World Conference on Women in Beijing, where a Platform for Action was adopted calling for 'gender main-streaming'. Gender main-streaming is defined as analyzing all policies and policy measures from the initial proposal stage to evaluate their effects on women and men, and ensure they reflect the agenda of gender equality (Paragraphs 202, 204). The *Vision of Gender Equality*, submitted in the summer of 1996, placed 'Forming a Society with No Gender-related Prejudice' at the top of its policy outline, echoing the Beijing Declaration of the World Conference on Women.

The 1995 recommendation of the Prime Minister's Advisory Council on the Social Security System

Let us now consider the stance taken by other government advisory councils toward the male breadwinner model-based livelihood security system. The recommendation *Toward a Twenty-first Century Society Where People Can Live with a Sense of Security: Recommendation for Reconstruction of the Social Security System* issued by the Prime Minister's Advisory Council on the Social Security System on 4 July 1995 provides a good example. This recommendation reiterated the importance of restructuring Japan's social security system on the basis of gender equality. In the section, 'Social Security and the Economy', it addressed the overall picture of how social security costs are borne, including what it called the 'shadow burden', with the following words:

> Costs to stabilize citizens' lives have to be eventually borne by someone. Even if the public burden for social insurance or taxation, for example, was increased, if the social security system is thereby strengthened, there will be a decrease in the burden on individuals (including user payments for medical treatment or welfare services, private insurance premiums, or maintenance, care and child-rearing borne by family members) and in the burden of fringe benefits on companies. Conversely, if the public burden were to be reduced, the burden on individuals and companies would increase.
> (Shakai hoshō seido shingikai 1995: 8–9)

Since the latter part of the 1970s, the Japanese government, led by the Ministry of Finance, had affixed the label 'national burden' to the sum of social security contributions and taxes; the ratio of this sum to national income was called the 'national burden ratio'. The bureaucracy was constantly sounding the alarm that having a stronger social security system, which it labelled 'high-welfare', would unavoidably entail a 'high burden', and thus lead to loss of economic vitality. The highest policy priority became preventing the national burden ratio from reaching 50 per cent – even though Japan faced the prospect of having one of the world's oldest populations by the first half of the 21st century.

It was this stance that was subjected to critique in the Advisory Council's recommendation of 1995. The latter redefined social insurance contributions and taxes as a 'public' rather than a 'national burden', pointing out that the 'public burden' constituted only a portion of the expenditures necessary to assure acceptable living standards for the Japanese populace. The proper definition of the 'burden on the nation', according to the Advisory Council, includes not only the public but also the private (corporate and individual) burden. The public burden and private burden are held to exhibit an inverse relationship: when the public burden is high, the private burden (on both individuals and corporations) is small.[5] The 1995 recommendation also states that 'It is simply not feasible to dictate a numerical target for the public burden in advance, divorced from a consideration of benefit levels.' As an *Asahi Shinbun* editorial noted at the time, 'This gives cause to re-evaluate the course followed by the government since the Report of the Provisional Commission for Administrative Reform 12 years ago.'

Following the route of simply limiting the national burden ratio amounts to ignoring the fact that individuals and corporations are then forced to bear the costs of sustaining and stabilizing living standards through other mechanisms than taxation and social security contributions. Most ignored were burdens that are not in the form of cash payments. In contrast, the 1995 report addressed not only monetary burdens but also 'the family burden of maintaining, caring and child-rearing'. 'Maintaining' also encompasses the burden of cash outlays for living expenses (economic provision), but a substantial component of this burden is domestic tasks of actually supplying, feeding and clothing family members (functional provision). The functional provision element of the 'family burden of maintaining, caring and child-rearing' overwhelmingly falls on women, who carry out these tasks without any monetary compensation. The route of 'limiting the national burden ratio' breezes by this dimension of the issue without a glance. Against this, the 1995 recommendation of the Advisory Council on the Social Security System called, at least implicitly, for a paradigm shift.

Toward the establishment of the Long-Term Care Insurance Law

The general election held in October 1996 resulted in the formation of the second Hashimoto cabinet, the first government to consist solely of LDP members since the advent of the Hosokawa government three years and three months before. (There was an extra-cabinet coalition with the Social Democratic Party of Japan and the New Party Sakigake, to be sure.) After forming his cabinet, the Prime Minister launched his 'Six Major Reforms'. How were the 1995 recommendation of the Advisory Council on the Social Security System and the *Vision of Gender Equality* reflected in the social security structural reform component of this plan? What the Hashimoto administration actually legislated were the long-term care insurance system (passed into law in December 1997 and effective from April 2000) and a partial revision of the Child Welfare Act (June 1997) with the aim of countering the falling birth rate. The 1998 *White Paper on Health and Welfare* identified the policy challenge for social security structural reform as 'maintaining the vitality of society and economy' in the face of growing social security expenditures entailed by an aging society with fewer children. To this end, the white paper noted, 'steps should be taken to make the social security benefits and premiums more efficient and rational' (Koseishō 1998: 227). In other words, the framework for policy choice was regarded as a trade-off between increasing social security expenditures due to an aging, low-fertility society and the maintenance of socio-economic vitality.

Meanwhile, the chairpersons of eight advisory councils related to social security convened and, in November 1996, issued an interim report titled 'Direction of Social Security Structural Reform'. In it, the Ministry of Health and Welfare invoked with particular emphasis the target of 'keeping the national burden ratio below 50 per cent at the peak of population aging' as a benchmark of structural reform. Constraints were also imposed on social security by the Law of Fiscal Structure Reform (enacted on 28 November 1997), which assigned top priority to fiscal reconstruction. (Under this law, the national burden ratio including the fiscal deficit, a new definition, must remain below 50 per cent.) As we saw above, the 1995 recommendation of the Advisory Council on the Social Security System had drawn attention to the inconsistencies of a policy route guided by capping the national burden ratio, but a change of chairpersons (from Mikio Sumiya to Kenichi Miyazawa in September 1995) and the step of bringing together the eight social security advisory council chairs led to this point in the 1995 recommendation being entirely ignored.

Fiscal reconstruction itself was subsequently shelved. For FY1997, the Hashimoto government raised the consumption tax rate from 3 per cent to 5 per cent, raised the user payment for those insured by health insurance from 10 per cent to 20 per cent,[6] and revoked a special tax cut. These measures raised the national burden by a total of 9 trillion yen. In the summer of 1997, the plunge of the Thai baht touched off the Asian currency crisis. Towards the end of the year, Japan's economy experienced an abrupt slowdown, and financial institutions including Yamaichi Securities, Sanyō Securities, Hokkaidō Takushoku Bank and Tokuyō Bank failed (went bankrupt, voluntarily closed their doors or had their operations acquired by other firms). In response, the Hashimoto government in March 1998 revised the Law of Fiscal Structure Reform, and in April released 16 trillion yen through a comprehensive economic stimulus plan. Ultimately, the LDP suffered a crushing defeat in the Upper House election of July 1998, and Hashimoto resigned as Prime Minister to be replaced by Keizō Obuchi and his cabinet. Obuchi suspended the fiscal reconstruction initiative, vigorously pushing through financial stabilization and economic stimulus measures instead. Even so, social security structural reform remained entangled with the goal of keeping the national burden ratio, including the fiscal deficit, below 50 per cent.

Let us examine the Hashimoto reforms in more detail, starting with long-term nursing care for the elderly, which was considered 'step one' of social security structural reform. In its 1998 *White Paper on Health and Welfare*, the Ministry of Health and Welfare stated that women having to change jobs, quit jobs or take time off work to care for elderly or ailing relatives represented a 'great loss' to 'society as a whole' and a 'major impediment to women's employment'. This is evidence that the Ministry had an appropriate awareness of the problem's seriousness (Kōseishō 1998: 235–6).

In July 1995, an interest group called the Women's Association for a Better Aging Society (Kōrei shakai o yoku suru josei no kai 高齢社会をよくする女性の会), chaired by Keiko Higuchi, presented two demands to the Council on Health and Welfare for the Elderly (*Rōjin hoken fukushi shingikai* 老人保健福祉審議会): first, that the long-term care insurance system make individuals rather than households the the unit of the system; and second, that it primarily provide services rather than cash benefits (Kōrei shakai o yoku suru josei no kai 1995). The intention behind these demands was to forestall any tendency by the governmental institutions responsible for implementing the policy from relying one-sidedly on cash benefits, while neglecting to develop the infrastructure to deliver nursing care services – an outcome which would further tie down women to care giving duties at home in exchange for only a nominal cash benefit.

The Long-Term Care Insurance Act as passed into law did not, in the end, adopt the cash benefit approach, providing benefits in the form of a graded system of authorized care services with cash value equivalents instead. This outcome was a victory for the Women's Group for a Better Aging Society. On the other hand, on the matter of designating units of the system, the law established a category called 'Class 2 insured' persons made up of those above the age of 40 and under 65. Class 2 insured persons who are dependent family members of an employee are covered by long-term care insurance without having to pay insurance contributions up to age 65. Although the assumption is that few people in this class will actually draw benefits, it is nevertheless in principle an extension and expansion of the gender bias embedded in the designation of the household as the unit of the system.

Dealing with declining fertility

Concerns over Japan's falling birth rate were also addressed by the *White Paper on Health and Welfare* for 1998, which was highly covered by the media. Part 1 of this document presented as its major policy objective the creation of a 'society where men and women can treasure the dream of living together and bringing up children'. Part 2, however, which addressed structural reform of the social security system, was less clear in the way it approached the problem of declining fertility and on countermeasures to be taken. It thus is questionable what degree of consistency between the *White Paper*'s first and second parts had been sought to begin with.

The policy objective offered in Part 1 of the *White Paper* took its cue from a report titled *Basic Thoughts on the Declining Birth Rate* issued by the Council for Population Problems (*Jinkō mondai shingikai* 人口問題審議会) in October 1997. According to this report, the main factor behind the falling birth rate was an increase in the proportion of never-married people in the population. To address this, it suggested that 'correction of stereotyped gender roles and employment practices and provision of support to increase the compatibility of childcare and working' would emerge as 'key'. The 'fundamental way of dealing with the problem', the report went on to suggest, was 'above all' 'creating a new employment environment in which the barriers by gender and age are removed' (Jinkō mondai shingikai 1997: 24). In other words, it argued that moving beyond the male breadwinner model was key to dealing with Japan's declining fertility. The assessment of the policy challenge presented in *Basic Thoughts on the Declining Birth Rate*, then, was accurate. But what policy instruments did the White Paper propose to deal with this challenge?

One proposed policy instrument was described as an increase in 'community-level assistance for childcare' to open the doors to 'a wider choice of childcare and other services offered either by public services or private corporations' (Kōseishō 1998: 222). This was instituted via the partial revision of the Child Welfare Act and related laws in FY1997. Key provisions of the revamped childcare system were the abolition of the placement system, under which children were assigned to childcare facilities by municipal authorities, and its replacement by a system allowing parents or guardians to choose their own preferred facilities. In addition, the existing method of determining childcare fees based on household income (an ability-to-pay basis) was revised to reflect childcare service costs, based on factors such as the age of the child (a pay-for-services-rendered basis). Concomitant with the revision of the law, it was planned that all childcare facilities should be upgraded to accommodate infants, while facilities should be given the freedom to offer extended hours and drop-in care at their own discretion, and permitted more flexibility in setting the number of children they will admit and standard operating hours (Kōseishō 1998: 156).

To what extent did these changes to the system bring about the desired policy outcomes, as expressed in the policy objectives described above? In order for there to be choice in childcare services, there must be adequate provision of those services. But many areas of Japan suffered from an absolute shortage of childcare facilities, as had been pointed out from the moment the revisions to the law were enacted. Without an infrastructure in place capable of providing public childcare services of sufficient quantity and quality at a reasonable price, deregulation and enhanced flexibility alone could hardly be expected to bring genuine choice in day-care or nursing care services. In fact, the waiting lists for places in childcare facilities subsequently failed to shorten, prompting the Koizumi cabinet to announce, in June 2001, its 'zero-waiting list strategy' for childcare facilities.

The 1998 *White Paper on Health and Welfare* considered Japan to be a society where men and women were 'unable to treasure the dream of living together and bringing up children'. Yet it must also be pointed out that this document lacked serious reflection on the role of national government policy in bringing this state about. For this reason, the impetus for policy change contained in it remained weak. Indeed, Part 1 of the *White Paper* devotes four pages to the question of whether a system of eligibility for benefits on an individual, rather than household basis should be introduced. But despite its acknowledgement that the present system 'is strongly household-oriented' and 'without doubt has various problems', the text limits itself to listing pros and cons and to calling for a national dialogue on the matter. This is emblematic of how the task of breaking away from the male breadwinner model failed to be accorded the required urgency in the context of social security structural reform.

The introduction of long-term care insurance and the Basic Law for a Gender-Equal Society

Ultimately, the centrepiece of social security reform during the 1990s was the Long-Term Care Insurance Law, passed in 1997 and implemented in April 2000. Ito Peng, who compared trends in social policy in Japan and South Korea in the 1990s, has emphasized that in Japan an 'expansion in social welfare spending' could be seen. On these grounds she argued that Japan's approach to welfare had departed from an East Asian 'productivist' or 'developmental state' welfare model. According to Peng, Japan's social security expenditures as a percentage of GDP nearly doubled during the 1990s, and total expenditures on 'social care' doubled as well (Peng 2004: 401, 416–17). However, even in the statistics that Peng cites, social security benefit outlays as a share of GDP rose only from 10.8 per cent to 15.2 per cent, which can hardly be described as 'doubling'.

Looking back further, the ratio of social security expenditures to GDP had also risen by 5 percentage points in the 1970s, but only 1.5 percentage points in the 1980s. Moreover, these statistics divide social security benefit expenditures into three categories: pensions, healthcare and other social welfare spending. Lumped in under 'other social welfare spending' are unemployment benefits paid by employment insurance and temporary disability benefits paid by workers' accident compensation insurance (in addition to expenditures on social welfare services, long-term care, various forms of public assistance excluding medical assistance, child allowances and other miscellaneous allowances, and accident and illness allowances covered under health insurance). This 'other social welfare spending' category was stuck at only 11 per cent of total social security benefit expenditures through the 1990s, jumping to 14 per cent only in 2000. The 2000 uptick in the share going to 'other social welfare spending' was due to a drop in medical outlays and the implementation of the Long-Term Care Insurance Law (National Institute for Population and Social Security Research 2001; 2002).

Its shortcomings notwithstanding, the introduction of a public long-term care insurance scheme was a step away from reliance on unpaid care work within the family by women and toward socialization of this burden. In this sense, it can be seen as 'de-familialization'. However, in the second half of FY1999, the ruling parties pushed through an 18-month exemption from premiums for Class 1 insured persons aged 65 and over. Considering that the long-term care insurance scheme had been trumpeted as bringing about a 'clear-cut relationship between benefits and premiums', this policy intervention amounted to an abandonment of the core principle of the reform at the point of its implementation. One politician involved in this revision was Shizuka Kamei, chairman of the LDP's Policy Affairs Research Council (PARC), who commented that a public long-term care insurance scheme could come at the expense of 'Japan's beautiful tradition of children taking care of their parents' (Japan Times, 5 November 1999: 3). This can only be described a repudiation of any regime that supports work/life balance and de-familialization. Although Hashimoto's Six Major Reforms certainly included elements for gender equality, they fell far short of being advanced consistently throughout the entire reform process.

Even so, it is important not to discount that in 1999 the Basic Law for a Gender-equal Society was passed, enshrining in law 'non-discrimination on the basis of gender' as a fundamental principle. This law sets out 'not only to correct from a perspective of gender equality the systems and customs that have been premised on fixed role divisions between women and men but also to shift the household-based thinking remaining in the systems and customs to individual-based thinking, establishing a social framework that will function neutrally whichever way of life the individual chooses' (Article 4), and calls for work/life balance on the basis of shared responsibilities among family members and 'social support' (Article 6). The adoption of these principles meant that a basic law of the land in Japan now endorsed gender-neutrality, rather than a social system built on the male breadwinner model, putting its weight behind work/family balance.

In summary, the path followed by Japanese social policy in the 1990s veered between the three routes identified by Esping-Andersen: it coincided with the work/life balance (Scandinavian) route in supporting employment for men and women and socializing long-term care; the market-oriented (neoliberal) route with respect to labour market deregulation; and the male/breadwinner (conservative) route with respect to an increasing dualism of the labour market as the advance of non-regularization in employment affected mostly young people and women. The 1990s thus turned out a 'lost decade' in social policy as well.

The restructuring of employment and marriage

Restructuring of employment

Nikkeiren's proposals and the shift to performance-based employment practices

As restructuring of Japan's social policy kept being postponed, important changes were occurring in the key subsystems of livelihood security: the corporation and the family. Let us begin by considering the changes in the employment regime during the 1990s.

First, from the early 1990s onward, public laments bewailing a 'collapse of Japanese-style employment practices' and 'the end of lifetime employment' were ubiquitous. In the mid-1990s, the Japan Federation of Employers' Associations (Nikkeiren) issued a series of reports including the *Interim Report of the Research Project on New Japanese-Style Management Systems and Practices* and *Japanese-Style Management in the New Age*. These documents broadcast a call for the restructuring of Japanese-style employment and Japanese-style management. According to Nikkeiren, lifetime employment and the seniority wage system had once been effective practices, both during the period of high economic growth and, since the mid-1970s, in a period of relatively low growth. But the reports concluded that these systems now needed an overhaul because of the rapidly changing business environment in Japan.

Nikkeiren presented a vision of 'multi-tracking' employees into three groups in the future. The first group was dubbed 'long-term accumulated ability utilization-type' employees, representing a reformulation of traditional long-term employment. The second group of 'advanced specialist ability utilization-type' employees, on the other hand, would include workers possessing specialized training and abilities in various fields, who are not necessarily employed long-term. The third group, labelled 'flexible employment type', would encompass temporary workers dispatched as the labour needs of companies dictated, to handle a range of tasks from routine to highly specialized duties. From the employee side as well, this category could range from by-employment to temporary provision of special skills. The multi-tracking proposal did not stop at defining these three groups, however. Even within the 'long-term accumulated ability utilization-type' employees, the proposal called for multi-tracking of promotions, and for assignments and compensation based on ability and performance. Wages would rise with seniority only up to a certain level of qualifications, and beyond that level a compensation scheme based purely on a competence rank system or annual salary system would come into play, with the intention of widening pay differentials based on actual job performance and outcomes delivered (Nihon keieisha dantai renmei (Nikkeiren) 1994; Nihon keieisha dantai renmei (Nikkeiren) 1995).

Looking at overall employment patterns in Japan at that time, however, multi-tracking, diversification and fluidization would appear much better suited as terms to describe the existing system than indicate a model for the future. After all, classic Japanese-style employment practices had pertained only to regular employees in large corporations and in the public sector to start with. This overwhelmingly male group never composed more than 20 per cent of the total workforce. In the early 1990s, it was calculated that it accounted for around 12 million out of a labour force of 50 million (Takanashi 1994: 21). Even among the full-time employees of large corporations, women were typically employed for only several years while still 'young and fresh'. They were also not included in lifetime employment and seniority wage systems. Neither, needless to say, were employees of SMEs, day labourers and part-timers.

The point of explicitly calling for multi-tracking, diversification and fluidization of employment practices in the early 1990s then was solely to further differentiate among the minority of already privileged male regular employees of large companies. The seniority wage system increased wages on the basis of age and tenure, ostensibly for the purpose of enabling male workers to meet the needs of supporting their wives and children through the life cycle. If men participating in the seniority wage system, in other words, male breadwinners were to become the exception rather than the norm, this would inevitably impose changes in patterns of life and employment on women and young people as well as men in their working prime. Companies employing women and young people at wages below the subsistence level would no longer be able to justify this practice on the basis of their traditional excuse that these categories of worker were dependents supported by a male breadwinner. There is no evidence that Nikkeiren or other encompassing interest organizations representing corporate management realized this contradiction.

In line with Nikkeiren's proposals, the seniority system in pay and other treatment in Japan was subsequently weakened. In other words, there has been a shift towards performance-based evaluation.[7] The 2002 *White Paper on Welfare and Labour* analyzed male employment and found that the age-wage profile, which represents the relationship between age bracket and wage level, has been flattening out. On a cohort basis, between older groups and the group born in 1951–5, its slope levels out abruptly (Kōsei-rōdō-shō 2002: Figure 2.1–5). In other words, men of Japan's 'baby boom' generation who were born between 1947 and 1949 were able to slip into the group of cohorts enjoying a favourable age-wage profile, but younger generations were not.

However, in the 1990s it became clear that nominal wages, especially for men of middle-age and above, were exhibiting downward rigidity, and it was argued that the flattening trend of age-wage profiles 'was brought to a halt' (Hattori and Maeda 2000: 5). Nakashima, Matsushige and Umezaki analyzed micro data from a firm that introduced a performance-based wage system in 1995. Their results show that, contrary to the intentions behind the system's introduction, by 2000 the effects of seniority on wages among middle management-level employees had actually increased, but their wage dispersion had narrowed. (Among one section of workers in their late twenties and late thirties it had widened.) The narrowing of wage dispersion was especially prominent for workers in their forties and older (Nakashima, Matsushige and Umezaki 2004). Despite the advocacy of Nikkeiren and others, the shift to performance-based pay and promotion did not automatically dismantle the seniority system and expand wage differentials among middle-aged and older workers. Still, according to Keisuke Nakamura, the introduction of performance-based pay is gradually eroding seniority-based wages in the higher management ranks. The seniority wage system, in that case, is meritocratic in the sense that it is based on appreciation of the job performance potential of employees (Nakamura 2006).

The various types of company benefits were not exempt from change either. According to the results of the *General Survey on Working Conditions* (formerly the *General Survey on Wages and Working Hours Systems*), the proportion of companies providing family/dependent allowances, housing allowances and other livelihood support rose through 1996, but from 1997 through 1999, family/dependent allowances fell. Among companies with 1,000 or more employees, the decline was from 91.4 per cent in 1996 to 79.6 per cent in 1999. Housing allowances rose

1.5 per cent across all firm sizes, but once again declined among those with 1,000 or more employees: from 67.0 per cent in 1996 to 56.5 per cent in 1999 (Rōdōshō seisaku chōsabu 1997: 40; Rōdōshō seisaku chōsabu 2000: 35).

What kinds of family allowances were most widely offered by companies? As of 1997, among companies offering such benefits, 76.6 per cent offered a spousal allowance, making it the most widespread benefit; 63.0 per cent offered an allowance for children under the age of 18; and 35.8 per cent offered an allowance for children over the age of 18 but still in education. At 49.9 per cent of the companies offering a spousal allowance, there was an eligibility ceiling on the spouse's income, in the majority of cases that ceiling being the same as that for tax exemption and spousal deduction purposes: 1.03 million yen (Rōdōshō seisaku chōsabu 1998: 25–6). Moreover, according to a fall 2001 study by the Council for Gender Equality of the Cabinet Office, among listed companies with a system of providing family allowances, 61.5 per cent limit the benefit based on the spouse's income, with 78.4 per cent of them applying the 1.03 million-yen ceiling (Danjo kyōdō sankaku kaigi eikyō chōsa senmon chōsakai 2002: 14). The system of corporate family allowances propped up the male breadwinner model, and these benefits were particularly generous at big corporations. But in the latter part of the 1990s, there was a conspicuous retrenchment.

On the other hand, there was little change evident in long-term employment. As tenure of employment grew among male workers aged 50 and over, against the backdrop of rising designated retirement ages, it dropped among young male workers (Kosei rōdō-shō 2002: Figure 2.1–10). Here we see the importance of cohort factors among middle-aged and older versus younger workers. In other words, men of Japan's baby boom generation ('block generation') born immediately after the end of the World War II were able to slip into a demographic bracket with a favourable age-wage profile and enjoy long employment tenures, but younger generations were confronted with faint hope that their wages would rise with seniority, and their average job tenure has been shrinking.

Non-regularization of the workforce and the gap in employment conditions

Employment of non-regular workers, including part-time and temporary employees, has continued to expand without any rectification of their employment conditions. Let us review the trend in the ratio of non-regular workers to all workers (excluding executive officers) according to the Detailed Tabulation of the *Labour Force Survey*. Among women, the proportion of non-regular workers rose from 32.1 per cent in February 1985 to 46.4 per cent in February 2002; by the first quarter of 2008, it had reached 54.2 per cent. Over the same time span, the figure among men went up from 7.4 per cent, to 11.7 per cent and finally to 18.7 per cent. By age bracket, as Figure 3.1 shows, after 1990 women aged 20–4 and 45-plus experienced a leap in the prevalence of non-regular work. Among men, by contrast, there was no striking shift toward non-regular work until the mid-1990s. But since then it became increasingly prevalent among younger age brackets (Figure 3.2).[8]

The 1990s – Japan's lost decade 73

As the ratio of part-time workers rose, so did the number of cases of workers who took part-time work not of their own accord, but because they had no other option. Moreover, the gap in wages between full-timers and part-timers grew. Normalizing hourly wages for full-time workers of each gender to 100, at the start of the 1990s hourly wages for part-timers were 72.0 for women and 57.8 for men. By 2003,

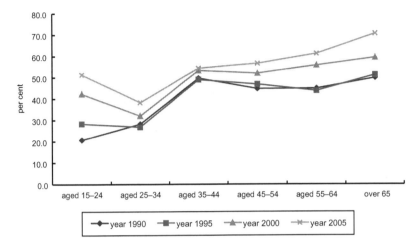

Figure 3.1 Proportion of non-regular employees, female, by age group

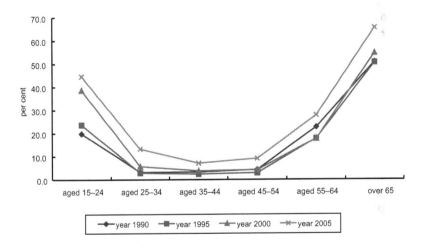

Figure 3.2 Proportion of non-regular employees, male, by age group

Source: Labour Force Survey (the Special Survey and the Detailed Tabulation), conducted by the Statistics Bureau, Ministry of Internal Affairs and Communications.

Note: Figures for 1990, 1995 and 2000 are for February of each year according to the Labour Force Special Survey, while figures for 2005 are January–March averages according to the Detailed Tabulation of the Labour Force Survey. For the population aged 15–24, figures excluding 'students' are shown from August 2000: 27.0 per cent for women and 19.7 per cent for men as of August 2000; 39.8 per cent for women and 28.9 per cent for men as average between January and March 2005.

those figures had fallen to 65.7 and 49.9, respectively (Danjo kyōdō sankaku kaigi eikyō chōsa senmon chōsakai 2004: Shiryō 38–2, 68–2).

Let us briefly review Japanese-style employment practices. Although companies have been scaling back their number of regular employees and the employment conditions of these workers have been changing, Japan's many non-regular workers have faced a lack of job security and poor employment conditions that are the flip-side of conventional Japanese employment practices. This dualism is exhibited in highly interesting results from a series of simulations conducted by the Mitsubishi Research Institute, first released in August 2002. These results show that if the hourly wages of part-timers with the same job and responsibilities as regular employees were raised to a normalized value of 77.6 (from 59.3 as the figure stood when the simulation was conducted), employment would actually increase by making the labour of regular employees relatively more of a 'bargain'. Alternatively, assuming that the wage gap remains static, with no reduction of working hours by regular employees, the simulation projected a decrease of 480,000 regular employees and an increase of 230,000 part-timers between 2002 and 2006.[9] On the other hand, reducing regular employee hours in combination with ameliorating the wage gap between part-timers and regular employees would boost employment by 710,000 regular employees and 300,000 part-timers over that five-year period (Mitsubishi sōgō kenkyūsho: 2002). The study concluded that because companies could cover increased wages for part-timers by increased production, no rise in costs would result.

But in fact the wage gap between full- and part-time workers did not shrink; it actually grew. Enmeshed by Japan's conventional employment practices, companies forged ahead with reductions in the number of regular employees, and in doing so became a risk factor in increasing employment (and livelihood) insecurity.

The tax and social insurance contribution burden

The increasing proportion of the workforce made up of non-regular employees suffering from poor employment conditions obviously constricts the tax and social security contribution base. Nonetheless, the tax and social security contribution burden per full-time worker cannot be assumed to have significantly increased during this period. The effective tax rate (income tax divided by income) for personal income tax using CPI-adjusted real earnings rose only slightly from the end of the 1980s through 1993; in the late 1990s, it started falling (Naikakufu 2002: Figure 2.1–4). The ratio of health insurance premiums to earning barely budged and the ratio of Employees' Pension Insurance (EPI) contributions rose from 1985 levels of 12.4 per cent for men and 11.4 per cent for women to 14.5 per cent for both with the reform of 1994. From April 1995, it was 17.5 per cent (with 1 per cent taken from bonuses). Then, starting in April 2003, it became 13.58 per cent as a result of the switch to calculating on an annual earnings basis that included bonuses (as opposed to 18.35 per cent on a current monthly standard earnings basis). Over a span of almost 20 years, the contribution rate thus rose by six percentage points. During that time, there was a cap of 620,000 yen on current monthly standard earnings for calculation purposes, so for high-wage earners with total monthly incomes exceeding this ceiling, the rise in the pension contribution ratio was not as large as the figures would suggest. For individual workers, the declining income tax rate and the rising pension contribution can be seen as offsetting.

It is clear, however, that a fall in individual income tax rates does not necessarily mean a fall in labour costs for employers. A rise in pension contribution rates, of which employers are responsible for paying half, entails a rise in legally mandated welfare expenses, and therefore labour costs.

How then do labour costs break down? The Ministry of Health, Labour and Welfare's annual *General Survey on Working Conditions* (formerly the *General Survey on Wages and Working Hours Systems* of the Ministry of Labour) compiles the labour costs of 'ordinary workers' in every three or four years. What interests us here is that the definition of ordinary workers in this case encompasses most part-time workers.[10] Tables 3.1 to 3.3 summarize the results of the five surveys conducted since 1991. Labour costs are composed of cash earnings, legally mandated welfare expenses (the share of social insurance contributions for which the employer is responsible), other welfare expenses not mandated by law, lump sum retirement allowance expenses and other items. In the 2002 survey, the composition of labour expenses was: cash earnings, 81 per cent; legally mandated welfare expenses, 9 per cent; lump sum retirement allowances, 5 to 6 per cent; and other welfare expenses not mandated by law, 2 to 3 per cent. Legally mandated welfare expenses further break down to about 30 per cent for medical insurance premiums, about 55 per cent for EPI contributions, and the remainder primarily for labour insurance consisting of unemployment insurance and worker's accident compensation insurance. Child allowance contributions were 0.7 per cent.

Between one-fourth and one-third of medical insurance premiums are transferred to the medical expenses of the elderly in the form of contributions to the Old-age Health Scheme. A large portion of social insurance contributions for the EPI are also directed to benefits for pensioners, including those classified as self-employed. In other words, companies' legally mandated welfare expenditures (the share of social insurance contributions borne by the employer) are applied not just to their employees, but to providing livelihood security to the elderly population at large. Who then is ultimately bearing the employers' share of social insurance contributions? There are three possibilities. First, this burden could be shifted to workers through reduced cash earnings (the pass-back scenario). Second, the companies themselves could bear the burden. Third, consumers could bear the burden through higher prices (the pass-through scenario). According to Toshiaki Tachibanaki, in advanced industrial countries between 20 and 60 per cent of the employers' burden was shifted to workers (the first channel), while the remaining 40 or 80 per cent was borne by the companies themselves (the second channel). But in Japan, it seems that companies actually absorb the costs (Tachibanaki 2005: 99–100).

Average monthly labour cost per ordinary employee rose with each iteration of the survey through 1998, but as Table 3.1 shows, the 2002 survey revealed a sharp drop of 10.4 per cent from the previous survey. Particularly noteworthy is that employee benefit expenditures (labour costs other than cash earnings), which had

Table 3.1 Average monthly labour cost per ordinary employee (yen)

	Total labour cost	Cash earnings	Labour costs other than cash earnings
1991	459,986	382,564	77,422
1995	483,009	400,649	82,360
1998	502,004	409,485	92,519
2002	449,699	367,453	82,245
2005	462,329	374,591	87,738

Source: Compiled by the author from the Outline of the *General Survey on Working Conditions 2006* (Kōsei-rōdō-shō, Tōkei jōhōbu 2006)

Note: For the years before 1999 the year of the survey refers to figures current as of the last day of December of the stated year; after 2001, the figures are as of the first of January of the stated year.

been growing faster than cash earnings through the 1998 survey, contracted more than cash earnings did in the interval leading up to the 2002 survey: the change in cash earnings was –10.3 per cent, whereas the change in labour costs excluding cash earnings was –11.1 per cent. In particular, employee benefits not mandated by law had already edged into the negative by the 1998 survey, and by 2002 had plunged a further 23.5 per cent. In the 1998 survey, costs for lump sum retirement allowances (including company pensions) that had shown 32.7 per cent growth up to the 1998 survey had dipped by 5.3 per cent by the 2002 survey.

The change in legally mandated welfare expenditures was –10.5 per cent, corresponding to the –10.3 per cent change in cash earnings. Breaking this figure down into specific components, health insurance premiums dropped 7.4 per cent, while EPI contributions were curtailed more sharply, down 11.9 per cent (Rōdōshō seisaku chōsabu 1996: 30–7; Rōdōshō seisaku chōsabu 1999: 36–43; Kōsei-rōdō-shō daijin kanbō tōkei jōhōbu 2002: 38–41).

Moreover, from 2000 the long-term care insurance system came into effect and long-term care insurance premiums were levied on top of medical insurance premiums. Long-term care insurance premiums come into effect for employees above 40 years of age who are covered by medical insurance, at a rate in the 1 per cent range. It is hard to conceive that the burden of medical insurance premiums, if the long-term care insurance premiums are not counted in, could have shrunk more than cash earnings. It appears that the EPI contribution burden was throttled back more than medical insurance premiums. As stated above, health insurance and EPI contribution rates were stable between 1998 and 2002. Despite this, monthly EPI contributions per regular worker declined more than cash earnings. This suggests that the proportion of workers not covered by EPI, namely part-timers, rose sharply.

Table 3.2 Labour costs other than cash earnings (average monthly labour cost per ordinary employee, in yen)

	Legally mandated welfare expenditures	Welfare expenditures not mandated by law	Expenditures for in-kind allowances	Expenditures for retirement allowances	Expenditures for education and training	Other labour costs	Total
1991	38,771	13,340	2,190	18,453	1,670	2,998	77,422
1995	42,860	13,682	2,207	20,565	1,305	1,741	82,360
1998	46,868	13,481	1,683	27,300	1,464	1,724	92,519
2002	41,937	10,312	1,266	25,862	1,256	1,613	82,245
2005	46,456	9,555	989	27,517	1,541	1,679	87,738

Source: Compiled by the author from the Outline of the *General Survey on Working Conditions 2006*

Note:
1 'Other labour costs' includes recruitment and relocation expenditures, internal company publications, work apparel (excluding apparel that is mandatory to wear on the job), etc.
2 For years before 1999 the year of the survey refers to figures current as of the last day of December of the stated year; after 2001, the figures are as of the first of January of the stated year.

Table 3.3 Legally mandated welfare expenditures (average monthly labour cost per ordinary employee, in yen)

	Medical and long-term care insurance premiums	Pension contributions	Labour insurance premiums	Child allowances	Contributions for the employment of the handicapped	Other legally mandated welfare expenditures	Total
1991	12,796	18,795	6,684	247	77	171	38,771
1995	13,739	22,575	6,074	318	71	84	42,860
1998	14,369	25,887	6,036	333	58	185	46,868
2002	13,303	22,814	5,365	302	88	64	41,937
2005	15,746	23,831	6,363	317	62	138	46,456

Source: Compiled by the author from the Outline of the *General Survey on Working Conditions 2006*

Note:
1 Before 1998, medical and long-term care insurance premiums refers solely of medical insurance premiums.
2 Other legally mandated welfare expenditures include legally mandated compensation, instalment premiums for the coal mining pension fund and mariner's insurance premiums.

Restructuring of marriage and the family

Toward no-fault divorce

But what kind of changes transpired with respect to the Japanese family? The first point to consider is that from the early 1990s onward, women whose life planning was contingent on being supported by their husbands became exposed to a substantial new risk independent of the scale and direction of the restructuring of employment practices. A pivotal 1987 Supreme Court decision transformed the jurisprudence of divorce in Japan by affirming the principle of so-called 'no-fault divorce': judicial (non-consensual) divorce based on marital breakdown. The advent of no-fault divorce meant that potentially even a husband who abandoned his wife to cohabit with another woman could be granted a divorce on the grounds that an irreconcilable breakdown of the marriage had occurred.

Before the landmark 1987 ruling, Japanese courts would not grant a filing for divorce by an 'at fault' spouse (e.g. one who had committed adultery or malicious abandonment) even if the marriage had irrevocably broken down. Instead the legal doctrine of showing-of-fault divorce prevailed, under which it was held that a not-at-fault spouse should not be deprived of his or her status as a spouse so long as he or she wished the marriage to remain in effect. To dissolve a marriage against the will of the not-at-fault spouse was famously called 'treatment like a dog' in a Supreme Court ruling of 1952 (Supreme Court, 19 February 1952). Under this principle, the formal status of the wife remained very secure as long as she did not commit adultery or abandon her domestic responsibilities. Thus, there was a presumption that marriage was a lifelong institution, even if only as a sheer formality. Under a livelihood security system based upon the male breadwinner model, this view of divorce probably served reasonably well.

But the 1987 Supreme Court ruling changed the showing-of-fault divorce system that had been the law of the land for 35 years by granting a request for divorce from a man who had been separated from his wife and living with another woman for 36 years (Supreme Court, 9 September 1987). Soon subsequent rulings shortened the period of separation necessary for the divorce to be granted. By the first half of the 1990s, divorce filings by at-fault spouses who had lived separately for only eight years were being granted (Supreme Court, 8 November 1990; 8 February 1994). Western countries had switched to no-fault divorce one after another over a period stretching from the 1960s to the 1980s. In Japan, however, this legal doctrine was established only in the early 1990s.

Unsurprisingly, then, during the thirty-some years preceding this change, 90 per cent of divorces in Japan were consensual. Another 9 per cent were arranged through the family court, and only 1 per cent of divorces were granted through judicial decision. Nevertheless, the switch to no-fault divorce should be considered a restructuring of the institution of marriage, whose effects on the functioning of Japan's strongly gendered livelihood security system cannot be ignored. The 'new Japanese-style management system' envisioned by Nikkeiren's reports entailed fewer men in a position to actually perform their role as male breadwinner. And for women, even a marriage to a man falling under the privileged 'long-term accumulated ability utilization' type would come with no guarantee of his employment security. The bottom line, for both wives and husbands, was that marriage had ceased to be a station with lifelong tenure. Marriage had, in other words, become a riskier proposition (Fukushima 1995). Turning from the legal framework for divorce to statistical reality, we see that the divorce rate per 1,000 population, following a minor peak in 1982, declined through 1988, and then soared in the following years through 2002 (*Vital Statistics of Japan*).

Constricted consumption

The next indicator of change we will scrutinize is that of household finances. In the 1990s incomes were virtually stagnant, yet the financial assets of households (the sum of savings deposits, securities and insurance/pension reserves) grew by 400 trillion yen. The average savings balance per employee-headed household also grew by 3 million yen (Ministry of Internal Affairs and Communications *Family Savings Survey*). After 1999, there was a slight contraction in savings balances, but it was less than the degree of contraction in incomes. So the ratio of savings to annual income increased from 151.4 per cent in 1990 to 176.9 per cent in 1999. It dipped slightly to 176.2 per cent in 2000, then rebounded to 181.2 per cent in 2001. (The 2001 figures are from the *Family Income and Expenditure Survey*.) And this expansion of savings came at the price of constricted consumption.

For insight into this throttling back of consumption that exceeded what shrinking incomes alone would explain, we turn to a public opinion survey conducted by the Bank of Japan on the subject of people's attitudes toward their livelihoods. In response to a multiple-response question about why they tightened their spending, 61.7 per cent of respondents chose, 'Because I feel uncertain about my future job and pay prospects' and 57.2 per cent chose, 'Because I'm worried that my pension and social security benefits will shrink.' Since 1998, the percentage of people expressing worry over their future job and pay has been hovering about the 60 to 65 per cent level. But when it comes to worries over pensions and social security benefits, the rise is striking, from a level right around 50 per cent in 1998, to almost 60 per cent after 2001 (Naikakufu 2003a: 39–40).

Examining the figures by age bracket, the propensity to consume of people in their thirties fell precipitously from the 1980s to the 1990s (Naikakufu 2003a: 41–2). Those in their thirties during the late 1980s were born between 1949 and 1960. Those in their thirties during the late 1990s were born in the 1960s. Those born in the 1950s saw first-hand the steep rise in real wages experienced by the generation born during the war years and the baby boom that followed the war's end. This may have inspired a sense of confidence in their own futures. In contrast, those born in the 1960s were faced with a stagnant wage climate, which may well have stoked their anxieties about future income. One analysis based on micro data shows that among heads of households in their thirties who are not living with their parents or receiving financial subsidies from them, those who say they are anxious over the fate of their pensions devote more of the household budget to accumulating financial assets than those who say they are not anxious over pensions (Murata 2003).

Given that, Masako Murozumi argues that as incomes shrank from the late 1990s onward, even as social insurance premiums, repayments of housing loans and contributions to private insurances grew, households inevitably sacrificed consumer spending (Murozumi 2006: Chapter 2). But did households lack the option of sustaining or boosting income by increasing earners, that is, by deploying dependent spouses into the labour market as opposed to crimping consumption?

According to the *Family Income and Expenditure Survey*, the ratio of employee households' actual income earned by spouses of household heads (mostly wives) was in the 8 per cent range in the latter part of the 1980s, and rose into the 9 per cent range in the 1990s, but by 2003 it had still not broken past the 10 per cent mark. Even restricting the analysis to dual-earning nuclear families where the wife is also an employee, this ratio is only around 25 per cent. Time series analysis of data from the Institute for Research on Household Economics' *Japanese Panel Survey of Consumers* provides a key insight. A cohort of 1,500 women aged 24 to 34 as of 1993 were tracked in subsequent surveys. During the eight years between 1995 and 2002, among women in this group married to a husband under 35 who experienced a drop in income two or more years in a row, the wife's income did not rise to make up the difference (Higuchi/Ōta, Kakei keizai kenkyūsho 2004: 42–3).

Men lead the way in declining intent to marry

This brings us to developments in practices of family formation and the bearing and rearing of future generations. The year 1989 brought the so-called '1.57 shock'. The figure refers to the total fertility rate announced in that year. This statistic was notable because it fell below even the anomalously low figure of 1.58 registered in 1966 as a result of a specific cultural factor. 1966 was 'the year of the fire horse' in the East Asian sexagenary calendar. Traditional beliefs about girls born in the year of the fire horse can make them face obstacles in marrying. Concern over this possibility on the part of prospective parents is thought to have depressed the birth rate in that year. The 1.57 shock galvanized concern over declining birth rates in Japan, but the birth rate nonetheless continued to fall. (The total fertility rate for a year is the average number of children women will bear in their lifetimes assuming that they conform to the age-specific fertility rates calculated for each age group in that year.)

The *Population Projections for Japan* issued in January 2002, based on data from the 2000 *Population Census of Japan*, assumed a long-term future fertility rate of 1.39. According to this projection's medium variant, by 2050, 35.7 per cent of Japan's population would be over the age of 65. The medium variant of the previous projection, issued in 1997, assumed a long-term fertility rate of 1.61 and projected the elderly share of the 2050 population at 32.3 per cent. Over the five years between the projections, the anticipated pace of the aging of Japan's population had accelerated appreciably.

In response to the 1997 population projection, the Council for Population

Problems issued a report entitled *Basic Thoughts on the Declining Birth Rate*, as mentioned above. According to this report, the recent decline in the birth rate was due to an increasing proportion of never-married people in the population. Fertility of married women was not declining much, but younger people were delaying marriage to an older age, and the proportion of lifelong never-married people was rising, causing declining fertility overall. The 1998 *White Paper on Health and Welfare* probed the social factors beneath fertility decline, highlighting aspects of the situation such as the burden of child-rearing responsibilities in families falling overwhelmingly on women and an employment regime that prioritizes work over family and is oriented primarily toward male, regular employees who joined the company straight out of school, and community life diminished by the non-participation of employed men.

How did intentions to marry and appraisal of the benefits of marriage change among the unmarried? According to the 12th *Basic Survey of Birth Trends*, the share of unmarried men responding that they 'definitely intend to marry' dropped continually from the early 1980s through the latter part of the 1990s. Among unmarried women, it dropped during the 1980s but levelled off in the 1990s. Between 1997 and 2002, there was a slight uptick in the percentage of all men and the percentage of women in their twenties who said they 'definitely intend to marry'. Conversely, the share of unmarried women who agreed that 'there are advantages to marrying' was stable around the 70 per cent level from the latter part of the 1980s through 2002, and the share of men affirming that statement fell from survey to survey through 2002, when it reached 62.3 per cent.

In the 1990s, intent to marry declined more significantly among men than women and the number of men seeing advantages to marrying shrank. On this matter, although the date of the survey falls somewhat outside the period in question, we can gain insight from the Cabinet Office's 2003 public opinion survey *Research into the State of Young People*. It queried people's reasons for remaining unmarried, allowing multiple responses (up to three). The top-scoring response among both men and women was 'I haven't found the person I want to marry' (39.9 per cent of men, 43.1 per cent of women). Among men, the second most popular response was 'I can't afford it financially' (36.0 per cent), and women's second-most popular response was 'I want to keep pursuing my own hobbies and interests' (24.9 per cent). 'I can't afford it financially' ranked third among women, cited by 24.5 per cent of respondents. Another question asked 'What are the disadvantages of marriage?' Multiple responses (up to two) were permitted, with the most frequent among men being 'Less freedom to spend money however I want' (57.2 per cent). This response was also chosen by 39.0 per cent of women, whose top choice was 'Limitations on doing the things I want to do' at 39.2 per cent. Also scoring highly among women was 'More responsibilities for housework and child-rearing' (34.0 per cent), a response which scored much lower among men (9.7 per cent) (Naikakufu 2003a: 171, 174).

The results of this survey make it clear that men perceive financial concerns as a major hurdle to getting married. Among women, on the other hand, the disincentive to marriage is that having children makes it difficult to continue a career and entails loss of an independent income, in addition to the prospect of bearing most of the child-rearing responsibilities. Returning to the *Basic Survey of Birth Trends*, its data show that what unmarried women are increasingly looking for in a spouse is 'cooperation in housework and child-rearing' and 'understanding and support towards my career'. Women are more determined than ever to form dual-career families, but men, as evidenced by their financial anxieties, are still caught up in the male breadwinner norm. This can be interpreted as a gap in attitudes and expectations between women and men.

At the same time, despite women's growing determination to seek a dual-career family arrangement, the shift to non-regular work has been especially pronounced in the employment market for young women, thereby attenuating their capacity to contribute to the household budget. This labour market shift has also acted as a brake on marriage for men. Data from the Cabinet Office's 2003 *Research into the State of Young People* cited above showed that only 33.9 per cent of men who are regular employees chose the response 'I can't afford it financially' as their reason for remaining unmarried, compared to 44.4 per cent of men who are part-timers (Naikakufu 2003a: 171). On the other hand, the cohort survey tracking women who were aged 24 to 34 in 1993 reveals that among those who were unmarried as of age 25, those who were unemployed or non-regular employees were less likely to be married than those who were regular employees, and this difference persisted all the way through age 40 (Higuchi/Ōta, Kakei keizai kenkyūjo 2004: 78–9).

Deepening poverty and inequality

Finally, let us examine how the social trends we observed in this chapter were reflected in low incomes and income distribution as dimensions of social exclusion. First, according to large-scale opinion surveys conducted by Shōgo Takegawa and his colleagues in 2000, the majority of people believe that Japan is already an unequal society, and that inequality will widen in the coming years (Takegawa, ed. 2006: Ch. 9). What prevailing social conditions do these views reflect?

It should be noted that data shedding light on the persistence of low incomes are sparse in Japan. One vital source is the Institute for Research on Household Economics' *Japanese Panel Survey of Consumers*. Specifically, using its data through 2002 on a cohort of 1,500 women who were between 24 and 34 years of age in 1993, Masami Iwata has carried out a poverty dynamics analysis that shows 7.8 per cent experienced extended periods of poverty. Women with only a junior high school education, those heading lone mother households, or those with a husband whose employment was unstable were at a greater risk of becoming entrenched in poverty.

Meanwhile, a comparative statics analysis by Sawako Shirahase provides additional important insights. Shirahase has analyzed heads of household broken down by age bracket and other factors for the *Comprehensive Survey of Living Conditions* 国民生活基礎調査 in the years 1986, 1995 and 2001. Her first finding pertains to low income households. Low income is defined as below 50 per cent of the median equivalent disposable income of all households. First, among households headed by persons in their twenties or thirties, the rate of low income households clearly increased for nuclear families composed of a married couple and their children (as well as single householders, for those in their twenties). On the other end of the age spectrum, the rate of low income greatly decreased among households whose head is over 70 years of age (with the exception of three-generation households, where the rate slightly increased). Second, 42 per cent of households composed of a single woman are low income, and in cases where the householder is in her thirties or older, the rate of low income rises with age. In recent years, as other age brackets, in particular 60-plus ones, have seen a decline in the rate of low income (for 60-plus from 60 to 70 per cent in 1986 to the 40 per cent range in 2001), those in their twenties have seen an especially striking rise in the rate of low incomes (from around 19 per cent in 1986 to almost 29 per cent in 2001). As for inequality, measured by the Gini coefficients on the basis of equivalent disposable income, from 1986 to 2001 for groups in working age (through age 64) the Gini coefficients have risen, but from age 65 onward, they have declined. In other words, inequality has declined among the elderly, but increased among those of working age (Shirahase 2006: 59, 65, 69).

Dovetailing with the results of Shirahase's analysis are those of Aya Abe's *Kodomo no hinkon* ('Child Poverty'). According to Abe, the poverty rate for children is the proportion of children living in households where the total equivalent household income is below 50 per cent of the median value. Based upon analysis of the *Survey on the Redistribution of Income* and the *Comprehensive Survey of Living Conditions*, Abe puts the poverty rate for children at around 10 per cent in 1990, rising to 14 per cent by 2001 (Abe 2005: 125). According to a more recent analysis by Abe, the increase in the poverty rate of households with children was primarily due to a growth in the proportion of low market incomes among child-rearing households as a whole. There is a high poverty rate among households with young fathers, especially fathers in their twenties (Abe 2008), and even with both spouses working, these households find it especially difficult to escape poverty (Shirahase 2008). This reflects the deteriorating employment opportunities for young people in Japan's shifting labour market.

4 Japan in international comparison at the turn of the century

By the end of the 1990s, Japan had yet to begin moving beyond the male breadwinner model. How did its livelihood security system fare in international comparison at the turn of the century? This chapter will bring into relief the characteristic features of livelihood security provision in contemporary Japan based on data mainly from the late 1990s to the early 2000s. In some areas the first half of the 1990s will serve as the basis for comparison due to data source constraints.

Section 1 will take a quantitative and qualitative look at the interrelations between the four relations of production of goods and services as schematized in Table 2.1. Commodity production in Japan is dominated by wage labour in for-profit enterprises to an exorbitant degree compared to the other leading economies. My focus in Section 2 will therefore be on employment practices in for-profit enterprises and employment performance broken down by gender and age. It will be seen that employment performance for men in the latter part of their careers continues to be favourable compared to that for women and in other nations.

Section 3 puts Japan's welfare government to the test. As Section 1 reiterates, the Japanese government is small as a 'welfare government' albeit big as a 'construction government'. Although the burden of tax and social security contributions on household budgets in Japan is relatively light compared to other leading industrial nations, the burden placed on single-member households as opposed to married households is relatively heavy. Social security benefits are strongly weighted towards pensions and medical treatment costs. Support for families, starting with support for family formation, is weak. And Japan's public pension system is centred to a greater degree on male breadwinners than that of any other developed nation. Although the generosity of Japan's elder care services, whose primary recipients are women aged 75 and over, is in line with other nations, Japan exceeds all other OECD members in the meagreness of its programmes for future generations. The take-up rate of its livelihood protection (public assistance) scheme as the 'last resort' for people in need is extremely low, and lone mothers receive as good as no support to raise their children. Tax policies and social security schemes are meant to reduce income inequality and alleviate poverty. Japan's income transfer system at present however, has caused the poverty rate to rise for substantial numbers of people. Rather than functioning poorly, Japan's livelihood security system is at present functioning in reverse.

Quantitative and qualitative interrelations between the four relations of production

Small welfare and big construction government

Let us begin by taking a closer look at the relations of production represented by quadrant (2) in Table 2.1 on p. 31 (production of non-commodities using wage labour). Suitable proxy indicators for the relative weight of the government include the share of public sector employment, the overall tax burden (i.e. the total amount of taxes and social security contributions as a percentage of GDP), total government expenditure relative to GDP and so on. According to Japan's Ministry of Internal Affairs and Communications, per capita public sector employment among Western nations is highest in France with 89.7 state employees per 1,000 residents (2003), followed by the United Kingdom with 78.8 (2004), the United States with 78.4 (2004) and Germany with 57.9 state employees (2003). With only 33.6 state employees per 1,000 residents, Japan has a by far smaller public sector.[1] It should be noted that the number for Japan includes not only local as well as central government employees, but also employees of government-linked enterprises such as public corporations, independent administrative agencies, national university corporations and government-affiliated 'special corporations'.

In 2006, the Nomura Research Institute (NRI) issued a report, commissioned by the Economic and Social Research Institute of the Cabinet Office, that estimated the number of public sector employees, including non-regular and temporary workers, per 1,000 residents using full-time equivalents (FTEs) based on a 40-hour work week (the typical European work week being shorter). Using 2004 data, NRI found that France had the most FTE public employees per 1,000 residents (83.8), followed by the US (73.9), the UK (70.5) and Germany (67.0). Japan again came in last (42.2, based on 2005 data).[2] Regardless of whether one considers the share of public sector employees (in the broad sense of this term) in employment overall, or the percentage of GDP spent on their salaries and benefits (Nakamura 2004; Suzuki 2005), it is obvious that Japan's public sector is among the smallest of all OECD member countries.

What about the total amount of tax and social security contributions as a percentage of GDP? This constitutes what Japan's Ministry of Finance calls the 'national burden'. But it is also the government revenue. OECD data from 2000 shows that Japan's government revenues were the third lowest at 27 per cent of GDP. Only Mexico and Korea had lower ratios, the OECD average being 36.2 per cent. Looking at the data longitudinally, we can see a persistent upward trend in nearly all member states. Japan's government revenues, however, peaked in 1989 at 29.8 per cent and have been trending downward ever since (OECD 2007: 74–5, 98–9).

There has also been a significant shift in the percentage of revenue the Japanese government has collected from taxation as opposed to social security contributions. Beginning in 1990, taxes on income and profits as a share of GDP fell markedly. Total tax collections relative to GDP also consistently declined from 1990 to 2004. Social security contributions, on the other hand, consistently increased. In 2000, the amount of revenue from social security contributions surpassed revenue from taxes on income and profits. Among major developed nations, only Japan saw its share of government revenues from taxes on income and profits steadily contract from 1990 to 2004 (OECD 2007: 77, 100–3).

Since the late 1990s, tax rates on businesses and the wealthy have declined in Japan, resulting in a drop in the central government's direct tax revenues. The government has collected less tax from businesses and upper-income earners on the order of 10 trillion to 20 trillion yen per year, all the while bemoaning budget constraints. The share of direct taxes as a percentage of national tax revenues declined from approximately 74 per cent in the early 1990s to 60 per cent, levelling off in 1998.

The corresponding share of indirect tax revenue, the bulk of which comes from the consumption tax, grew from roughly 7 per cent to 20 per cent (Seikatsu keizai seisaku kenkyūsho 2007). Consumption tax in general is regressive and thus imposes a disproportionately heavy burden on households whose ratio of consumption to disposable income is high, such as elderly women living alone, lone mother households and low-income households with children.

Japan's total government expenditures as a percentage of GDP amounted to 36.6 per cent (central government, 7.8 per cent; local governments, 13.8 per cent; social security fund, 15.0 per cent) in 2001 according to Ministry of Finance reports based on the System of National Accounts (Zaimushō 2003: 9).

According to the same Japanese Ministry of Finance material, total government spending as a percentage of GDP in the UK, the US, Germany and France averages 40 per cent, of which the central government spends an average 16.0 per cent and local governments 11.4 per cent, while social security disbursements equal 12.7 per cent. In Japan, the central government's total expenditures are notably smaller, amounting to only 7.8 per cent of GDP. In contrast, Japan's social security fund expenditures equal 15 per cent of GDP, greater than the 12.7 per cent average of the four nations mentioned above. Japan's lead in this one category, however, is misleading because in the Western nations both central and local governments disburse a larger share of social security expenditure as tax-financed benefits, such as public assistance, child allowance and housing benefits, as opposed to as social insurance benefits.

Furthermore, if gross government expenditure is broken down by type, cash benefits (pensions, unemployment benefits, etc.) in the US, the UK, Germany and France average 15.2 per cent of GDP, considerably higher than Japan's 10.5 per cent. It is worth noting that government budgets for welfare programmes also include social transfers in kind, largely medical care provided through public health insurance.

Conversely, the Japanese government's 4.8 per cent rate of gross fixed capital formation stands out, being twice the 2.4 per cent average of the four Western nations. Government gross fixed capital formation is basically synonymous with public investments. And in Japan, it is only a slight exaggeration to say that public investments equal public works. In other words, small 'welfare government' in Japan is overshadowed by big 'construction government' at both the national and local levels. In 1997, for example, local governments accounted for 80 per cent of public capital formation in Japan, and these outlays exceeded 40 per cent of their total expenditures, surpassing the central government's roughly 30 per cent budget share spent on public works. As massive as Japan's construction government is at the national level, it is larger still at the local level.

Consequences of Japan's big construction government

Public works projects can also redistribute wealth away from metropolitan areas by increasing income and employment opportunities in rural areas. They can thus be seen as forming part of what John Campbell (2002) has called a 'welfare state in the broad sense'. According to a report published by the Policy Research Institute of Japan's Ministry of Finance, however, it should be noted that Japan's public works spending has stood out in international comparison only since the late 1970s, and was most pronounced during the 1990s. In the early 1970s, the UK, Germany, France and other Western European nations spent approximately 4 per cent of GDP on public works, not much lower than Japan's public works budget of slightly less than 5 per cent. (Western European nations, of course, had much more extensive social welfare programmes than Japan at that time.) Shortly thereafter, economic recession and government budget shortfalls led European nations to sharply scale back their public works spending. At the same time, the report points out, their awareness increased that the employment maintenance and job creation effects of public works spending are at best temporary (Zaimu sōgō seisaku kenkyūsho 2002: Figure 3.1).[3]

The hypothesis that Japan's 'construction government' is the functional equivalent of a welfare government must therefore be evaluated carefully. Empirical studies of public works spending in Japan since 1995 have shown that the massive outlays under its 'construction government' have actually generated smaller induced effects on employment and income than spending on medical and long-term care provision, welfare, and education and research (Tsuruta 2003; Iryō keizai kenkyū kikō 2005).

An exception to the 'renaissance of self-employment'

With regard to quadrant (3) of Table 2.1 (production of commodities using non-wage labour), let us take a closer look at the self-employed sector. As shown below in Figure 4.1, based on the Ministry of Health, Labour and Welfare's *White Paper on Working Women*, the percentage of Japanese workers who report being in the self-employed sector is not particularly high when compared to other developed nations (Kōsei-rōdō-shō 2006b). The share of female family members working in family businesses, on the other hand, is comparatively large (10.6 per cent). In Korea, by comparison, the percentage of the self-employed among female workers is 19.7 per cent, which is higher than the percentage of female family workers at 19.5 per cent.

Japan in international comparison 89

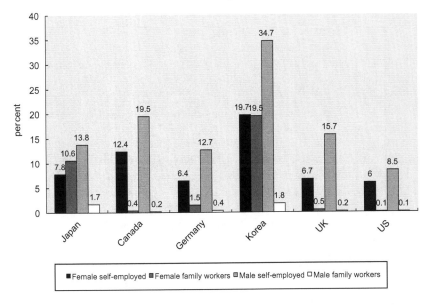

Figure 4.1 Percentage of self-employed and their family workers, by gender
Source: Kōsei-rōdō-shō 2006b

The self-employed sector merits attention because dwindling employment prospects for women and young adults have led people to pin their hopes on starting their own businesses. The growth of the self-employed sector since the late 1990s has drawn attention in several of the OECD member states. Chapter 5 of the OECD's *Employment Outlook 2000* analyzes this trend under the heading 'The partial renaissance of self-employment' (OECD 2000: 155). In the face of this trend towards increased self-employment, headlined by the service industry, knowledge professions and women in the developed world, Japan stands as an exception.

In 1973, 14 per cent of Japan's non-agricultural workforce were self-employed (excluding unpaid family workers), the third highest percentage among OECD members, behind Italy and Spain. In 1997, however, only 9.7 per cent of the non-agricultural workforce were self-employed, below the OECD average of 11.9 per cent. The number of self-employed workers in Japan increased during the 1970s, but began to dwindle in the 1980s. During the 1990s, the annual rate of decline stood at 1.4 per cent, the steepest drop among OECD member states.

The OECD member states showing the greatest relative and absolute growth in the numbers of self-employed were Canada, the UK during the 1980s, and Germany during the 1990s. Industrial sectors that experienced a rise in self-employment included financial intermediary services, real estate and other service industries (community services, social services and personal services). In terms of occupations, professional, technical and semi-professional occupations saw increased self-employment. The number of self-employed women also grew in most OECD member countries.

The number of self-employed women in Japan, on the contrary, levelled off in the 1970s and 1980s, to subsequently fall at an annual rate of 2.8 per cent in the 1990s, a decline not matched by any other OECD member nation (OECD 2000: 158–62). According to Yūji Genda (2003: 166), Japan's exceptional drop in self-employment was a result of falling business revenues during the prolonged recession of the 1990s.

As the OECD's *Employment Outlook 2000* also reports, a majority of OECD member nations had adopted policies to support self-employed workers beginning in the early 1980s. These governments created programmes to assist existing micro-businesses and to encourage unemployed workers, women and young adults to open their own businesses. No mention is made of self-employment policies in Japan.

The data on the scale of governments' efforts to promote self-employment in the field of public support to help unemployed people become self-employed show that Canada's government, for example, liberally spent 4 per cent of its budget for active labour market policies (ALMPs) during the late-1990s. Sweden and Germany spent 3.7 and 2.1 per cent of their ALMP budgets, respectively, for this purpose. One per cent to 6 per cent of all unemployed workers in these three countries participated in these programmes (OECD 2000: 178). Government outlays for active labour market programmes reached approximately 0.5 per cent of GDP in Canada, 1.3 per cent in Germany, and 2 per cent in Sweden. Japan, meanwhile, spent no more than 0.1 per cent of its GDP on such efforts while spending roughly 0.4 per cent of GDP on unemployment insurance benefits (OECD 2000: 224–9).

The preponderance of women in unpaid work

Quadrant (4) of Table 2.1 (production of non-commodities using non-wage labour) encompasses work within the household, such as domestic tasks, child-rearing and nursing care. As mentioned in Chapter 2, mainstream economics and conventional wisdom conceive of this type of work not as 'production' but as 'consumption'. The UN's System of National Accounts (SNA), for example, counts the labour of producing goods for self-consumption by family businesses as 'productive labour', but does not take domestic chores, child-rearing or nursing care into account at the same time.

The 'Platform for Action' adopted at the Fourth World Conference on Women held in 1995 at Beijing, called for 'recognizing the economic contribution of women and making visible the unequal distribution of remunerated and unremunerated work between women and men' (Beijing Declaration and Platform for Action, para. 206(f)). To achieve this goal, a method of placing a monetary value on the unpaid work that women put into family care, domestic work, environmental protection, mutual aid activities and so forth, was to be developed 'for possible reflection in satellite or other official accounts' (ibid.). A satellite account is a 'system of "ancillary" calculations around [the SNA] that allows other areas of interests to be explored' such as the environment, culture, education and other areas of significant social concern (Harrison 1993: 26). These accounts are designed to present information on economic activities in these areas in a systematic and integrated fashion.

In response to the Beijing Declaration, Japan's Economic Planning Agency (EPA) developed estimates of the wage equivalents of unpaid work. In 1997 it released a report on its estimates for the years 1981, 1985 and 1991. In 1998, it issued another report on its estimates of the value of unpaid work performed in 1996.

The EPA relied on the results of the Ministry of Internal Affairs and Communications' *Survey on Time Use and Leisure Activities* for estimates of how many hours people spent doing unpaid work such as housework (cooking, cleaning, laundry, etc.), caring for the aged and ill, child-rearing, shopping and community activities (neighbourhood clean-up days, road cleaning, consumer advocacy, citizens' movements, etc.).

The *Survey on Time Use and Leisure Activities* was first conducted in 1976 by the Management and Coordination Agency and has been repeated every five years since. It divides daily time use into three categories: (1) primary activities such as sleeping and eating that are physiologically necessary; (2) secondary activities that are defined as activities 'which each person is committed to perform as a member of the family or of the society', including 'commuting to and from school or work, work (for pay or profit), schoolwork, housework, caring or nursing, child care and shopping'; and (3) leisure activities.[4]

There are two chief ways of estimating the wage equivalents of unpaid work – the opportunity cost method and the replacement cost method. The opportunity cost method calculates lost income or the amount of wages for paid work someone forgoes to perform unremunerated work. Lost income estimates for an individual are based on the average hourly wages received by workers of the same gender and age group. The EPA (Keizai-kikaku-chō 1997: Table 1) estimated that the opportunity cost of unpaid work was approximately 20 per cent of GDP for the years 1981, 1986 and 1991.

In the same report, the EPA also included estimates of the opportunity costs of unpaid work in several other countries circa 1991. For example, the lost income from unpaid work was estimated to equal 69 per cent of GDP in Australia, 63 per cent in Germany (1992) and 54.2 per cent in Canada (1992) – figures more than twice as large as the estimates for Japan. The primary reason for this gap is that in other countries aggregated hours of unpaid work done by all citizens 15 years and older are longer than hours of paid work, whereas in Japan aggregated hours of unpaid work are about half of the hours of paid work. Using 1991 data, the EPA estimated that, on an average day, women spend nearly four hours performing unpaid work, while men spend 30 minutes (four hours and half per day in total). Work for pay, on the other hand, was estimated at nearly three hours per day for women and 5.75 hours for men (approximately eight hours and half in total). Thus, women, whose average hourly wage rate is less than 67 per cent of men's, are performing the vast majority of unpaid work in Japan. This is why lost income from unpaid work figures much lower in Japan than in other countries.

For 1996, the total estimated value (per year for the population 15 years and older) of unpaid work calculated with the opportunity cost method was 116 trillion yen, corresponding to 23.3 per cent of GDP. Shortly thereafter, the Ministry of Internal Affairs and Communications' Statistics Bureau initiated a plan to incorporate behavioural segmentation in the *Survey on Time Use and Leisure Activities* to get a more detailed picture of unpaid work. When the survey was conducted in 2001, the Statistics Bureau turned to Kōji Hamada, director of the Institute for Research on Household Economics, to calculate the monetary opportunity costs of unpaid work. He estimated the total amount of forgone wages to be 129 trillion yen (Hamada 2006). As Japan's nominal GDP was 498 trillion yen in 2001, the combined opportunity costs of unpaid work were equivalent to 25.9 per cent of GDP. Monetary value of unpaid work in Japan has thus not greatly increased in overall scale.

In 2006, the Statistics Bureau conducted a cross-national comparison of the time use of parents of preschool children employing the most recent data available. Figure 4.2 below charts the average amount of time in minutes that parents spent per day (averaged over the entire week including weekends) working and travelling for work, or performing housework and looking after their children. Wives in Japan reported spending 398 minutes per day on household chores and child care, the highest among all eight nations in the comparison group. As one might expect, Japanese husbands reported spending the least amount of time on domestic tasks at 78 minutes per day. They also spent by far the most time working and travelling for

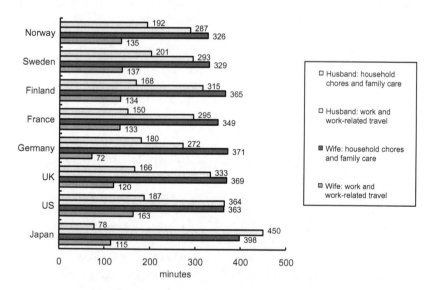

Figure 4.2 Daily time use of married couples with at least one child aged six and under (aged five and under for Japan and the US) (weekly averages for husbands and wives)

Source: Ministry of Internal Affairs and Communications, Statistics Bureau (2006): 26.

Notes:
1 For the US, persons aged 18 and over with children aged 5 and under, 'travel' classified by purpose.
2 Definitions vary by countries.

work at 450 minutes per day, indicating a trade-off between the length of working hours and the amount of time spent on housekeeping and child care.

Japan's extreme and apparently immutable gender imbalance in unpaid work reflects its high degree of gender inequality in the labour market. Sawako Shirahase (2006: 16) presents evidence of this inequality in her detailed analysis of international income data from the mid-1990s. Among seven nations – Japan, Germany, Italy, Sweden, Taiwan, UK and the US – the relative share of household income earned by women ranges from 52.7 per cent in Sweden to only 22.9 per cent in Japan.

Small scale of the social economy and gender biases

So far this chapter has discussed characteristics of the four relations of production of goods and services, as schematized in Table 2.1, from the viewpoint of their quantitative and qualitative interrelations and in international comparison. To sum up the main results: first, the Japanese government is small as a welfare government albeit big as a construction government. Second, the scale of Japan's self-employed sector is similar to other developed nations, but the number of women working in family businesses is relatively high. If one turns to self-employed persons other than unpaid family workers, several advanced countries experienced a 'partial renaissance of self-employment' headlined by the service industry, knowledge professions and women. Japan has proved an exception to this trend. Finally, we looked at the scale of unpaid work such as housework, child-rearing, nursing care and some community activities. According to the Japanese government's calculations, the amount of unpaid work is considerably smaller than in other industrialized nations because the time Japanese men expend on unpaid work is incomparably brief.

What, then, can be said about the scale of Japan's 'social economy' or 'third sector' that straddles the public and private sectors? Compared to other nations, scarcely any effort has been made in Japan to collect economic data in this area. Even for the relatively well-known cooperatives and mutual aid societies, available data are insufficient for an international comparison, although we do know that consumer cooperatives accounted for 2.7 per cent of all retail sales in Japan in 2004.[5] In terms of paid employment, a recent estimate by Akira Kurimoto, chief researcher at the Consumer Co-operative Institute of Japan, shows that the overall number of employees in cooperatives (consumer, agricultural, banks, insurance and so on) in 2007–8 is in the range of 570,000, amounting to 1 per cent of the total number of employees in Japan (Kurimoto manuscript).

In 2006, a report titled *The Social Economy in the European Union* was drawn up for the European Economic and Social Committee by the International Centre of Research and Information on the Public, Social and Cooperative Economy (CIRIEC). It shows that paid employment in the social economy as a percentage of total wage-earning employment in 2002–3 was 10.7 in the Netherlands, 10.6 in Ireland, 8.7 in France, 8.5 in Finland, 7.5 in Italy, 7.0 in the UK and so on, yielding an average of 7.0 per cent for the first 15 member countries of the European Union (Europe-15).[6]

94 *Japan in international comparison*

According to data compiled by the ICA's Gender Equality Committee for the late 1990s through early 2000s, 90 per cent of the members of Japan's consumer cooperatives are women (in 2003), which is the highest figure in the table. Yet, women comprise only 15 per cent of these cooperatives' employees (2000), an imbalance not seen in other nations.[7] Not only is the scale of the not-for-profit sector in Japan small (even if cooperatives and mutual aid societies are included), it also seems safe to infer that a gender-based division of labour – where 'consumption' is regarded as a female activity and paid employment is the domain of males – exists in consumer cooperatives as well.

As noted earlier, among the four relations of production, commodity production using wage labour in for-profit enterprises accounts for a larger share of the economy in Japan than in other nations. What are the characteristic features of employment in this sector?

Employment performance

Employment protection

General employment security

In September 2004, the International Labour Organization (ILO) issued its first ranking of nations using a new metric, the national Economic Security Index (ESI). The ESI is a composite based on seven socio-economic security indexes relating to income security, employment protection security, occupational health and safety, and 'voice representation security' including, but not limited to, the right to collective bargaining between labour unions and employer federations. Among the more than 90 nations ranked by the ILO, covering 86 per cent of the world's population, Japan ranked 18th (ILO 2004). The highest scores went to the Scandinavian nations followed by the countries of Continental Europe. The UK ranked 15th and the US ranked 25th, below Japan. Japan's overall ranking was depressed by its having the 26th highest score for employment protection and 22nd highest score for voice representation, but it was boosted by its 9th place on occupational health and safety.

All seven socio-economic security indexes combine 'input indicators (policy variables), process indicators (institutional variables), and outcome indicators (statistical reflections of the effectiveness of these policies and institutions)' (ILO 2004: 2).[8] National employment protection security refers to regulations banning arbitrary dismissals and requiring employee compensation in unfair dismissal cases. The input indicators used in calculating the national employment protection security index (EPSI) are: (1) ratification of the ILO's Termination of Employment Convention (no. 158); (2) existence of national legislation dealing with average notice period prior to redundancy, severance pay and definition of unfair dismissal; and (3) procedures for handling collective redundancies such as requiring consultation with employee representatives. The two process indicators in the EPSI are (1) the percentage of workers covered by collective bargaining agreements and (2) the existence of independent labour tribunals. Finally, the three outcome indicators are: (1) the share of all workers formally employed (wage workers); (2) the share of all workers employed in the public sector; and (3) the ratio of female to male wage workers (ILO 2004: 160–1).

Japan's lowest score on these measures was 0.105 for inputs. Its process indicator score was 0.833 and its outcome indicator 0.713, giving it an overall employment protection security score of 0.591. Japan's input score was lowered by its opting not to ratify the ILO's Termination of Employment Convention, which depressed its composite score. Most industrialized nations had process scores of either 0.833 or 0.667. Finland, which had the highest employment security ranking, had a process indicator score of 1.00, as did tenth-ranked Israel. Comparing outcome indicator scores alone moves Japan up only two slots to 24th place (ILO 2004: 401–2). In other words, the level of employment protection security in Japan is not great.

However, even if overall levels of employment security are low, they may still be high for one segment of the population. The security that one group of employees enjoys is often intrinsically linked to the fact that the protection of other groups is poor. The case of protection against dismissals for regular workers requires particular attention in this regard.

Protection of regular and deregulation of non-regular employment

The OECD has published estimates of the strictness of employment protection in member countries since the late 1980s (OECD 1999, 2004a). Detailed information on employment protection for each country, along with annual time series data from 1985–2008, is now available from the OECD's employment protection website.[9] Past values of indicators were revised in a 2008 update, which are now compiled from 21 items, as opposed to 18 items used in the 2003 update given in OECD 2004a. These 21 items, just like the previous 18 items, are classified into the following three categories: 'employment protection of regular workers against individual dismissal; specific requirements for collective dismissals; and regulation of temporary forms of employment'.[10] Sub-indicators were further constructed for 'strictness of regulations for regular contracts, temporary contracts and collective dismissals', each of these indicators being scaled from 0 to 6 (Venn 2009: 6).

Of the 28 OECD member countries evaluated in 2003, Japan had the 18th highest level of employment protection legislation for regular contracts with a score of 1.87 according to the 2008 update, placing it third in the G7 following Germany and France. This score had been unchanged since 1985. However, according to the 2003 update, Japan's score had been 2.4 and the tenth highest (OECD 2004a: 117). Japan is among six countries for which a different value for the regular employment indicator was given in the revision (Venn 2009: 43). Comparing values in OECD (2004a) with the data given on the OECD's employment protection website shows that the revision for Japan (–0.53) was substantial, whereas for other countries it was more or less trivial (–0.05 for Canada, 0.13 for Denmark, –0.07 for Greece, –0.14 for Poland and –0.14 for Spain). The 2008 revision to the Japanese figure for 2003 is explained by the fact that severance pay estimates previously incorporated into the indicator had been removed (Venn 2009: 43).

96 *Japan in international comparison*

The majority of regular, full-time workers who are protected against dismissals in Japan are 25 to 54 year-old men employed by large firms. Non-regular workers, such as part-timers, are overwhelmingly women, young adults and men over the age of 60. As Mari Miura has observed, firms facing the biggest hurdles in actually implementing restructuring dismissals are those with organized labour unions (Miura 2003: 122).

Non-regular employment is usually for a fixed period of time, i.e. temporary employment. According to the OECD's employment protection website, Japan's sub-indicator for 'strictness of regulation of temporary employment' was 1.0 in 2003 (based on the 2008 update), ranking it in the lowest group of OECD member states, or 21st out of 28 (as compared to 18th with a score of 1.3 according to the 2003 update). Among G7 states, Japan thus occupied the middle position, following France with a score of 3.63, Italy with a score of 1.88 and Germany with a score of 1.5. Calculating again the difference between the values given in OECD (2004a) with those according to the 2008 update, the revision is –0.3 for Japan, –0.3 for Germany, –0.22 for Italy and 0.2 for Portugal. The extent of changes in the case of non-regular employment is more substantial than in the case of regular contracts for all countries except for Japan. Japan's figure was revised because 'new information' had been obtained that 'there are no restrictions on renewal of temporary work agency contracts' (Venn 2009: 43).

Japan's temporary employee protection score was 1.81 until 1995. But this score has dropped over the years as a result of deregulation of the use of dispatched workers from temporary employment agencies. In 1985, use of temporary employees had been limited to 13 industrial sectors. This number grew to 26 in 1996, and in 1999 all restrictions were lifted.

Figure 4.3 shows change over time, from 1990 via 1999 to 2003, of the overall strictness of protection against dismissals for regular workers (vertical axis) and of the overall strictness of regulation for temporary contracts (horizontal axis). In the 'liberal' countries, scores for both categories had been low in the first place, but except for the US and Canada some modest increases in employee protection and regulation were seen. New Zealand and Ireland strengthened regulations governing employment of temporary workers, and New Zealand and Australia strengthened their labour laws' provisions for terminating regular workers.

Four nations – the Netherlands, Sweden, Germany and Norway – that had higher scores for their protection for regular workers, deregulated the use of non-regular workers. Spain and Finland weakened dismissal protections for regular workers without relaxing regulations for temporary workers at the same time. Countries that earned middling scores for their protections for regular workers – Italy, Belgium, Denmark and Japan – left those protections in place but substantially deregulated temporary employment. In terms of relative rankings, these changes brought Denmark, Italy, Belgium and Japan closer to New Zealand and Australia.

Whether viewed in absolute or relative terms, Japan had weak regulations on the use of temporary workers and yet continued to deregulate further in this area, whereas protections for regular workers remained unchanged at a middling score.

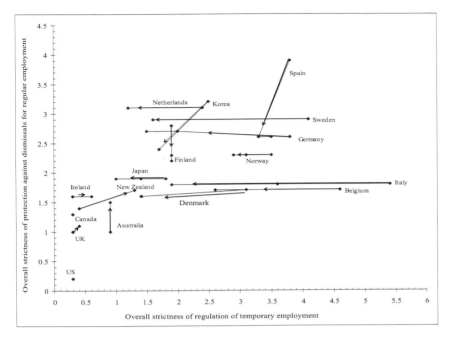

Figure 4.3 Labour market regulations in 1990, 1999 and 2003
Source: OECD's employment protection website, www.oecd.org/employment/protection.

Risk of unemployment, increasing part-time work and labour costs

Unemployment risk by gender and age group

The complement to employment protection is risk of unemployment. From the mid-1990s, Japan's unemployment rate has been rising, and it is higher for men than for women. When compared internationally by age and gender, the following points stand out. First, the unemployment rate for young workers (both men and women) aged 16 to 24 has risen in Japan while declining in other nations, especially in the European Union, where the unemployment rate of those aged 15 to 24 declined by one-fourth from 1995 to 2000 (OECD 2004: 297–305; European Commission 2001: 26). Second, for those aged 25 to 54, i.e. individuals in their 'working prime', Japan has a relatively low rate of unemployment, and a lower rate for men than for women. In contrast, the rate of male unemployment in Scandinavian and Anglo-Saxon nations exceeds that of women in the same 25 to 54 age bracket. Third, turning to Japanese men age 55 to 64, their employment rate is far and away the highest among OECD members. This brings us back to Esping-Andersen's analysis of the male breadwinner model in Continental Europe. Esping-Andersen found that countries that pursued 'familialistic' or male breadwinner-oriented welfare regimes adopted a 'labour reduction' route beginning in the 1980s, as mentioned earlier. This observation clearly does not apply to middle-aged and older men in Japan.

To what extent have workers been able to maintain their income? Comparing Japan with the other G5 nations (the UK, France, Germany and the US), the 2004 *White Paper on Labour Economics* found that real wages in Japan have been falling since 1997.[11] Real wages in the US had fallen in the early 1990s but recovered shortly after, while real wages in the three European nations rose during the same period (Kōsei-rōdō-shō 2004: figure 1(2)1).

Of the G5 nations, only in Japan have real wages declined since 1997. Trends in consumer prices have also diverged with Japan experiencing deflation since 1999, while prices in the other G5 nations have risen at an annual rate of approximately 2 per cent. In other words, nominal wages in Japan have dipped sharply on average.

Have the regular male workers in their prime earning years, the group with the greatest employment security, seen their pay checks dwindle as much as other groups? Evidently not. Trends in designated wage (base wage without overtime pay) levels in Japan are functions of three factors – changes in the base salaries of regular, full-time workers, changes in the base salaries of part-time workers and the percentage of all workers who are employed part-time. The base salaries of regular, full-time workers rose from 1997 to 2000. We can therefore conclude that the overall decline in average nominal wage resulted from the rising share of part-time workers in the labour force (Taguchi 2004: 480–1).

High rates of part-time employment and low wages

According to OECD data, in 2001 41.0 per cent of working women in Japan were employed part time, the fourth highest rate in the OECD after the Netherlands (58.1 per cent), Switzerland (44.7 per cent) and Australia (41.7 per cent). Moreover, 13.7 per cent of Japanese men in the labour force were working part time, the third highest rate in the OECD after Australia (15.8 per cent) and the Netherlands (13.8 per cent). By 2004, rates of part-time employment had risen to 41.7 per cent for Japanese women, giving Japan the third highest rate in the OECD after the Netherlands (60.2 per cent) and Switzerland (45.3 per cent). Japan continued to have the third highest rate of part-time male employment as the share of such workers grew to 14.2 per cent. Only Australia and the Netherlands had higher rates of part-time male employment at 16.1 per cent and 15.1 per cent, respectively. In these statistics, part-time employment refers to persons who usually work less than 30 hours per week, but only for Japan to less than 35 hours per week (OECD 2005a: 253). Relative to the size of their working populations, the Netherlands, Australia and Japan have the largest share of part-time workers, both male and female. The fact that the share of women working part-time continues to rise in countries that already have the highest rates is troubling.

One way to evaluate the disadvantages of working part time cross-nationally is to compare the median hourly wages of part-time and full-time female employees.

Scaling the latter to equal 100, the OECD reported that in 1995 median part-time wages were 93.1 in the Netherlands, 92.3 in Sweden and 87.5 in Germany. In Australia (1997), median part-time wages were 86.8, in the UK 74.5 (2000), in Japan 66.4 (2001) and in the US 62.5 (1996) (OECD 1999a: 24; Naikakufu 2003b: 28). As this list shows, although Australia and the Netherlands have higher rates of part-time employment, their part-time hourly wages are within 85 per cent of full-time hourly wages. The part-time/full-time wage gap in Japan is more than two to three times greater. And, as discussed in Chapter 3, it is widening.

Moderate labour costs and social security contributions

As pointed out in Chapter 3, Japanese enterprises have controlled labour costs by turning to non-regular employees. Table 4.1 presents an international comparison of social security contributions and labour cost as reported in the OECD's *Taxing Wages*. Columns 1 and 2 show the respective amount of social security contributions paid by workers and employers. Column 3 presents 2004 labour costs in US dollars with equal purchasing power. The labour costs are calculated using data from each nation on (production) workers' annual average pre-tax incomes and firms' social security contributions and general payroll taxes (OECD 1999b; OECD 2005d).

In Germany, the US, the UK and Japan, employers and employees contribute equally to social security schemes, but in the majority of member nations employers pay a greater share. Only in the Netherlands and Denmark do employees' social security contributions exceed that of their employers. Column 4 in Table 4.1 presents the ratio between workers' pre-tax income (labour costs excluding employers' social security contributions) and employers' social security contributions. This ratio is called the 'employers' net social security contribution rate'. In nations where employers pay more than workers, the values in column 4 are much greater than in column 2. Their values in column 4 are near the current burden rate for employers in Japan. But their gaps between columns 4 and 2 are wider..

In 2003, Japan changed how it calculates its social security contribution rates. Originally, rates were based on monthly pre-tax base salaries, not including bonuses or overtime pay. Starting in 2003, the rate calculations included annual bonuses.[12] The employers' net social security contribution rates in column 4 are thus nearer to the current rate of Japan based on annual income including bonuses.

Column 3 of Table 4.1 shows that Japan had the 17th highest labour costs of the 29 nations in the OECD in 1998. In 2004 Japan ranked 15th out of 30 OECD member states in labour costs (OECD 1999b; OECD 2005d). It is important to note that Japan's labour costs are not unusually high compared to other developed nations. In fact, Korea now ranks higher than Japan after its labour costs soared 57 per cent. However, in 1998, Japan's employers' net social security contributions rate was the sixth lowest in the OECD at 7.5 per cent. By 2004, Japan's employers' contribution rate had increased to 12.5 per cent, making it the 11th lowest in the OECD. Nations that increased their employers' net social security contribution rate between 1998 and 2004 were Turkey by 9.1 percentage points, Australia by

Table 4.1 Comparison of social security contributions as percentage of labour costs, 1998 and 2004

Country[1]	1 Social security contributions (% of labour costs)				2 Labour costs[3]		3 Net social security contribution of employer(%)[4]	
	Employees[2]		Employers					
	1998	2004	1998	2004	1998	2004	1998	2004
Belgium	10	10.7	26	23.0	40,995	46,261	35.1	29.9
Germany	17	17.3	17	17.3	35,863	42,543	20.5	20.9
Australia	2	0.0	0	5.7	29,590	40,630	0.0	6.0
Netherlands	23	22.2	14	14.0	32,271	39,614	16.3	16.3
Switzerland	10	10.0	10	10.0	32,535	38,213	11.1	11.1
Canada	5	6.2	6	10.1	32,211	37,856	6.4	11.2
Denmark	10	10.5	1	0.5	32,214	37,788	1.0	0.5
United States	7	7.1	7	7.1	31,300	37,606	7.5	7.6
Norway	7	6.9	11	11.5	31,638	37,550	12.4	13.0
Finland	6	4.9	21	19.4	29,334	37,174	26.6	24.1
United Kingdom	8	7.8	9	9.0	29,277	36,159	9.9	9.9
Korea	4	6.5	9	8.1	22,962	36,125	9.9	8.8
Luxembourg	11	12.1	12	11.9	31,102	35,767	13.6	13.5
France	9	9.8	28	28.2	28,198	35,443	38.9	39.3
Japan	7	10.3	7	11.1	27,664	35,103	7.5	12.5
Italy	7	6.9	26	24.9	32,351	35,005	35.1	33.2
Sweden	5	5.3	25	24.6	29,768	34,606	33.3	32.6
Austria	14	14.0	24	22.5	29,823	34,356	31.6	29.0
Iceland	0	0.2	4	5.4	22,545	32,194	4.2	5.7
Ireland	5	4.5	11	9.7	24,667	30,236	12.4	10.7
Spain	5	4.9	24	23.4	24,454	29,382	31.6	30.5
New Zealand	0	0.0	0	0.0	24,332	28,228	0.0	0.0
Greece	12	12.5	22	21.9	17,880	22,138	28.2	28.0
Turkey	8	12.3	11	17.7	15,825	20,003	12.4	21.5

(*continued*)

	1		2		3		4	
Country[1]	Social security contributions (% of labour costs)						Net social security contribution of employer(%)[4]	
	Employees[2]		Employers		Labour costs[3]			
	1998	2004	1998	2004	1998	2004	1998	2004
Czech Republic	9	9.3	26	25.9	15,781	19,395	35.1	35.0
Poland	0	21.1	33	17.0	13,051	17,319	49.3	20.5
Portugal	9	8.9	19	19.2	13,903	16,128	23.5	23.8
Slovak Republic		9.9		26.3		13,997		35.7
Hungary	8	9.9	32	26.9	9,916	13,229	47.1	36.8
Mexico	2	1.3	20	11.4	8,662	10,278	25.0	12.9

Source: OECD 1999b, 2005d.
Notes:
1 Countries ranked by decreasing costs in 2004.
2 Single individual without children at the income level of the average production worker.
3 Dollars with equal purchasing power.
4 Calculated as $(3) \times (2) \div 100 = A$; $(3) - A = B$; $A \div B \times 100 = (4)$.

6.0 points, Japan by 5.0 points, Canada by 4.8 points and Iceland by 1.5 points. Belgium, Poland, Hungary and Mexico, on the other hand, significantly lowered employers' net contribution rates, albeit from high levels ranging from Poland's 49 per cent rate to Mexico's 25 per cent rate in 1998. In short, the net social security burden placed on businesses in Japan in 2004 remained relatively light despite its rate increase.

Based on the data above, Japan's employment performance can be summarized as follows. First, the fact that men have a higher unemployment rate in average than women is a result of high levels of unemployment among workers age 16 to 24 and over age 54, although the employment rate of older male workers is higher than in other nations. Second, the base salaries of regular, full-time workers – the majority of whom are men age 25 to 54 – continued to rise despite falling prices and ongoing efforts to cut labour costs largely by denying women and young workers the opportunity to become full-time regular employees. In other words, despite Japan's recent economic challenges, employment performance for male regular workers age 25 to 54 remained high not only relative to Japanese women and other less favoured groups in Japan, but also in international comparison – a dubious achievement.

Main features of Japan's small welfare government

The tax burden and government expenditure structure

Light tax burdens disadvantaging single-member households

Let us first compare the incidence of the tax and social security burden on household budgets. Takafumi Uzuhashi (2002) compared rates of net burden (the sum of income tax, local tax and social security contribution, from which cash benefits are deducted) of dual-earner households, single-earner married households (male breadwinner and full-time housewife) and single-member households with equal incomes (assuming the number of children to be zero for all types of household) in Australia, Germany, Japan, Sweden, the UK and the US, using data from the 1999–2000 edition of the OECD's *Taxing Wages* series.

Uzuhashi found that in Australia, Sweden and the UK, the net burden of single-member households is generally equivalent to that of single-earner married households but higher than that of dual-earner households. The Australian burden rate for dual-earner households is nearly ten percentage points lower than for single-earner (married or single) ones. In the UK, dual-earner households pay 4 to 19 percentage points less than single-earner households; the lower the income level, the greater this discrepancy becomes. In Sweden, the net burden rate for dual-earner households is 2 to 7 percentage points lower. The burden rate falls further for dual-earner households with either higher income levels or greater parity between spouses' wages.

According to Uzuhashi, the burden rate gaps in Australia and the UK stem from their progressive tax structures (the UK has basic deductions for working wives and tax deductions for social security contributions), and the higher burden rate of single-earner married households in Sweden results from tax exemptions such as basic deductions. The system offering the strongest incentives for gender-equal dual earning is apparently that of Sweden.

In Germany, the US and Japan, by contrast, the burden rates of single- and dual-earner married households are roughly the same, but the burden rate of single-member households is higher. In Germany, the difference in the burden rates between married and unmarried households is more than 10 percentage points, and burden rates for unmarried people in the US are several points higher than for married people. In Japan, the difference amounts to 2 to 3 percentage points. Unmarried people in Germany and the US pay more owing to split taxation under progressive income tax schemes. (In the US, basic deductions apply to single-earner married households as well.) The Japanese results, on the other hand, are owing to different types and a larger scale of income deductions.

The most noteworthy aspect of this comparison of tax and social security rates is that personal tax rates in Japan are much lower than in other nations.[13] It may not be surprising to find much higher tax rates in Sweden and Germany, with rates ranging from 30 to 40 per cent in Sweden and 20 to 47 per cent in Germany, but Japan's rates of 12 to 19 per cent also fall at the lower end of the 10 to 35 per cent tax range of the (neo-)liberal welfare regimes of Australia, the US, and the UK. Social security contributions in Japan are levied generally at a same rate of 10 per cent, i.e. regardless of income level, which is half of Germany's rate, but higher than Sweden's rate of less than 7 per cent, and the UK's of approximately 8 per cent (Uzuhashi 2002). Although its social security contribution rate thus differs relatively little from these other nations, Japan's income tax rates are markedly lower. In absolute terms, the burden rate of Japanese single-member households is only 2 or 3 percentage points higher than that of married households, but due to Japan's low tax rates, the relative difference between the tax rates of married and unmarried people in Japan is similar to that in Germany and the US.

Preponderance of pensions and medical care in social security benefits

As noted already in Section 1 of this chapter, the scale of Japan's welfare government is among the smallest in the OECD. A recent OECD Working Paper offers a comparison of public social expenditures (a close approximation of social security benefits) in 2005 as percentages of GDP in four categories: pensions (old-age and survivors' pensions), income support to the working-age population, health care and social services other than health care (Adema and Ladaique 2009). Under the small welfare governments of Turkey, Japan and Greece, the largest share of public social expenditure is taken up by pensions.

The relatively large welfare governments of Italy, Poland and Portugal have social expenditure structures that are similarly concentrated on pensions. Sweden, Denmark, Finland and Norway, on the other hand, dedicate a smaller share of their social expenditure to pensions and medical care. Income support to the working-age population and service benefits other than health care occupy a greater share of public social expenditure in these Scandinavian countries than in the large spending Western European countries such as France, Austria and Germany (Adema and Ladaique 2009: 26).

Yukiko Katsumata (2005) has conducted a comparative analysis of trends in OECD members' spending, relative to their GDP, on social programmes for the elderly and families with dependent children. Along with Spain, the US, Italy and Korea, Japan spent the smallest share on families relative to its spending on the elderly, and this gap continued to expand throughout the 1990s. Taking into account the varying severity of the aging society problem across nations, Katsumata also compared nations' social spending per eligible elderly person or child 15 or younger, finding that from 1980 to 2000 Japan's per capita spending on the elderly declined, while spending per child remained flat. These spending patterns confirm that in Japan an 'expansion of social care' (Peng 2004) did not occur during the 1990s.

Given that expenditures on the elderly have been decreasing on a per capita basis, it is obvious that their livelihood security is low, despite the fact that the elderly population as a whole receives the majority of social security benefits. The relative poverty rate of elderly Japanese circa 2000 was among the highest in the OECD (see Table 4.4 on p. 121 below). Relative poverty is defined by the OECD as having an income less than 50 per cent of the median equivalent income. In 14 OECD member states, the average Gini coefficient (which measures disposable income inequality remaining after redistribution of wealth through taxes and social security disbursements) for the age 18 to 64 population is slightly higher than for the population age 65 and older. The reverse is true in Japan and this difference is by no means trivial. In a comparison of Japan and eight Western nations, only Japan and the US had higher Gini coefficients among elderly people than among their working-age populations according to data from the mid-1990s (Yamada 2005).

In her study of Taiwan and the G7 nations, Shirahase (2009) finds that only the elderly in Japan and Taiwan are experiencing greater income inequality than their younger compatriots. The bottom line is that although Japan directs most of its social security benefits to the elderly, large income inequalities persist in this group and its relative poverty rate is high.

Public pensions schemes

Generous support of male breadwinner households

Government policies in Japan particularly favour male breadwinners after they retire and their widows through the public pension system, the scheme that consumes the greatest share of public social spending. Table 4.2 presents a comparison of pension schemes in Japan, the US, the UK and Germany circa 2000.

Figure 4.4 shows estimates by the Ministry of Health, Labour and Welfare's Pension Bureau of average pension benefit levels by type of household in July 2002. The Pension Bureau calculated how much an average worker with a 40-year employment history was likely to receive in pensions, including Basic Pension, as a percentage of his or her wages at the time of retirement in four different ways: according to whether the average monthly wage amount would be for full-time workers or for full-time and part-time workers combined; and according to whether it would be based on monthly wage equivalents for annual nominal income (annual income including bonuses divided by 12) or base wages (nominal monthly income). In this section, I focus on base income replacement rates (pensions as a fraction of pre-retirement base income) for full-time workers for two reasons. I exclude part-time workers because they are mostly not covered by the Employees' Pension scheme. Second, in 2002, when the Pension Bureau estimated what the average pension rate would be, insurance contributions in Japan were assessed on base wages alone, making nominal monthly income – a close approximation of both monthly wage amounts and monthly standard remuneration – the logical choice for comparisons. Figure 4.4 illustrates the favourable treatment given to male breadwinner households in Japan and the US.

In the Pension Bureau's calculations, only households in which wives themselves never paid into a pension fund at any time in the 40-year period were defined as male breadwinner households. Pension benefits levels for male breadwinner households in the US are much higher than for all other household types, but the number of American wives who were never employed during a 40-year span is

Table 4.2 Public pension schemes in Japan, the US, the UK and Germany (from the perspective of women's lifestyle choice)

	Japan	The United States	The United Kingdom	Germany
Historical backgrounds for public pension schemes	1942: Workers' pension scheme introduced for male blue collar workers. 1961: Universal coverage of public pension schemes for Japanese citizens. 1973: Price indexation and wage indexation introduced. 1985: National pension scheme reformed. Introduction of the Basic Pension scheme. 1994: Pension eligibility age raised from 60 to 65. Wage indexation changed to net income indexation.	1935: Pension scheme established for employees in commercial/industrial enterprises. Coverage gradually expanded thereafter. 1972: Price indexation introduced. 1983: Pension eligibility age to be raised in steps to 67 by 2007.	1946: Comprehensive National Insurance scheme established. 1975: Wage and price indexation introduced and State Earnings Related Pension (SERPS) established. 1980: Wage indexation abolished. 1986: Benefit level of SERPS reduced. Shift to occupational pension and/or individual pension schemes encouraged. 1999: Stakeholder pension introduced. 2000: SERPS to be replaced from April 2002 by the State Second Pension (S2P) favouring low income earners.	1889: Lifetime/old-age pension scheme introduced. 1957: Wage indexation introduced. 1992: Wage indexation changed to net income indexation. 1999: Lowering of contribution rates for employers and employees. 2000: Reduction of pension benefits. Earnings replacement rate lowered from 70 to 67 per cent. Introduction of savings-type pensions.
Relationship with occupational/ private pension schemes	Occupational/private pension plans also widespread.	Defined-benefit/ contribution-type occupational or private pension plans widely used.	Occupational pension plans and private pension plans widely used.	Occupational pension schemes available for workers in the private sector.

(continued)

	Japan	The United States	The United Kingdom	Germany
(Contributions)				
Who pays the pension contribution?	Non-employees other than dependent spouses of full-time employees (Class 1): individual based. Full-time employees (Class 2): individual-based (Class 3 status mitigates pension contribution payments for married couples).	Individual-based	Individual-based	Individual-based
Criteria for requirement of pension contribution	Class 2: three-quarter criterion. Class 1: if three-quarter criterion not met, 1.3 million criterion if spouse of an employee	Employees: income. Self-employed: earnings of $400 or more in a year. Non-working: ineligible for membership.	Employees: earnings of £67 or more per week. Self-employed: earnings of £3,825 or more per year. Low income earners: membership optional.	Employees who work for 15 hours or less per week or earn 620 DM or less per month may join the public pension scheme on an optional basis. Other workers are required to join. Self-employed optional membership (compulsory in some professions). Unemployed: membership optional.
Calculation base for collecting contribution	Income	Income	Income	Income

	Japan	The United States	The United Kingdom	Germany
Relationship between pension contribution and calculation base	Class 2: proportional to income Class 1: flat rate	Proportional to income	Employees: proportional to income. Self-employed: flat rate, if income exceeds a certain level, income proportional contribution is applicable (without corresponding benefit).	Proportional to income
Preferential measure(s) for child care	Employees (regular): contribution reduced, but counted as full contribution during child-care leave. Non-regular employees and self-employed: no preferential measures.	None	Home responsibility protection: if income falls below lower earnings limit due to child care (for a child under age 16), the required number of contribution years (qualifying years) for full pension is reduced (The actual number of qualifying years must not be less than 20 or a half of the standard number of qualifying years).	If a person raises a child younger than 3 years old, he/she is considered to have paid pension contributions at the same amount as the average pension insured person. Preferential measures are also applicable if the income falls short of the average wage.
Income-splitting between husband and wife	None	None	None	Splitting of pension benefits (income-splitting) possible on an optional basis for couples married 25 years or longer.
Who receives the pension benefits?	Individual-based (However, the pension scheme includes Class 3 status and survivor's pension benefits for senior spouses.)	Individual-based (However, the pension scheme includes spouse benefit as well as survivor's benefits for senior spouses.)	Individual-based (However, the pension scheme includes the benefit for wives based on husband's contribution.)	Individual-based (However, the pension scheme includes survivor's pension benefits for senior spouses.)

(*continued*)

	Japan	The United States	The United Kingdom	Germany
Class 3 insured person status, or spouse's pension schemes	Class 3 status guarantees Basic Pension benefits for homemakers even if they did not pay own pension contributions.	A pensioner's spouse who is 65 years or older receives pensioner's spouse benefit (50 per cent of the pensioner's pension benefits).	A pensioner's wife who is over age 60 (pension eligibility age to be raised in steps to 65, the same as for men, from 2010 to 2020) receives a spouse benefit (60% of the pensioner's Basic Pension benefit).	None
Survivor's pension for senior spouses	Class 2 insurants must enrol in survivor's pension scheme (the Basic Pension scheme does not include a survivor's scheme for senior spouses). The survivor receives three quarters of the Employees' Pension benefit (the second tier) of the deceased spouse, if the survivor remains unmarried after bereavement. The survivor has the option of receiving her or his own Employees' Pension benefit, or the survivor's benefit, or half of the sum of both benefits.	The insured person must enrol in the survivor's pension scheme. A widow(er) is entitled to survivor's benefits (100% of the old age benefit of the deceased) if aged 60 or older (50 or older for disabled persons) and unmarried after bereavement. Survivor's benefits are continued for widow(er)s who remarry after age 60.	In the case of bereavement on or after 9 April 2001, a widow(er) may receive a pension benefit based on the contribution of the deceased (Mandatory). A widow(er) may be able to receive a 2nd tier pension (50-100% of the 2nd tier pension of the deceased depending on when the deceased reached or would have reached the pension age). A man who was widowed before 8 April 2001 can claim only widowed parent's allowance.	A bereaved spouse is able to receive survivor's pension benefits if he/she is at least 45 years old. (Mandatory)

	Japan	The United States	The United Kingdom	Germany
Survivor's pension benefits for young bereaved spouse or his/her child	Basic Pension: A widow receives survivor's Basic Pension if she has a child under age 18 (Mandatory). Employees' Pension: A widow receives survivor's benefit (three quarter of the second tier benefit of the deceased) irrespective of her age or having a child (Mandatory). A widower under age 55 at bereavement is not entitled as a survivor, and cannot claim survivor's benefits while he is under age 60.	A widow(er) receives Mother's/Father's benefit (75% of pension benefit of the deceased) if (s)he remains unmarried after bereavement and raises a child who is either under age 16 or disabled (Mandatory).	A widow(er) receives widowed parent's allowance if he/she is raising at least one child under age 16 or a student aged 16 to 18, or if she is expecting her husband's baby (Mandatory). A widow(er) aged over 45 and under pension age at the time of bereavement and not raising children can receive bereavement allowance (rate depending on age at the time of bereavement) for 52 weeks from the date of bereavement (Mandatory). Bereavement allowance stops at remarriage.	If a bereaved spouse raises a child 18 years old or younger, he/she can claim the same benefits as mentioned above (Mandatory). If a bereaved spouse has no children, survivor's benefits are paid at a smaller amount (Mandatory).
Pension benefit structure	Minimum + income-related portion (2nd tier portion is only applicable to Class 2 insured)	Income-related portion only	Minimum + income-related portion (2nd tier portion is only applicable to employees.)	Income-related portion only
Structure of 'Minimum' portion	Flat rate (Basic Pension)	None (Livelihood subsidy is provided to low-income earners.)	Flat rate (Basic Pension)	None (Livelihood subsidy is provided to low-income earners.)

(continued)

	Japan	The United States	The United Kingdom	Germany
Relationship between contribution and pension benefits	Basic Pension: flat rate (However, the duration of contribution is also taken into consideration.) Employees' Pension (second tier): Proportional to income.	Proportional to income	Basic Pension: flat rate (However, the duration of contribution is also taken into consideration.) Employees' Pension plans (2nd tier): Proportional to income	Proportional to income
Redistribution	Redistribution via the Basic Pension scheme	Applicable multipliers for income level will be lowered at two different income-level points (bend-point system)	Redistribution via the Basic Pension scheme	None
Pension-splitting between husband and wife (at divorce)	The pension scheme does not provide a pension-splitting option. In the case of divorce after April 2007 the income-related portion may be split on an optional basis. Employee's Pension benefits accrued during enrolment in Class 3 after April 2008 are split half and half (Mandatory).	If they have been married for 10 years or longer, a divorced person receives the pension benefits based on the ex-spouse's contribution (50 per cent of ex-spouse's pension benefits).	A divorcing couple files jointly to either divide 2nd tier pension benefits based on a judicial court ruling or by a mutually agreed splitting-ratio. If not remarried, a divorced person is also able to receive spouse's pension benefits (60 per cent of Basic Pension benefit for ex-spouse) based on the ex-spouse's contribution.	A divorcing couple may split their pension rights, divide their future pension benefits, or decide the splitting rate by mutual agreement. (In the latter two cases, a divorced person is not able to gain independent pension rights from his/her former spouse.)
(Reference) Replacement rate gap among households	(Basic Pension + 2nd tier portion) male breadwinner households > dual-earner households	male breadwinner households > dual-earner households	male breadwinner-income households > dual-earner households	male breadwinner-income households = dual-earner households = male single-member households = female single-member households:

	Japan	The United States	The United Kingdom	Germany
(Reference) (cont.) (numbers in the parenthesis are estimates)	[male breadwinner household: 64.6%; dual-earner households: 50.5%; male single-member households: 46.5%; female single-member households: 56.9%]	[male breadwinner household: 65.0%; dual-earner households: 44.9%; male single-member households: 43.3%; and female single-member households: 47.1%]	[male breadwinner household: 42.9%; dual-earner households: 36.2%; male single-member households: 34.8%; female single-member households: 38.2%]	43.0%
(Reference) Pension eligibility age	Basic Pension benefits: 65 years Employees' Pension benefits: 60 years	65 years (Pension eligibility age to be raised in steps to 67 by 2007.)	Men: 65 years Women: 60 years (Pension eligibility age to be raised in steps to 65 by 2020.)	Male pensioners: 63 years (Pension eligibility age to be raised to 65 by 2009.) Female pensioners: 60 years old (Pension eligibility age to be raised to 65 by 2018.)
(Reference) Dependence of pension benefits on tax revenues	One third of Basic Pension benefits financed from tax revenues.	Taxes levied on high-income earners' pension benefits to fund pension account.	None	Federal government grants subsidies for pension expenditures.

Notes:
1 This table was prepared based on Pension Fund Association, 'Overseas Pension Schemes', Tōyō Keizai Shinpōsha and hearing sessions conducted by the Specialist Committee on Impact Survey.
2 Japan's pension scheme has the following pensioner statuses:
 Class 1 insured person status: Falls short of the three-quarter criterion but satisfies ¥1.3 million criterion if spouse of employee. (This category is for insurants not falling under Class 2 or Class 3, such as the self-employed.)
 Class 2 insured person status: Satisfies the three-quarter criterion. (This category consists of employed workers, i.e., members of employee's pension schemes.)
 Class 3 insured person status: Falls short both of the three-quarter criterion and the ¥1.3 million criterion. (Dependent spouses of employed workers fall under this category.)

('Three-quarter criterion' means set working hours that are three quarters or more of a full-time worker's. ¥1.3 million criterion' means that worker's annual income is ¥1.3 million or more.)

112 *Japan in international comparison*

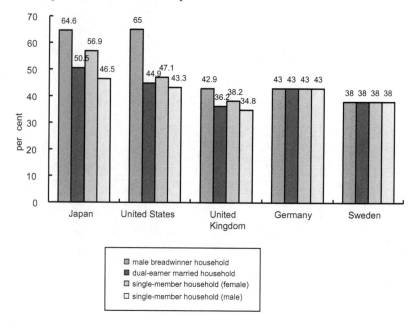

Figure 4.4 Pension benefit levels by type of household (earnings replacement rates in per cent)

Source: Shakai hoshō shingikai, Nenkin bukai: Seventh meeting, Material 1, p. 4.

presumably small. Male breadwinner households in Japan receive pensions on a level that is 7.6 to 18 percentage points higher than for other households, whereas in the UK the difference is 6.5 percentage points on average. Germany's pension benefit levels are uniform across all households at 43 per cent.[14] As a point of comparison, the pension benefit level in the high-cost/high-benefit Swedish welfare state is 38 per cent for everyone.[15]

Pension benefit levels are flat in Germany and Sweden because pensions are not used as vehicles for inter-household wealth redistribution. Instead, pensions are achievement-based – the higher the earnings, the higher the contribution (and thus the pension) will be. Given the fact that both Germany and Sweden have strong social democratic political parties, it is more than a little ironic that their pensions are achievement-based while the US and Japan have redistributive pension schemes. It must be noted, however, that redistribution in Japan as well as the US favours male breadwinner households over single-member and dual-earner ones.

Belated introduction of pension splitting and generous support for widows

Second, pension splitting after divorce was first introduced in Germany in 1976. In that year, Germany's civil code (*Bürgerliches Gesetzbuch*) was revised, and divorce laws changed from an at-fault system to a no-fault one (Hirowatari 1990:

297–9). Under the German system, not only public but also occupational and individual pensions are divided. Pension splitting for still-married couples who have been married for 25 years or more was introduced, if both parties agree, as part of Germany's 2001 pension reforms (Josei no raifusutairu no henka tō ni taiō shita nenkin no arikata ni kansuru kentōkai 2002: V-5–7). The UK enacted pension sharing after divorce in 1999. Japan, as discussed in Chapter 5 below, introduced pension splitting at long last in 2004. The US Social Security Administration will grant spouse benefits, equal to one-half of the primary wage earner's benefits, to divorced people if their marriages had lasted at least ten years and if they had not remarried. As the payment of spouse benefits to ex-wives does not reduce the primary wage earner's benefits, nor preclude a subsequent spouse from receiving benefits, this policy supports male breadwinner households at the expense of single-member and dual-earner ones.

Third, in several nations the requirements for receiving surviving spouse pension benefits are either gender neutral or moving towards gender neutrality. Young surviving spouses without dependent children are either ineligible for pension survivors' benefits, or eligible only for a limited time at a rate lower than that for spouses with dependent children. Japan's surviving spouse pension system, however, treats widows much more favourably as regards eligibility requirements, payment levels and benefit entitlement periods (Josei no raifusutairu no henka tō ni taiō shita nenkin no arikata ni kansuru kentōkai 2002: 163–4).

Japan's gender differential in eligibility requirements is highly pronounced. As mentioned earlier in Chapter 2, under Japanese law a widower is not eligible for survivors' benefits unless he was at least 55 years old at the time of his wife's death. Widows who had annual salaries below 8 million yen at their husbands' time of death are eligible for lifetime survivor's pension benefits regardless of their age or whether they have children. Widows with children younger than 18 are also eligible to receive the Basic Pension for survivors. Widows of men who only contributed to the pension fund for a short period of time, receive benefits calculated as if their husbands had paid into the fund for 25 years (300 months).

In short, the pension systems of Japan and the US show the most rigid male breadwinner orientation. Wives who are financially dependent on their husbands are 'rewarded' by a Basic Pension as Class 3 insured persons in Japan and by spouse benefits in the US. The US pension system has no provisions whatsoever for dependent children. In Japan, the more a woman works outside the home, the *lower* the level of her household's pension benefits will be. The German pension system is the most consistent in expressing that husbands and wives work in tandem as a couple through its provisions for pension splitting at divorce and in marriage. It also provides generous preferential measures for child care to persons with dependent children, demonstrating the high value the government places on women as mothers.

Elder care systems

Japan's long-term care insurance scheme has been lauded as the 'largest and most comprehensive' system of care for the frail elderly that takes a social insurance approach (Campbell 2008). But is this in fact the case?

Eligibility and spending

From 2001 to 2004, the OECD studied elder care programmes in 19 member nations including Japan, and published its findings in a 2005 report entitled *Long-term Care for Older People*. The core of the OECD's study was a questionnaire survey conducted by the OECD Health Project in cooperation with selected specialists in each nation. Nearly all statistics on expenditures and implementation were taken from 2000 data. Because complete data were not available for seven nations in the study, for some comparisons I include only 12 nations – Australia, Canada, Germany, Ireland, Japan, the Netherlands, New Zealand, Norway, Spain, Sweden, the UK and the US. For the case of Japan, I also refer to 2005 statistics since Japan launched its long-term care insurance programme only in 2000, while the other nations' programmes had been in place already for at least five years at that time.[16]

Twelve of the 19 nations in the OECD study rely solely on general taxation as their 'source of fund' for long-term care. Japan is one of the seven nations that also use insurance contributions, the others being Germany, Hungary, Luxembourg, the Netherlands, Switzerland and the US. As 50 per cent of Japan's long-term care insurance funding comes from general taxes, its system can be seen as taking a middle position in this regard. In the social insurance approach, those who fail to pay contributions are not eligible to receive benefits in principle. In Japan, in 2005 the proportion of contributions actually paid to the amount assessed was 90 per cent in the general collection category, which suggests that cases of ineligibility are not negligible.[17]

Japan is among the 11 nations in the OECD study that provide only benefits in kind to its long-term care insurance beneficiaries; the remaining eight nations also provide cash benefits. Ten of the 19 nations use means testing (valuation of assets and income levels) to determine eligibility. Japan and eight other nations do not disqualify people based on their wealth. On the other hand, 14 nations provide long-term care benefits to people regardless of their age and five limit eligibility for at least some benefit types to the elderly. Australia applies age restrictions only to one type of home care, New Zealand restricts institutional care coverage to the aged, and the US has minimum age requirements for Medicare benefits. Only Japan and Korea limit eligibility for all forms of long-term care benefits to the elderly (ibid.: Table 1.1).

How does Japan's spending on long-term care compare to spending in other developed nations? In 2000, Japan's public and private spending on long-term care amounted to 0.83 per cent of its GDP, the fourth lowest among the 14 nations listed above (ibid.: Table 1.2). According to the Ministry of Health, Labour and Welfare's

2005 *Annual Report on the State of Long-term Care Insurance*, 6.3957 trillion yen was spent on long-term care services including 601.4 billion yen charged to beneficiaries.[18] Another 85.2 billion yen was used for long-term care assistance under the public assistance programme, partial subsidy to costs of the Long-term Care Insurance Act for atomic bomb victims and family long-term care leave benefits. In total, 6.4809 trillion yen was spent on long-term care in 2005, an amount equal to 1.29 per cent of Japan's nominal GDP of 501.7 trillion yen. The US spent a similar percentage of its nominal GDP on long-term care. The two nations thus fell exactly in the middle of the 12 nations' spending ranking.

Utilization rates and the quality of institutions

Another measure of the comprehensiveness of long-term care insurance is the percentage of people over age 65 receiving long-term care benefits. In 2000, 3.2 per cent of people 65 and older were receiving institutional care, a lower percentage than all but two of the other 14 nations – Korea and the Netherlands. In Japan, 5.5 per cent of older people received home care benefits in 2000, placing Japan in eighth place out of 15 nations. The seven nations ranked below Japan were, in ascending order, Korea, the US, Hungary, Luxembourg, Switzerland, New Zealand and Ireland (OECD 2005e: Table 2.3).

In 2005, 790,000 people were beneficiaries under institutional care and 2.58 million received home care in Japan (monthly average), comprising 3.1 per cent and 10.0 per cent of the total of 25.88 million Class 1 insured persons (age 65 and older).[19] The percentage of elderly people living in nursing homes was slightly lower than in 2000. The percentage of elderly people receiving home care in Japan was the sixth highest among the 15 nations. The growth rate of home care in Japan has been impressive, but the figure in 2005 is not outstandingly high in international comparison.

A final measure of the adequacy of long-term care benefits is the average number of residents per patient room in nursing homes. The OECD has published statistics from eight nations on this topic – Australia, Germany, Japan, Korea, the Netherlands, Norway, Sweden and the UK (OECD 2005e: Table 4.5: 4). Around 2002, Norway topped the rankings with an average of 1.08 residents per room. In last place was Korea with a 2.9 average. Japan came in seventh with a 2.8 average. With the exception of the Netherlands, five nations had averages below 2.0, meaning that roughly half of their nursing home residents had private rooms. In the Netherlands, 55 per cent of nursing home residents either had private rooms or shared with one other person. This contrasts sharply with Japan where 73 per cent of residents were in rooms with 4 or more people.

In 2005, according to the *Survey on Care Service Facilities*, the average capacity per room was 2.4 persons in Japan on 1 October. Even though the number of single rooms has increased, a 2.0 capacity average has not been reached. The survey found that 67.7 per cent of all capacity is in rooms with four or more people. The ratios of occupancy to capacity were 98.2 per cent in welfare facilities for the elderly, 90.5 per cent in health care facilities for the elderly and 92.7 per cent in medical facilities for convalescent care for elderly persons.[20] Actual occupancy is thus approaching full capacity.

In brief, given Japan's middling or worse performance in several aspects of long-term care, it must be said that the assertion that its long-term care system is the 'largest and most comprehensive in the world' greatly overstates the actual situation.

Support for raising the next generation and the 'last resort'

Poor work/life balance and negative income redistribution

As for support for raising the next generation, let us look at Table 4.3, which shows individual and summary indicators of work/family reconciliation policies and relevant flexible work arrangements. This table was adapted from Table 4.9 of the OECD 2001 *Employment Outlook* (OECD 2001).[21] The indicators are scaled to have mean zero and standard deviation unity. The composite index of summary indicators for the 18 nations in the comparison group range from Sweden's 3.3 down to Greece's −3.4. Japan is second to last with a composite index of −2.9. The next lowest group are the Southern European nations of Italy, Spain and Portugal. The Anglo-Saxon countries occupy the middle ranks, and the Continental European nations are scattered throughout. The highest-ranking nations are Sweden, Denmark and the Netherlands.

Japan has negative scores for all summary indicators except for voluntary part-time working. It has the lowest score (−2.1) for child care coverage for children older than three and voluntary family leave in firms (−2.1) among the 18 nations. Akira Kawaguchi (2004) found that total fertility rates in 2001 were most correlated with the extent of available child care for children under three. Notwithstanding the Japanese government's efforts to increase provision of child care through its 1994 'Angel Plan' and the 1999 'New Angel Plan', at the turn of the century Japan's policies and arrangements to support child-rearing were at the low end among OECD members.

Support for lone mother households

How do Japan's policies to support lone mother households compare with policies in other nations? In her 2000 work *Lone Mothers Between Paid Work and Care*, Majella Kilkey compared policy arrangements and outcomes as of May 1994 in 20 nations, including Japan, concerning the guarantee of three social rights in the case of 'lone mothers' (mothers without male partners): their social rights attached to care-giving, their social rights attached to paid work and their social rights attached to transition between periods of care-giving and paid work. The treatment of lone mothers, as Kilkey argued, serves as a 'touchstone' of the evolution of a society's state, market and family interactions, its class-based and racial inequalities, and its gender relations (Kilkey 2000: 70). As Tarō Miyamoto (2002: 3–5) has pointed out, the welfare state is the node in which these various relationships and inequalities intersect.

Table 4.3 Summary indicators of work/family reconciliation policies and relevant flexible work arrangements

All indicators scaled so as to have mean zero and standard deviation unity, across the countries included a)

Country	Child-care coverage for under-3s	Child-care coverage for over-3s	Maternity pay entitlement b)	Total maternity/ child-care leave	Voluntary family leave in firms c)	Flexi-time working	Voluntary part-time working	Composite index d)	Employment rate for women aged 30-34
	(1)	(2)	(3)	(4)	(5)	(6)	(7)	(8)	(9)
Sweden	1.3	0.4	2.3	0.0	−1.9	0.6	0.2	3.3	76.7
Denmark	2.1	1.0	1.3	−0.1	−0.4	−0.3	−0.1	2.9	78.8
Netherlands	−1.0	1.3	0.0	−0.4	0.3	1.0	2.5	2.7	71.5
Australia	−0.5	−0.7	−1.4	−0.7	−0.1	2.6	1.3	1.9	64.2
United Kingdom	0.5	−0.7	−0.7	−0.9	−0.2	0.5	1.1	1.3	69.4
Germany	−0.8	0.3	−0.1	1.6	1.5	0.7	0.8	1.3	68.6
United States	1.6	−0.1	−1.4	−1.6	−0.8	2.0	−0.5	1.2	72.0
Canada	1.1	−1.2	−0.7	−0.8	..	−0.5	0.2	0.2	71.8
Belgium	0.3	1.3	−0.4	−0.4	0.4	−0.1	0.2	0.2	70.8
France	0.3	1.4	0.0	1.6	0.2	−0.2	−0.3	−0.1	65.6
Finland	−0.1	−0.3	1.9	1.6	−0.6	−0.6	−1.2	−0.3	70.7
Austria	−1.1	−0.2	0.0	0.5	1.5	−0.6	0.3	−0.6	72.6
Ireland	0.7	−0.9	−0.5	−0.9	−0.5	−0.9	−0.2	−1.1	69.1

(continued)

All indicators scaled so as to have mean zero and standard deviation unity, across the countries included a)

Country	Child-care coverage for under-3s	Child-care coverage for over-3s	Maternity pay entitlement b)	Total maternity/ child-care leave	Voluntary family leave in firms c)	Flexi-time working	Voluntary part-time working	Composite index d)	Employment rate for women aged 30-34
	(1)	(2)	(3)	(4)	(5)	(6)	(7)	(8)	(9)
Italy	−1.0	1.2	0.2	−0.5	1.2	−0.9	−0.7	−1.9	52.6
Portugal	−0.7	0.1	0.8	0.9	−0.1	−0.9	−1.3	−2.2	75.7
Spain	−1.0	0.6	0.0	1.6	0.6	−0.8	−1.0	−2.5	49.3
Japan	−0.6	−2.1	−0.7	−0.6	−2.1	−0.9	0.3	−2.9	52.6
Greece	−1.1	−1.4	−0.7	−0.9	1.1	−0.5	−1.6	−3.4	57.1
Correlation with the employment rate for women aged 30–34	0.59	0.20	0.36	−0.04	−0.18	0.26	0.25	0.68	

.. Data not available

Source: OECD 2001: Table 4.9.

Notes:
1 This is designed to put the indicators onto a common scale. A value of zero implies that the country concerned is at the average value for the countries in the table.
2 Calculated as the product of the duration of maternity leave and the earnings replacement rate.
3 Average of data for the sick child leave, maternity leave and parental leave.
4 Calculated as the sum of the indicators in columns 1, 3, 6 and 7, plus half of that in column 5.

Of the 20 nations included in her study, Kilkey found that Japan provided quite low support to lone mothers for undertaking full-time caring, and that its support for lone mothers to undertake paid work was middling. Kilkey thus placed Japan in the same group as Southern European nations and France (Kilkey 2000: 248, 262). Even in this group, Japan, together with Italy and Spain, is outstanding in that its public assistance system does not exempt lone mothers from the obligation to undertake paid work for undertaking full-time care. It also does not offer family or child allowances without income restrictions.

Jones (2007: 24) compares relative poverty rates in households with children and a head of working age, circa 2000, and finds that 58 per cent of working single parents in Japan lived in relative poverty, second only to Turkey among 26 OECD nations. This figure is higher than the 52 per cent of non-working single parents in Japan. This relative poverty rate of Japanese non-working single parents is not especially high compared to other OECD members. During this period in Japan, the relative poverty rates of children were higher on the level of disposable income (equal to market income plus cash transfer payments minus taxes and social security contributions paid) than on the level of market income (wages plus income from self-employment and assets) for all types of household, except for households with a single adult who is not working (Whiteford and Adema 2007: 24–5). In other words, lone mothers in Japan suffer negative redistribution if they work. They may pay more in social security contributions even when their earnings remain below the income tax threshold.

Japan's track record in providing public assistance or livelihood protection as a 'last resort' is also dismal. Japan's government spent only 0.2 per cent of GDP on public assistance in 2003, a rate as low as that of the UK.[22] This minimal level of expenditure is due not to benefit levels but to a very low take-up rate. (The 'take-up rate' is the number of eligible people who actually receive benefits.) The OECD reported in its *Benefits and Wages 2004* that Japan's benefit levels were the sixth highest among 23 OECD nations in 2002; benefit levels being defined as the maximum amounts of benefits as percentages of average full-time gross earnings of workers in the manufacturing sector of the country as a whole (OECD 2004b: 29–31).

A Keio University research group led by Kōhei Komamura has found that the OECD's relative poverty metric can substitute for the Japanese government's livelihood protection standards in identifying the number of households in Japan that need public assistance (Yamada *et al.* 2008). Under the OECD formula, the relative poverty rate in Japan was 15.3 per cent around 2000. However, only 0.84 per cent of Japan's population received public assistance in 2000 according to data on livelihood protection programmes published by the Social Security and Population Problem Research Institute.[23]

Determining Japan's take-up rate from 1965 to 2009 is complicated by the Ministry of Health and Welfare's decision not to conduct official estimates of national poverty rates throughout this lengthy period. According to the estimates of several scholars, Japan's public assistance take-up rate falls somewhere between 10 and 20 per cent. In contrast, the UK's public assistance take-up rate is approximately 80 per cent. In the US the take-up rate for the Aid for Dependent Children and food stamp programmes are 60 to 67 per cent, while the take-up rate for social assistance in Germany is estimated at 37 per cent (Tachibanaki and Urakawa 2006: 125).

What are the causes of the great discrepancy between apparent need and actual aid in Japan? One important factor is that people are not adequately informed of public assistance programmes. Social stigma associated with receiving non-contributory welfare benefits additionally deters people from applying for aid. For those who are able to overcome those obstacles, programme eligibility requirements other than income caps, such as asset utilization rules and the government's expectation that applicants should look to family members for assistance first, further reduce enrolment rates. In short subsidiarity as a principle and in application is extremely pronounced.

Aggregate effect of Japan's tax and social security schemes

Japan as a frontrunner in social inequality and relative poverty

In the final section of this chapter, we review the efficacy of Japan's small welfare government in ameliorating poverty and income inequalities. The OECD's 2006 *Economic Survey of Japan* provides important data in this regard, which were examined by Kiyoshi Ōta soon after their publication. Table 4.4 summarizes a more detailed tabulation by Ōta, which positions Japan in comparison to 14 OECD nations at the start of this century. As noted above, the OECD's definition of relative poverty is income below one-half of the median equivalent income. As the table indicates, if one calculates relative poverty and income inequality using market income, Japan does fairly well. However, if the calculation is based on disposable income, Japan comes into the highest (worst) ranks. Using disposable income levels, the relative poverty rate is 15.3 per cent for the entire population, 13.5 per cent for those of working age, and 21.1 per cent for the elderly.

In 1999 among the working age population, the ratio of people in Japan receiving benefits from the government was 11.4 per cent (the average among the 16 OECD nations being 19.7 per cent). Out of this number, 5.1 per cent were recipients of old age pensions and 1.6 per cent were recipients of survivor's pensions. In other words, over half of the working-age beneficiaries of government cash transfers were collecting pensions. Single parents and social assistance recipients amounted to no more than 0.3 per cent of the working-age population, a small fraction of the 16 OECD nations' 2.6 per cent average. As stated earlier, in 2000 Japan's relative poverty rate for the working-age population was 13.5 per cent based on disposable income (the OECD average was 8.4 per cent). Japan was thus the only OECD nation in which the number of government benefits beneficiaries was smaller than the number of people living in relative poverty (Jones 2007: 21, 23–4).

Around 2000, people in the lowest income quintile received 15.7 per cent of the Japanese government's cash transfers. In contrast, people in the lowest income quintile in 27 OECD nations received an average of 22.8 per cent of their

Table 4.4 Japan's ranking for Gini coefficient and relative poverty rate among 14 OECD countries (around 2000)

	Type of income and ranking	Age bracket		
		Total population	Working age population 18–65 years	Elderly population over 65 years
Gini coefficient	Market income A	11	12	7
	Disposable income B	5	5	2
	Change in rank from A to B	–6	–7	–5
Relative poverty rate	Market income a		9	
	Disposable income b	2	2	3
	Change in rank from a to b		–7	

Source: Ōta 2006: Table 2–1.

Notes:
1 Compiled from OECD data (2006), etc.
2 14 OECD countries are: Australia, Canada, Denmark, Finland, France, Germany, Italy, Japan, Netherlands, New Zealand, Norway, Sweden, UK, US.

governments' cash transfers. The tax burden of the lowest income quintile in Japan was 7.4 per cent, substantially higher than the average 4.0 per cent tax burden of their counterparts in 27 OECD nations. Moreover, the government net transfer (benefits received minus taxes paid) received by the poorest fifth of Japan's population were a mere 1.3 per cent of their households' disposable income (the OECD average being 4.0 per cent). The Japanese government paid more in benefits to the highest income quintile than the lowest, which received 80 per cent of what the top quintile received. In the comparison OECD group of nations, the lowest income quintiles received on average 2.1 times more in benefits than the highest income quintiles (Jones 2007: 22).

Increase in the poverty rate due to the tax and social security system

Figure 4.5 is made from the data in OECD's 2009 *Employment Outlook*. It shows the percentage by which relative poverty was reduced through net social transfers in households with one, two or more employed household members. The degree to which poverty is reduced is measured by the difference between poverty rates before and after social transfers, as a percentage of the poverty rate before social transfers. The poverty rates before and after transfers are calculated on market income and disposable income, respectively. The Japanese government's cash transfers do less to reduce poverty than any other nation's aside from Mexico. Worse still, Japan has the dubious distinction of being the only state whose social transfers have resulted in a deepening of poverty, by 7.9 per cent, for households with all adults working (two-earner couples or single persons including lone

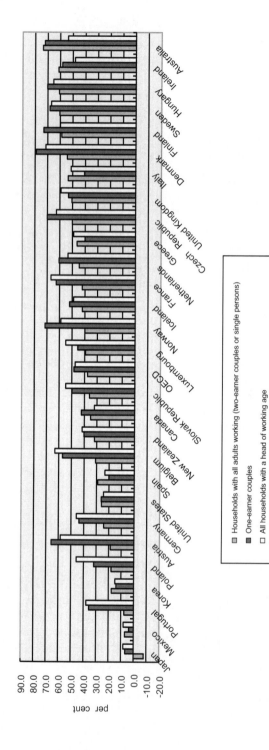

Figure 4.5 Percentage reduction of poverty rates among the working-age population, operated by net social transfers, mid-2000s

Source: OECD Employment Outlook 2009

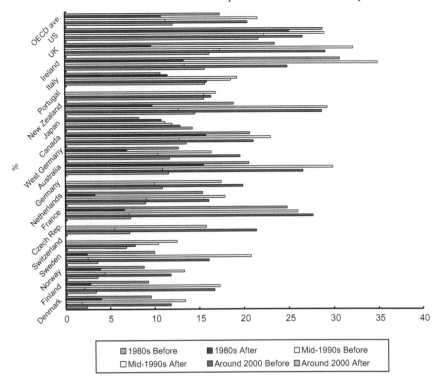

Figure 4.6 Child poverty rates, before and after taxes and transfers, in the 1980s, mid-1990s and around 2000

Source: Whiteford and Adema 2007: Table 2.

Note: 'Before' denotes market income poverty before deduction of direct and payroll taxes (social security contributions) paid by individuals and households, and 'after' reflects disposable income poverty after the subtraction of taxes and the addition of cash transfers. Countries from the US to Denmark are ranked by decreasing 'after' rates of child poverty around 2000.

parents) (OECD 2009: 186). It thus should come as no surprise that social transfers reduce poverty among single-earner married households, i.e. male breadwinner households, by 6.7 per cent.

According to OECD data, in 2000 the relative poverty rate of children in Japan was the seventh highest among 19 countries at 14.3 per cent. Moreover, a comparison of the 1980s, the mid-1990s and circa 2000 shows (Figure 4.5) that only in Japan it has increased with figures consistently higher after tax and social security transfers than before (Whiteford and Adema 2007: 18). In Italy, negative redistribution was seen to a slight extent in the 1980s, but a positive redistribution, although thin, took place in the mid-1990s. Around 2000, redistribution was weak in Italy, Portugal and Switzerland, but not reversed. The fact that Japan's tax and social security system have increased the poverty rate for children clearly means that its livelihood security system is functioning in reverse.

5 Taking stock of the Koizumi reforms

The cabinet of Junichirō Koizumi came into office in April 2001 under the slogan of 'structural reforms'. Ministries and central government agencies had already been restructured in January of the same year, as a result of the administrative reforms initiated by the Hashimoto government in the latter half of the 1990s. These reforms included the establishment of a new Cabinet Office and the merger of the Ministry of Health and Welfare with the Ministry of Labour into the Ministry of Health, Labour and Welfare. In the Cabinet Office, four Councils related to important policy matters were created: the Council on Economic and Fiscal Policy (CEFP), the Central Disaster Prevention Council (CDPC), the Comprehensive Science and Technology Council and the Council for Gender Equality. The Prime Minister chaired the first three Councils, and the Chief Cabinet Secretary chaired the Council for Gender Equality. The aim of the Hashimoto administrative reforms had been to strengthen the leadership role of the prime minister. Prime Minister Koizumi became the first to flex the resulting new muscle of the office.

The Council on Economic and Fiscal Policy lost no time in preparing an outline of its basic policy for economic and fiscal management and structural reform, later dubbed the *honebuto* 骨太 or 'robust' policy. The first *honebuto* policy statement was adopted by cabinet decision on 26 June. The fifth among the 'seven reform programs for structural reform' enumerated in this document, the programme for 'lifestyle restoration' (*seikatsu ishin* 生活維新), included, in addition to the Koizumi cabinet's 'zero-waiting list for day-care facilities' strategy, the objective of building 'a society that is friendly to working women' (*hataraku josei ni yasashii shakai* 働く女性に優しい社会). To this end, it called for a revision of tax and social security schemes to make the individual rather than households the unit for tax and social security purposes, and for abolishing gender discrimination in employment. However, concrete steps that would be taken were left unspecified.

Several moves by the government in 2002 suggested the possibility of a shift away from the rigid male breadwinner orientation of Japan's livelihood security system. In September 2002, the Ministry of Health, Labour and Welfare announced its 'Plus One Plan' to counter declining fertility, of which a major plank was 're-examining work styles including those of men' (Kōsei-rōdō-shō 2002a). Furthermore, in early December 2002, the Ministry proposed a reform of the Basic Pension scheme for Class 3 insured persons. A document entitled *Directions and*

Issues Regarding the Framework for Pension Reform (hereinafter referred to as *Directions and Issues*), which included several proposals for reforming the Class 3 insurant scheme, was published as a 'springboard' for discussion (Kōsei-rōdō-shō 2002b). Then, in the *Outline of Tax System Reform* adopted by cabinet decision on 17 January 2003, it was announced that the special deduction for spouses under the income tax system would, as a rule, be abolished effective from January 2004.

These moves were of course not coincidental, but interconnected. As mentioned in Chapter 3, in the 1990s the Equal Employment Opportunity Law had been amended and strengthened, and policy measures were introduced to support the ability of men and women with family responsibilities to work. Setting aside the questions of actual budget allocation and of the strength of these policy measures, elements of a work/life balance model were thus embraced. Finally, the Basic Law for a Gender-equal Society was promulgated and enacted in June 1999. This law held out the prospect that 'social systems and practices', in other words, the livelihood security system, would be made more 'neutral' as compared to the prevailing male breadwinner model (Article 4), and that work/life balance would be strengthened (Article 6).

These guiding principles of the Basic Law for a Gender-equal Society became quite explicitly reflected in cabinet-level policy once the Koizumi administration was launched. The Council for Gender Equality in the Cabinet Office, which was composed of 12 ministers representing each of the central ministries and 12 specialists from the private sector, was assigned the task of monitoring the progress of measures implemented by the government and its ministries to bring about a gender-equal society and of examining their (secondary and ripple) effects. I served as the chairperson of a Committee of Specialists of this Council to examine policy effects from April 2001 to July 2004. This institutional setup enhanced the possibility of promoting gender equality through policies spanning the jurisdictions of multiple ministries and agencies. Thus by FY2002, there were signs from various quarters suggesting that the government was moving towards a change of the model on which the Japanese livelihood security system was based.

But to what extent were these signboard policies of the Koizumi administration accompanied by real achievements? In this chapter we will trace the social policy reforms enacted during the Koizumi administration and investigate what changes occurred in Japan's livelihood security system in the 2000s. Section 1 focuses on the pension reform of 2004, presenting an overall review of the process and content of measures to address the declining birth rate, as well as reforms of long-term care insurance and health care. The results of this analysis reveal that a decisive shift away from the male breadwinner model was deferred. In its last *honebuto* policy statement, the Koizumi administration took pride in having achieved a 'muscular economic structure'. Section 2 of this chapter will assess what effect this had on income and employment. Section 3 will highlight how, as a basic reorientation of the livelihood security system was postponed, the social security system not only underwent a hollowing out, but even turned into a mechanism for social exclusion. Section 4 will recapitulate the main points of this chapter in conjunction with those of Chapters 3 and 4.

The social policy reforms of the Koizumi administration

The honebuto *policy and gender equality*

The *honebuto* policy statement 2001 proclaimed that it would 'reform regulations, practices and institutions hindering Japan from achieving its potential' to remedy the economic stagnation of the 1990s. The policy was dubbed 'restoration for the new century' (*shinseiki ishin* 新世紀維新). Taking the basic stance that 'without reform, Japan cannot grow', it advanced structural reforms in domains such as economics, public finance, administration and society at large. After pointing to a drastic solution to the problem of nonperforming loans as 'the first step to reviving the economy', the following seven-point structural reform programme was rolled out (Cabinet decision of 26 June 2001).[1]

To revitalize Japan's economy/society:

1 Privatization and regulatory reform. (Introduction of free market principles into such fields as health, nursing care, social welfare and education.)
2 'Supporting challengers' programme for individual and corporate innovation and entrepreneurship. (Promotion of business start-ups and ventures based on creative ingenuity.)

To enrich people's lives and provide a safety net:

3 Strengthening of social insurance. (Creation of a social security system that people understand and trust.)
4 The 'doubling knowledge assets' programme. (Prioritization of four sectors including the life sciences, IT and the environment.)
5 The 'lifestyle restoration' programme. (Elimination of waiting lists for day-care facilities, accelerated construction of barrier-free facilities, etc.)

To strengthen government functions and conduct a thorough review of how responsibilities are allocated:

6 Increased devolution of authority and revitalization of non-metropolitan regions. (Mergers of municipalities and rationalisation of government subsidies.)
7 Fiscal policy reform. (Review of earmarked revenue sources and long-term plans related to public works.)

Based on the pamphlet 'Let's Change Japan' issued to promote the *honebuto* policy, the items above can be further concretized as follows: Item (1) specifically referred to privatization of the special public corporations and postal services; Item (2) advanced consideration of tax schemes that give preferential treatment to equity investments; Item (3) emphasized controlling the growth of medical expenses; and item (6) advocated review of the local tax allocation system.[2] Although on the whole these programmes followed the neoliberal route, promotion of gender equality was included by way of the slogan 'a society that is friendly to working women'.

The second *honebuto* policy statement of June 2002 called for a design of the pension system 'in accordance with the ideal of a gender-equal society'. The concrete details of pension reform, however, remained nebulous; it was merely stated that 'social insurance for part-time workers will be expanded and the scheme of Class 3 insured persons will be reviewed'.

The Directions and Issues *regarding pension reform of December 2002*

Was the call of the second *honebuto* policy statement for a pension system 'in accordance with the ideal of a gender-equal society' adequately met by the pension system reform of 2004? Let us begin with a brief overview of the reform process. The Pension Working Group of the Council on Social Security of the Ministry of Health, Labour and Welfare, began its deliberations on pension reform in January 2002. In December 2002, the Ministry issued its *Direction and Issues Regarding the Framework for Pension Reform* as a basis for discussion, and in March 2003 the Pension Working Group's *Opinions on Reforming the Pension System* were submitted. I had been a member of this Pension Working Group since January 2002. In the general elections held in November 2003, pension reform was a major campaign issue addressed by the manifestoes of all political parties. The Ministry of Health, Labour and Welfare's proposal announced its plan after the elections were over. Subsequently, following deliberations by the ruling parties, the government introduced its bill in February 2004.

First, what kind of proposals did the Ministry of Health, Labour and Welfare's *Direction and Issues* of December 2002 contain? The centrepiece of its plan was 'fixed insurance contribution rates'. Although the contribution rates have to be raised and the levels of benefits cut, due to the increasing number of pensioners and decreasing number of the working-age and contributing population, fixed insurance contribution rates would be adopted, meaning that the ceiling of the future levels of contribution would be determined by law, and the level of benefits be made commensurate with the scope of the contribution burden, subject to automatic adjustment in line with shifts in demographic and wages and price trends. This automatic adjustment was referred to as 'macro-economic indexation'.

Previously, the revision rate (indexation rate) of benefits under the Employees' Pension Insurance scheme had been based on the growth rate of per capita take home (net) earnings in the case of persons receiving a pension for the first time (de novo beneficiaries), and on the rate of price inflation for existing pensioners (de facto beneficiaries). In the proposed reform, the 'indexation adjustment rate' was to be subtracted from the revision rate. The 'indexation adjustment rate' is the difference between the rise in net earnings per capita and the growth rate of aggregate net wages, and thus corresponds to the rate of fluctuation in the working population. Even if the net pay of wage earners increases, aggregate wages (and insurance contribution collections) decrease if the number of workers declines. The fixed insurance contribution rates system attempts to make benefits reflect that. In more concrete terms, assuming that the ceiling of the insurance contribution rate is FY2022's 20 per cent, then, based on projections of population and wages/prices, the level of benefits of the future 'model pension' (after FY2032) would be estimated at 52 per cent of net pay (as opposed to 59 per cent before the reform). This 'model pension' reflects a pure instance of the male breadwinner model insofar as it assumes a husband to have been enrolled for 40 and his wife for zero years. As illustrated in Chapter 4, this scenario offers the highest replacement rate of pension benefits to pre-retirement income.

Directions and Issues also addressed the declining fertility rate, participation of women in society and changes in work patterns. It also included a proposal to review the system of Class 3 insured persons. Four options were presented: (1) splitting pension rights between husband and wife; (2) having Class 3 insurants also pay social insurance premiums; (3) reducing Basic Pension benefits for Class 3 insured persons; and (4) expanding Employees' Pension Insurance benefit eligibility to part-time workers and shrinking the number of Class 3 insured persons (Kōsei-rōdō-shō 2002b). Options (2) and (4) would impose a greater burden on male breadwinner households, where only the husband is working outside the home. Option (4) would also raise the burden on employers hiring part-time workers. Option (3), on the other hand, would be problematic because it reduces Basic Pension benefits, which were seen as a pre-existing entitlement. It thus seems safe to assume that option (1) was conceived of as the only feasible one under this Plan.

The Pension Working Group's Opinions on Revising the Pension System *of September 2003*

The *Opinions on Revising the Pension System*, issued by the Pension Working Group in September 2003, offered as its 'basic perspective on pension reform' systems that would accommodate various work styles and maintain neutrality towards the 'life course' (choices about lifestyle and working arrangements throughout the course of life) of an individual. Issues related to gender and pension had up to that point been dealt with as the 'women and pension issue' and relegated to being a side issue. In the *Opinions*, on the other hand, such issues were treated as part of the 'basic perspective' of the whole reform initiative. In that sense, pension reform had come to provide the stage for 'gender main-streaming' to occur.

A related point that deserves attention is reference to the so-called 'model pension' under the 'individual discussion items' of the pension reform proposal. Besides the conventional 'husband as sole provider' household, taking other types of household such as 'dual-earner' and 'single-member households' as models in designing benefits was unequivocally pronounced 'appropriate'. Among the 'individual discussion items', three plans were mooted for revamping the treatment of Class 3 insured persons: (1) splitting of pension rights between husband and wife; (2) having Class 3 insurants also pay insurance premiums; and (3) reducing Basic Pension benefits of Class 3 insurants. The Ministry of Health, Labour and Welfare proposal of November 2003 settled on the first plan. With regard to surviving spouse pensions, it was proposed to make benefits for young widows without children expire after a set term, among other policies prioritizing employment assistance. In cases of divorce, the proposal included a scheme for transferring (from husband to wife with the consent of both parties) the contribution record for EPI premiums in an agreed upon ratio.

What is the significance of splitting pension rights between husband and wife? If pension splitting renders surviving spouse pensions unnecessary, contribution rates and pension benefits between male breadwinner households and dual-earner households would also be equivalent given equal wages. In that sense, the system would become more neutral against women who choose employment. This proposal thus evinced an intention to break away from the male breadwinner model. On the other hand, as long as the Basic Pension system is maintained, the male breadwinner household will retain a higher benefit level (relative to nominal monthly household wages) regardless of adjustments in contributions and benefits, and inequality in benefit levels among household types will remain.

In fact, there were two schools of thought within the Pension Working Group that advocated overhauling the entire system. One proposal, made by several members of the group, was for a unified system, including also self-employed and non-working persons, offering benefits proportionate to income combined with supplemental benefits (minimum guarantee for non-contributors) for low income or no-income persons that would be funded out of taxes rather than insurance contributions. This system would eliminate the uneven, vertically divided and two-tiered structure of the Japanese system, thus approximating the Swedish pension system introduced in the reform of 1999. It differed from the Swedish model, though, in basically adhering to pension splitting by dividing the household income between husband and wife (Ōsawa 2003; Ōsawa 2004). This opinion met with critique on the grounds that a unified income-proportional scheme would reduce pension benefits for low income women below even the current level.

I was one of the proponents of the unification proposal. The reasoning behind it was that the prevailing system of an uneven, vertically divided structure not only makes it more likely that workers fall through the cracks of coverage under conditions of increasingly fluid employment patterns, but that it creates powerful incentives for employers to engage in further non-regularization of employment or try to extra-legally evade the mandate. (Examples of this will be described later.) A system of vertically segmented social insurance schemes is among the characteristic enumerated by Esping-Andersen for a 'conservative' welfare regime (or male breadwinner model in the diction of this book). Unification in itself would signify a break away from the male breadwinner model.

The other school of thought advocating an overhaul of the system proposed funding the Basic Pension entirely out of taxes (currently one-third of the Basic Pension benefits is borne by the national treasury; this is scheduled to be raised to one-half). Representatives of employers and the labour unions were in agreement on this view. They disagreed, however, on what taxes should be used as a source of funds. Due to this lack of consensus within the Working Group, accomplishing an overhaul of the system failed to materialize as a feasible option in the 2004 reform initiative.

The pension reform of 2004

What, then, did make it into the government pension reform bill of 2004? First, the ceiling fixed on the contribution rate was set at 18.3 per cent in FY2022 as opposed to 20 per cent as envisaged by the Pension Working Group. This was a reflection of the opinion of the business community and the Ministry of Finance that 20 per cent was too high. Macro-economic indexation would be applied to the fiscal years 2005–23. Assuming that the working population contributing to the pension regime would decline by 0.6 per cent per annum and the average future lifetime of the pension beneficiary population would grow annually by 0.3 years, the total of 0.9 per cent was taken to be the 'indexation adjustment rate'. The pension revision rate was fixed at the figure obtained by subtracting the indexation adjustment rate from the rate of price inflation. At the same time, the future pension benefit level would be set at 50.2 per cent for the 'model pension' of the male breadwinner household (husband being the sole breadwinner) with 40 years of enrolment. Figure 5.1 shows changes in pension benefit levels by different household types affected by the reform. The figure clearly demonstrates that the reform did not effectively change the structure whereby the longer the wife has subscribed to the Employees' Pension Insurance scheme, the lower the household's pension benefit level becomes.

Some specific provisions should be noted. First, the expansion of eligibility for employee pensions to part-time workers was postponed for five years in response to protests from the restaurant industry, chain stores and other businesses that employ many part-time workers. Second, although splitting of pension benefits in case of divorce was finally introduced, there was no consistency, since the option of pension splitting does not apply to couples who remain married as well.[3]

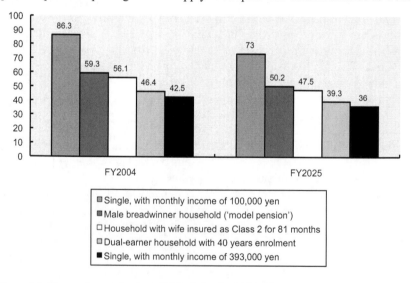

Figure 5.1 Change in pension benefit levels by the 2004 reform

Source: Shakai hoshō shingikai, Nenkin bukai: 27th Meeting, Discussion Paper No. 1; 12–13.

Third, surviving spouse pension benefits for widows were reined in to a certain extent but the embedded gender bias was not remedied.[4] In the case of pension splitting for married couples in particular, no provision was made for persons who continued their marriage. A newspaper article reported that there were voices at the Pension System Research Committee of the Liberal Democratic Party who 'stressed the importance of traditional family values' and insisted that 'married couples should be considered as one unit for pension benefits' (*Asahi Shinbun* 22 January 2004). This can be read as signs of resistance to the shift to individuals as the benefit-receiving unit and any break away from the male breadwinner model as advocated by the *honebuto* policy, reflected in the *Opinion* of the Pension Working Group, and announced as its objective by the Ministry of Health, Labour and Welfare.

In short, the government plan for a pension reform in 2004 maintained the uneven, vertically divided structure of the system centred on male breadwinners, and failed to go beyond minimal revision of individual policy items. Not only was the break from the male breadwinner model once again deferred, but measures against 'hollowing out', as will be discussed in Section 2, were shelved for the time being as well.

In response to this government bill, the Democratic Party of Japan proposed a bill for a unified, income-proportional system plus minimum security pension, based on its own manifesto at the time of the 2003 general elections. The DPJ plan was similar to the unified compensation-proportional system proposed by members of the Pension Working Group. In the end, the government bill was passed and adopted in the Japanese Diet on 5 June 2004 in a regular session of the House of Councillors (Upper House) that was boycotted by all opposition party members with the exception of the Communist Party. During deliberations on the bill, Prime Minister Koizumi's much taunted leadership was not in evidence.

Actually, the Prime Minister had appeared in television broadcasts before deliberations on the bill in the Diet began, announcing that the ruling and opposition parties would cooperate and that 'unification is desirable'. This caused considerable consternation in the parties forming the government. Also after Diet deliberations had begun, Koizumi asserted that 'the government bill will lead to unification', which further contributed to the deliberations going nowhere. In addition, from late April 2004 onward, cases of parliamentarians not enrolled in or paying contributions to the National Pension (Basic Pension) scheme began to be reported in the press almost daily, with the result that substantial deliberations on the bill all but ceased. Those suspected of not paying contributions included former cabinet members, vice ministers and parliamentary vice ministers, and 14 leading politicians of the New Kōmeito beginning with party president Takenori Kanzaki. They also included DPJ party president Naoto Kan (the allegations later proved to be mistaken), former DPJ party president Yukio Hatoyama and DPJ deputy party president Ichirō Ōzawa. After Chief Cabinet Secretary Yasuo Fukuda took responsibility for being one of the negligent parliamentarians and resigned, questions were also raised about Prime Minister Koizumi's pension history. At a meeting of the Committee on Audit and Oversight of Administration in the House of Representatives on 2 June 2004, Koizumi was questioned by Katsuya Okada of the DPJ about his enrolment in the Employees' Pension Insurance scheme despite the fact that he had not been employed at the company in question. Koizumi responded, 'People lead all kinds of lives, there all kinds of companies, and there are all kinds of employees.' He went on to say he had relied on the good offices of 'a generous, warm-hearted company president' and had 'nothing to be ashamed of'.

A different vector in the Outline of Measures to Cope with a Society with Fewer Children

In July 2003, the Basic Law for Measures to Cope with a Society with Fewer Children was passed from a private member's bill, and in June 2004 the *Outline of Measures to Cope with a Society with Fewer Children* was drafted on its basis. This document was influenced by the outlook of the LDP's Research Commission on Declining Birthrate Issues chaired by former Prime Minister Yoshirō Mori. The LDP's Research Commission on Declining Birthrate Issues had been established in 2003. In May 2004 it had announced an interim report towards drafting the *Outline*, putting forward the following principles: 'Laws and other factors that have created a basis for the trend towards self-centredness are to be reconsidered', and: 'Fostering a social atmosphere in which people will naturally feel that marriage and childbearing are an intrinsic part of life' (*Asahi Shinbun* 8 June 2004).

As mentioned already in Chapter 3 above, advisory council reports and white papers issued by the government in the latter half of the 1990s had included the idea of 'work/life balance' as a vector in addressing fertility decline. 'Work/life balance' meant a review of the ingrained gender division of labour and of male-centric employment practices in addition to respect for diverse lifestyle choices. Against this, the *Outline of Measures to Cope with a Society with Fewer Children* harboured a different vector. Former Prime Minister Yoshirō Mori said in an open discussion in Kagoshima City on 26 June 2003 that 'women who do not bear a single child are celebrating their freedom and enjoying life, and it is truly bizarre that they expect to be taken care of by taxes in their old age'. Seiichi Ōta, Chairman of the Liberal Democratic Party's Administrative Reform Promotion Headquarters, was at the same forum and went so far as to say, 'At least gang rapists are still vigorous. Isn't that at least a little closer to normal?' (*Asahi Shinbun* 1 August 2003).

Statements such as these by powerful figures within the Liberal Democratic Party reveal aversion to the freedom and autonomy of women; they even come close to suggesting that rape could be considered the norm for men. In not a few cases these have been looked upon as revivals of a 'traditional' Japanese belief in the 'predominance of men over women' (*danson johi* 男尊女卑), or as a resuscitation of conservatism. It should be noted, however, that such statements are indicative rather of the 'crisis' faced by conservative politics that had been riding high in the last quarter of the 20th century. In Europe as well, the various reforms along the neoliberal route that conservative parties pursued from the 1980s made it difficult also for their own constituencies to 'conserve their livelihood', thus eroding the very basis in which 'traditional values' had their support. Precisely for this reason, conservative outbursts have focused on issues of public safety and nationalism, sounding alarm over problems with immigrant foreigners, and singing the praises of family values (gender relations) deemed 'traditional' (Noda 2006). The Koizumi administration included promotion of gender equality among its basic policies, but it made no effort to rein in such moves by elements within the LDP.

Structural reform of long-term care insurance and health care – evaporation of the unification drive

The long-term care insurance system was revised in 2005. In a pamphlet issued by the Ministry of Health, Labour and Welfare in March 2006, entitled 'Outline of the long-term care insurance reform – Amendment of the Long-term Care Insurance Law and revision of remuneration for long-term care services', the background to the amendment is explained as follows. Total expenditures for long term-care insurance rapidly grew from 3.6 trillion yen in 2000 to 7.1 trillion yen in the FY2006 budget, requiring major hikes in contribution rates under the existing system and calling into question the sustainability of the system. In addition, the number of elderly persons needing long-term care was expected to increase as the 'baby boom' generation born in 1947–9 would reach old age in 2015.[5] The keystone of the amended system, therefore, was to be a shift from the previous 'long-term care' model to one of 'long-term care plus prevention'.

Specific points of revision were, among others: (1) mild cases (persons 'requiring assistance' or Care Level 1) were to be moved to a new category of 'prevention benefits' providing a fixed sum to pay for those benefits on a monthly basis; (2) expenses for meals and living quarters (hotel costs) at long-term care facilities, including short-stay costs, were to be excluded from insurance coverage and borne by the beneficiary; (3) a network of new services, such as 'localized services', was to be established.

If benefits are restrained through benefit limits for mild cases and increases in the user payment burden for treatment at long-term care facilities, women are affected to a disproportionate degree. Women account for 70 per cent of persons requiring long-term care and 71 per cent of beneficiaries of long-term care services (Kōsei-rōdō-shō 2006c).

What about structural reform of the health care system? In 2002 the Koizumi administration introduced a health care reform under the slogan 'splitting the burden three ways' (*sanbō ichiryō zon* 三方一両損). 'Three ways' referred to the three parties involved: doctors, patients and insurants. By reducing remuneration for medical treatment, increasing the patient's payment from 20 to 30 per cent (the patient being an insurant) and raising insurants' premium rates, each party would take a share of the 'pain'. Next, on 28 March 2003, a cabinet decision 'On the basic policy regarding the health insurance system and the medical treatment fee system' was adopted. This decision aimed at the establishment of a new health care system for the elderly and a reshuffling and unification of the national and other health insurances by 2008. In October 2005, the Ministry of Health, Labour and Welfare prepared its 'Draft Proposal for Structural Reform of the Health Care System', and the amended law was enacted in June 2006.

The three main pillars of the reform were as follows: (1) An increase of the user payment for elderly patients (from 10 to 20 per cent, or from 20 to 30 per cent of the total cost if the patient has an income on par with a working-age person) and review of expenses for room and board (hotel costs) at long-term medical care facilities, in addition to 'adjustment' of health care costs in the medium to long term. (Income on par with a working-age person was defined as 5.2 million yen for a married couple and 3.83 million yen for a single-member household.); (2) Creation of a new health care system for the elderly. This would include establishment of a 'latter-stage elderly health care system' for persons over 75 years of age and the creation of a fiscal adjustment system among insurers for the health care expenses of persons 65–74 years of age. The 'latter-stage elderly health care system' would require elderly persons to pay insurance premiums equivalent to 10 per cent of medical expenses incurred above the user payment amount; (3) Consolidation of insurance schemes at the prefectural level. This consolidation would encompass not only the national health insurance, but would include transformation of government-run health schemes into public corporations and the creation of new regional health care associations.

Under the 'latter-stage elderly health care system', the user payment would be subtracted from the medical expenses and the remainder would be borne as follows: 50 per cent by the government (shared at a ratio of 4:1:1 between the national, prefectural and municipal levels), 40 per cent would be covered by latter-stage elderly support funding from insurers covering persons under age 74, and the remaining 10 per cent would be borne by the insurance contributions collected from the 'latter-stage elderly'. At the same time, revision of the maximum and minimum levels of standard monthly compensation and the scope of 'standard bonuses' were expected to increase the premium burden of typical working-age insurants. It was not only the elderly who would have to bear a greater burden.

The Ministry's draft proposal was greeted with immediate critique from the Japan Association of City Mayors, the National Association of Towns and Villages and the All Japan Federation of National Health Insurance Organizations. Their central point was that unification of public health insurance schemes was necessary for maintaining the integrity of the public health insurance schemes as an 'insurance for all' (*kokumin kai-hoken* 国民皆保険), and that the draft proposal was inadequate if measured against this task. The cabinet decision of March 2003 referred to above, stated as its second basic policy point that it would 'provide for equality in benefits and fairness in the distribution of the burden among health insurance schemes and aim for unification of the latter'. The Japan Association of City Mayors, the National Association of Towns and Villages and the All Japan Federation of National Health Insurance Organizations unanimously voiced their disapproval that this basic policy of unification had disappeared from the Ministry of Health, Labour and Welfare's draft proposal. As the proposal was not clear about future fiscal consequences for municipalities, the organizations retorted that they could 'never approve' of having to manage such a system (Zenkoku shichō kai, Zenkoku chōson kai and Kokumin kenkō hoken chuōkai 2005).

Under the amended law, premiums are collected by the municipalities, even though the financial management of the system is conducted by the 'regional federations' (*kōiki rengō* 広域連合) in which municipalities participate on a prefectural basis. The law stipulates that premiums for individuals with low income are to be subsidized from public funds, but the basic setup is as specified by the draft proposal.

In light of the developments leading up to the 2004 pension and subsequent health care system reforms, it appears that from 2003 to early 2004 Prime Minister Koizumi and his administration had been intent on unifying the social insurance schemes that had been characterized by an uneven, vertically divided structure, both in the case of public pensions and of health insurance. Unification, not merely the separate objective of 'a society friendly to working women', would have meant a break away from the male breadwinner orientation of the system as such. These intentions, however, soon faded away.

Real-life consequences of the 'muscular economic structure'

Effects on income, employment and relative poverty

The *Basic Policy for Economic and Fiscal Management and Structural Reform 2006*, adopted by cabinet decision on 7 July 2006, was the last *honebuto* policy statement of the Koizumi administration. Its opening lines were: 'The Japanese economy has emerged from the long tunnel of stagnation and has been transformed into a muscular structure. The situation at last presents a bright outlook for the future.'[6]

What did this 'muscular economic structure' mean in terms of people's livelihoods? Let me state the main points of my argument first. The Japanese economy resumed growth in February 2002. During the following 69 months lasting until October 2007, it experienced its longest period of growth since World War II. During this time corporate earnings increased in real terms. However, real incomes of employees did not rise. Total unemployment, certainly, continued to decline after reaching a peak of 5.5 per cent in the summer of 2002, and the overall number of employed increased. But this was overwhelmingly due to an increase in the number of non-regular workers. In particular, non-regular employment of women increased after 2000 at an accelerating speed. Also, despite the decline in the unemployment rate, the proportion of long-term unemployment among unemployed men has risen. Even during economic recovery, the degree of exclusion from the core labour market for women has deepened due to non-regularization, while increasing numbers of men have suffered exclusion in the form of persistent unemployment. One outcome of these trends has been a rise in relative poverty.

Figure 5.2 is based on the 2008 *White Paper on International Trade* issued by the Ministry of Economy, Trade and Industry. As the figure shows, during the period of economic recovery from 2002 to 2007, real incomes of employees showed no increase whereas real corporate earnings did. In contrast, during the economic

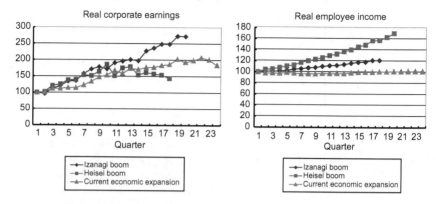

Figure 5.2 Changes in corporate earnings and employee income (bottom of the recession=100)

Source: Ministry of Economy, Industry and Trade (2008): Column 7.

Note: Izanagi boom (57 months from Nov. 1965 to July 1970), Heisei boom (51 months from Dec. 1986 to Feb. 1991), current economic expansion (69 months from Feb. 2002 to Nov. 2007).

recovery of the latter half of the 1980s (the so-called Heisei boom), growth in real incomes of employees surpassed real corporate earnings.

The *2008 Annual Report on the Japanese Economy and Public Finance*, on the other hand, shows year-on-year changes in regular salaries differentiated into three factors: regular salaries of general (full-time) workers, regular salaries of part-time workers and the ratio of part-time workers. At almost every point in time during this period, regular salaries declined compared to the previous year. This clearly demonstrates that this development is primarily due to the rise in the proportion of part-time employment (Naikakufu 2008: Figure 1.3–20).

Figure 5.3 shows the proportion of non-regular employees over a fairly long time period. The extent of non-regularization of female employees from the latter half of the 1990s to the first half of the 2000s is striking. As illustrated in Chapter 3, analysis by age group demonstrates that the greatest growth of non-regular employment since the 1990s was among women aged 15 to 24 and over 45. Among men, on the other hand, non-regularization was not salient until the mid-1990s. It advanced in the first half of the 2000s, but was reined in from 2005 onward.

With regard to unemployment, the unemployment rate (seasonally adjusted) declined to 3.9 per cent in 2007 after reaching a peak of 5.5 per cent in the summer of 2002. But during the same period, the prevalence of long-term unemployment among unemployed men increased. The Detailed Tabulation of the *Labour Force Survey* show trends in duration of unemployment by gender from 2001 to 2006. Figure 5.4 indicates that the proportion of unemployed men who were unemployed for more than one year was about 30 per cent in 2001 and grew to about 40 per cent in 2006. In the case of women during the same time period, the figure hovered around 22 per cent (18 per cent in 2001). The duration of unemployment was longer for men and lengthened further during this period, whereas for the majority

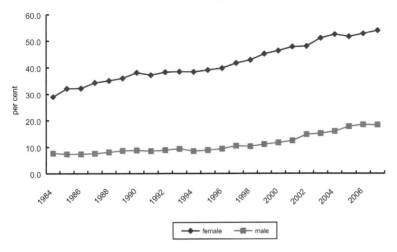

Figure 5.3 Trends in proportions of non-regular employees, by gender

Source: *Labour Force Survey* (the Special Survey and the Detailed Tabulation)

Note: Figures from 1984 to 2001 are figures for February of each year according to the Labour Force Special Survey. Figures from 2002 and after are the average of January–March figures according to the Detailed Tabulation of the *Labour Force Survey*.

of women unemployment lasted less than six months. The incidence of long-term unemployment among women thus did not grow.

The breakdown of unemployed persons by duration of unemployment for major countries in 2006 is shown in the *Databook of International Labour Statistics* published by the Japan Institute for Labour Policy and Training (JILPT). Duration of unemployment was short in the Anglo-Saxon countries, long in Southern Europe and Continental Western Europe, and in-between in the Northern European countries. Japan's situation is similar to Spain's. In South Korea, by contrast, unemployment rarely exceeds six months, similar to the situation in the Anglo-Saxon countries. In terms of the distribution of unemployment duration in 2006, Japan's situation can thus be said to approximate that prevailing on the European continent and in Southern Europe.[7]

As already noted above, during the period of economic recovery the degree of exclusion of women from the core labour market deepened due to increased non-regular employment, and increasing numbers of men have been suffering exclusion in the form of persistent unemployment. The implications of this are: if employee incomes do not grow, consumption will not grow either. During the period of economic recovery from February 2002 to October 2007, the breakdown of contributions to real GDP growth by demand sector shows that a staggering 60 per cent was due to exports while private sector consumption accounted for no more than approximately 36 per cent. During the 1980s, by contrast, private sector consumption was responsible for almost half of the economic growth (METI 2008: Figure 2.2–23). The 'muscular economic structure' in which the

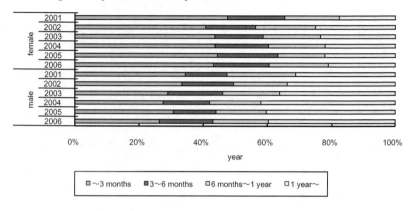

Figure 5.4 Trends in duration of unemployment in Japan, by gender

Source: *Labour Force Survey* (the Special Survey and the Detailed Tabulation)

Koizumi administration took pride was one in which corporate earnings increased but employee incomes did not: an economy of sluggish consumption and growth dependent on exports.

Rise in the relative poverty rate and characteristics of Japan's relative poverty bracket

Sluggish growth of employee incomes was not all. In the Lower House elections of 30 August 2009, the Democratic Party of Japan (DPJ) swept into power with an overwhelming victory. After the new administration was installed, Minister of Health, Labour and Welfare Akira Nagatsuma announced on 20 October 2009 the results of a study on relative poverty. According to his figures, the relative poverty rate of the whole population had declined modestly from 15.3 per cent in 2000 to 14.9 per cent in 2003, and then risen to 15.7 per cent in 2005. The relative poverty rate for children under 18 in those years had been 14.5 per cent, 13.7 per cent and 14.2 per cent, respectively.[8] Minister Nagatsuma explained that this was the first time the Japanese government had measured relative poverty, but this is not in fact the case. Material provided by the Council on Economic and Fiscal Policy (CEFP) in April 2009 and the FY2009 *Annual Report on the Japanese Economy and Public Finance* issued in late July of that year had already provided data on relative poverty rates up through the mid-2000s (Naikakufu 2009: Figure 3.2–6, Figure 3.2–14).

At a meeting of the Council on Economic and Fiscal Policy on 22 April 2009, four expert members from the private sector jointly presented material titled *On the Current State of Income Disparity*. It contained calculations of relative poverty rates in different countries, based on the *OECD Factbook 2009*, through the mid-2000s. The figure for Japan was 14.9 per cent, coming in fourth highest after Mexico, Turkey and the US.[9] The same material also demonstrated, on the basis of data from the *OECD Factbook 2009* for the years 1985, 1994, 2000 and 2003, that the relative poverty rate for children in Japan was higher if measured in terms of disposable as opposed to initial income (Keizai zaisei shimon kaigi 2009: 8). This data confirms prior analyses by researchers. Aya Abe, for instance, has shown that at seven points in time at three-year intervals between 1984 and 2002, the taxation system in every case and the social insurance system in most cases have worked to elevate the poverty rate for children. The exceptions were in 1984 and 2002 where at least the social security system, but not the tax system, contributed to alleviating child poverty (Abe 2006; Abe 2008).

The document *On the Current State of Income Disparity* cites the increase in the numbers of elderly households and single-member households as causes of greater disparity. It also drew attention to the fact that from 1999 to 2004, households whose head was aged 50–64 or that were comprised only of two or more adults – household types that had relatively low poverty rates in the past – saw a rise in poverty rates. However, as this document also emphasized, Japan's relatively poor households are in international comparison characterized by a high proportion of households with an actively employed person for households whose head is of working age (18–65). According to OECD averages, 37.3 per cent of relatively poor households with a head of working age have no household member who is actively employed, and 17 per cent have two or more actively employed members, being households where both spouses work, etc. In Japan's case the proportions are reversed, at 17.3 per cent and 39 per cent respectively (or 18.2 per cent and 32.8 per cent according to the *National Survey of Family Income and Expenditure*) (Keizai zaisei shimon kaigi 2009: 9). This data indicates that even the employed in Japan face a high risk of becoming poor and that it is difficult even for dual-earner households to break out of poverty. This clearly suggests that the working poor are a significant presence in Japan and the feebleness of women's earning power.

It may be the case that employed individuals living in relative poverty in Japan are working short hours despite the fact that they count as employed. The distribution of incomes of full-time workers, however, reveals that in Japan wages at the bottom of the wage ladder are indeed low. The *OECD Employment Outlook 2009* offers an international comparison of the situation at the bottom of the wage ladder and countries' minimum wage regimes. The basis of the comparison are the ratios between the income of a full-time worker in the lowest decile of the earnings distribution and the median disposable income for a single person without children. Of the 19 countries in the comparison, the lowest ratio belonged to the US at 0.6, followed by Canada at 0.62, then Japan at 0.63. The highest ratio was Denmark's at 1.42, followed by Germany and Sweden at 1.09, then Finland at 1.01 (OECD 2009b: 198). After taxes and social insurance premiums are paid (since the comparator is the median disposable income of a single person), in the US, Canada and Japan, the lowest decile of workers falls wholly into the relative poverty bracket.

What is more, in these countries the legal minimum wage was even lower. Minimum wages, as a ratio to the median disposable income of a childless single person, were 0.4 in the US, followed by Japan at 0.46 and Canada at 0.5 (OECD 2009b: 198). Some countries in Europe do not have a legal minimum wage, but in their cases a floor on wages is frequently set by collective agreements between organized labour and management.

Hollowing out and reverse functioning of the social insurance system

Erosion of Employees' Health and Pension Insurance coverage

How did increasing non-regularization of employment and the rise in relative poverty affect Japan's social insurance systems? To summarize the main point ahead, the social insurance system for employees started to contract while its fiscal condition was aggravated. At the same time, social insurance for non-employees (unemployed or self-employed individuals and their family workers) and part-time workers bloated in a state of fiscal fragility, thus falling into dysfunction. The entire social insurance system has been hollowed out.

The coverage of workers' accident compensation insurance, besides direct employees as explained in Chapter 2, has always included contract workers provided they are required to work certain hours under the immediate direction of a business. The coverage of employment insurance has repeatedly been expanded trying to keep up with the growing numbers of part-time and temporary employees (Kanai 2010). The area where coverage has shrunk is the Employees' Health and Pension Insurance schemes. In the case of employment insurance whose coverage has been expanded, the growing number of unemployed who do not (are unable to) receive unemployment benefits represent a hollowing out of the system, as will be described below, as well.

Let us first review the scope of eligibility for social insurance as of the end of FY2006 (the end of March 2007). Persons eligible for health insurance numbered 127,300,000, amounting to 99.7 per cent of Japan's total population of 127,720,000 at the time. Social insurance coverage also extends to foreign nationals in Japan, and although such coverage is not the same as for Japanese nationals, speaking of 'insurance for all' is not an overstatement. The breakdown of eligible insurants according to health insurance schemes was as follows: government-managed health insurance 28.2 per cent (insured persons 15.2 per cent, their dependents 12.9 per cent); society-managed 23.8 per cent (insured persons 12 per cent, their dependents 11.8 per cent); mutual aid association-managed 7.5 per cent (association members 3.5 per cent, their dependents 4 per cent); and National Health Insurance 40.3 per cent (Kokuritsu shakai hoshō jinkō mondai kenkyūsho 2008). In the case of pension schemes the breakdown of eligible insurants in FY2006 was as follows: 21,230,000 Class 1 insured persons under the National Pension scheme; 38,340,000 Class 2 insured persons (33,790,000 under Employees' Pension Insurance, 4,570,000 insured persons under mutual aid associations' pension schemes); and 10,780,000 Class 3 insured persons (Shakai-hoken-chō 2008).

Figure 5.5 shows changes in the proportion of insured persons in Employees' Health and Pension Insurance schemes by gender. Coverage of male employees by each scheme shows a faint downward trend that is negligible. Coverage of female

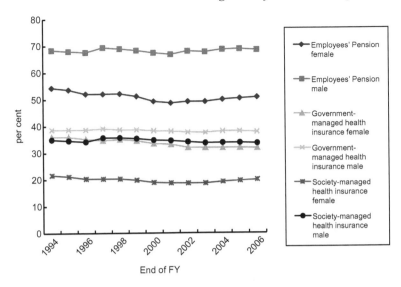

Figure 5.5 Coverage of employees' social insurance schemes, proportion of insured to number of employees, by scheme and gender

Source: *Labour Force Survey*; Kokuritsu shakai hoshō jinkō mondai kenkyūsho 2008

employees under Employees' Pension Insurance, on the other hand, declined in the latter half of the 1990s to rise only slightly after 2002, as the economy recovered. In the case of government-managed health insurance, coverage of female employees consistently decreased during this period.

Let us look at the state of pension coverage in a little more detail. Data from the *Comprehensive Survey of Living Conditions* showing the proportion of Class 2 insured persons (under Employees' Pension Insurance and mutual aid association schemes) in the population by age for 1995, 2000 and 2004, is presented in Figure 5.6. The proportion of female Class 2 insured persons is low and declined in the twenties age bracket while slightly increasing in the thirties and forties brackets. Among men, the proportion of Class 2 insured persons declined in the twenties and thirties age brackets between 2000 and 2004.

If the number of Class 2 insured persons decreases, the number of Class 3 insured persons, who are dependent spouses of Class 2 insurants, naturally decreases as well. Recently, however, the number of Class 3 insurants has continued to decline despite an uptick in the number of Class 2 insurants. After reaching a peak of 12,200,000 in 1995, the number of Class 3 insured persons declined to 10,790,000 in 2006. Figure 5.7 narrows down the data to insured persons aged 20–9, among whom there was a marked downturn in the proportion covered under Class 2, and shows self-reported public pension status broken down by gender. Among both men and women the share of Class 1 insured persons increased, among men the proportion of Class 2 insured persons (under Employees' Pension Insurance and mutual aid association schemes) decreased, and among women a decline in the

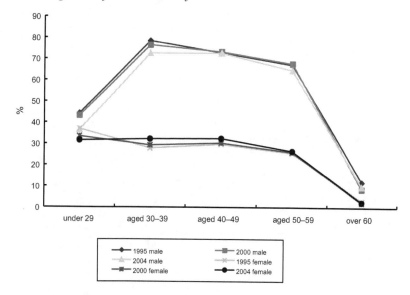

Figure 5.6 Coverage of Employees' Pension Insurance and mutual aid pension, by gender and age group, years 1995, 2000 and 2004

Source: *Kokumin seikatsu kiso chōsa* (Comprehensive Survey of Living Conditions), various years.

Note: Based on the understanding of policyholders themselves. Errors are small provided employers did not submit false data to social insurance offices.

proportion of Class 3 insurants is apparent. In 1995, classification into Class 1 by default was introduced for those who have reached age 20 and become eligible but fail to enrol themselves. In 1997, the basic pension identification number system was introduced to ensure universal, automatic enrolment. Subsequently the number of those failing to enrol in the system has shrunk dramatically. Hence, those who replied 'not covered' in most cases are people who are not aware of their enrolment by default as Class 1 insurants – possibly because they are not paying contribution rates.

Employees' Pension Insurance goes into the red

With the number of, and payments from insured persons decreasing, contribution revenues diminished from 1997 onward. By 2003 revenues were down 1.44 trillion yen, 7 per cent from 1997. (Subsequently, the contribution ratio was raised.) Starting in 2002, benefit expenditures exceeded revenues from contributions, and in FY2003 the deficit was actually 3.5 trillion yen. It was reported that the scheme was drawing down its reserve fund for the first time since its inception (*Asahi Shinbun* 7 August 2004). The reserve fund had been 138 trillion yen in 2002, but shrank to 130 trillion yen in FY2006 (Shakai-hoken-chō 2008).

The shrinking of the reserve fund was due not only to decreasing contribution revenues but also to huge losses on stocks and bonds as investment management of

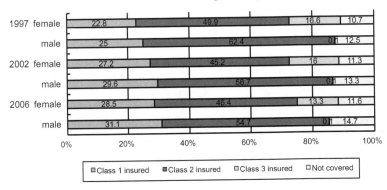

Figure 5.7 Coverage of the public pension scheme for those aged 20–9, by class and gender, in 1997, 2002 and 2006

Source: *Kokumin seikatsu kiso chōsa* (Comprehensive Survey of Living Conditions), various years.

Note: Based on understanding of policyholders themselves. Respondents who said 'not insured' include Class 1 insured persons *ex officio* applied.

its assets increased. From FY2001 onward there were major changes in the fund's management. Up through FY2000, public pension reserve funds had been required to be deposited with the Ministry of Finance's Trust Fund Bureau and, along with the reserve funds of the postal savings and postal insurance scheme, provided the source of funds for the Fiscal Investment and Loan Program (FILP) (*zaisei tōyūshi* 財政投融資 or *zaitō* 財投). In 1996, Prime Minister Hashimoto took on reform of FILP as part of his administrative and financial system reform package (Noble 2006). In June 2000, an amendment to the Trust Fund Bureau Law was passed, to go into effect on 1 April 2001. The FILP funds deposited with the former Trust Fund Bureau were to be returned as their terms expired (with the process completed by 2008), and the returned pension reserve funds to be managed at the Minister of Health, Labour and Welfare's discretion. In actual practice, they were entrusted to the Government Pension Investment Fund (GPIF) (*Nenkin tsumitatekin kanri un'yō dokuritsu gyōsei hōjin* 年金積立金管理運用独立行政法人) as an independent administrative corporation.

In FY2007 stock prices began to fall in connection with the subprime loan problem in the US, and in the fall of 2008 a global financial crisis was triggered by the Lehmann shock. The fiscal management of the pension reserve funds incurred losses of 5.8 trillion yen in FY2007, rising to 9.35 trillion yen in FY2008. In FY2008, the reserve fund monies invested in the securities market exceeded 90 trillion yen. From FY2009, the even larger sum of 140 trillion yen was set aside for 'independent management' and thus exposed to the price volatility of stocks and bonds (GPIF Home page, Status report of each fiscal year).[10]

The swelling ranks of young temporary or part-time workers among Class 1 insurants

How did declining coverage by Employees' Health and Pension Insurance (particularly for women) affect social insurance of the non-employees and part-time employees? The number of Class 1 insured persons under the National Pension scheme increased between FY1995 and the end of FY2003 by more than 3.3 million (slightly decreasing thereafter). Because employees whose weekly work hours are less than three-fourths of a full-time employee, are neither eligible for Employees' Pension Insurance nor Employees' Health Insurance, anyone whose work hours are reduced below this threshold must switch from Class 2 to mainly Class 1. (Spouses dependent on a Class 2 insured person switch to Class 3). According to a survey by the Social Insurance Agency in 1996, 39.3 per cent of Class 1 insured persons were self-employed (business owners and family members employed in their own businesses) and 24.9 per cent were ordinary workers and temporary or part-time workers. By 2005, however, the self-employed share had dropped 10 percentage points to 28.3 per cent, and ordinary and temporary or part-time workers accounted for 37.2 per cent (Shakai-hoken-chō 2006: Reference 3).

What is the actual situation of Class 1 insurants under the National Pension scheme? Every year, the ranks of Class 1 insurants are joined by persons reaching age 20 as well as persons switching from Class 2 or 3. Those turning 60, on the other hand, leave. For more than a decade, the 5 to 6 million persons entering Class 1 have included 3 to 4 million persons transferring from Class 2. The reasons for their transfer can be assumed to be unemployment, a switch to part-time employment, resignation (including phony resignations) from a workplace, etc. In other words, they are those who have dropped out of regular employment.

The age composition of Class 1 insured persons shows an increase of persons in their 20s (from 22 per cent to 32 per cent), the 20 to 39 age bracket comprising a majority in that Class since FY2000 (Shakai-hoken-chō 2002, 2008[11]). This trend is confirmed in the 2006 *White Paper on the Labour Economy* (Kōsei-rōdō-shō 2006: 208–10). Considering the decrease of the population aged 20 to 29 since the latter half of the 1990s due to Japan's declining birth rate, the increase in the proportion of Class 1 insurants occupied by that age group can only be attributed to a massive surge of part-time employees among the younger generation. In brief, the typical Class 1 insured person is a relatively young 'freeter' (freelancer or underemployed person) rather than a middle-aged or elderly self-employed person. This trend will accelerate after 2007 when the baby-boomers start to reach 60 and leave the National Pension scheme.

On 25 July 2003, there were extensive reports in the media that the compliance rate for contributions to the National Pension scheme by Class 1 insurants was only 62.8 per cent in FY2002, the lowest in its history. (The compliance rate is the ratio of months' worth of contributions paid to those required over the course of a year.) Since then the percentage recovered to 67.1 per cent in FY2005, only to decline again in FY2006 and 2007 and reach a new record low of 62.1 per cent in

FY2008 (Shakai-hoken-chō, 2008).[12] The breakdown of the compliance rate for contributions by Class 1 insured persons in FY2002, for example, was as follows: 52.6 per cent for those formerly in Class 2, 78.9 per cent for those formerly in Class 3 and 42.5 per cent for those automatically enrolled upon reaching 20 years of age (Shakai hoshō shingikai nenkin bukai, 22nd Meeting, Material 3–1). The payment compliance rate thus is low indeed for insurants in their twenties, but they are outnumbered by insurants who switched from Class 2 by a factor of three. It is important to realize that, on the whole, it is the group of temporary or part-time employees who have dropped out of Class 2 that is depressing the payment compliance rate in Class 1.

In sum, it is a hollowing out of Class 2 pension insurance owing to widespread non-regularization of employment that is causing the hollowing out of the public pension system in its entirety. The so-called 'pension for all' (*kai-nenkin* 皆年金), in which Health and Welfare bureaucrats have taken pride, is threatened to become universal in name only.

Health insurance for all in name only

Health insurance coverage of the total population reached close to 98 per cent in 1965 and has since been maintained at 99 per cent and more (*Shakai hoshō tōkei nenpō* each year). As the proportion of employees in the working population increased, the proportion of those covered by the Local Governments' National Health Insurances (*Shichōson kokuho* 市町村国保) managed by municipalities (towns and villages) on behalf of their citizens declined. This trend reversed course in the early 1990s. Insured persons covered by the Local Governments' National Health Insurances started to increase in 1993 in terms of both insured households and individuals (reaching 47,380,000 insured persons by the end of FY2006). Their share of all health insurants grew from a 1990 low of about 35 per cent to 40.3 per cent by the end of FY2006. Among Employees' Health Insurance schemes, many society-managed health insurance schemes (*kumiai kenpo* 組合健保) were dissolved after 1998, due to worsening finances. At their peak, health insurance societies numbered more than 1,800 in 1997, but by the end of FY2006 that number was down to 1,541 (a 14.4 per cent reduction). Government-managed health insurance has been in the red since FY1993 and is drawing down its reserve fund.

In the 1960s, more than 60 per cent of insurants under National Health Insurance were self-employed. From the 1980s onward, the proportion of 'non-employed' increased, reaching a majority (50.9 per cent) in 2001 (Kokumin kenkō hoken chūōkai 2003). The non-employed included pensioners but also a substantial number of people of working age who had become unemployed, in other words, both 'alumni' and 'dropouts' of the Employees' Health Insurance schemes. The capacity of both of these groups to pay insurance premiums is limited, and the compliance rate of national health insurance contributions (taxes) declined year after year reaching 90.1 per cent in 2004 (Kōsei-rōdō-shō 2008). The number of municipality-run schemes exceeded 3,200 through 2002. Subsequently the number decreased, as many cities, towns and villages merged administratively in 2004 and

2005, reaching just over 1,800 in 2006. Although the municipalities grew in scale, most of the Local Governments' National Health Insurance schemes administered by them were in the red. In March 2003, the Japanese government announced a policy to integrate National Health Insurance into prefectural-level units ('Basic Policy Regarding the Health Insurance System and Medical Treatment Fee System' adopted by cabinet decision on 28 March). This initiative resulted in the health care reform of 2006 described above, although consolidation of national health insurance on a prefectural basis was not realized.

However, the fiscal fragility of National Health Insurance stems from structural problems that are difficult to resolve regardless of whether the system is reorganized on a prefectural basis. According to the All-Japan Federation of National Health Insurance Organizations, the average yearly income of households belonging to local government-administered National Health Insurance schemes was estimated to be 1.53 million yen in 2001, significantly lower than that of insured persons in government-managed health insurance, at 2.37 million yen and in society-managed schemes, at 3.81 million yen. If considered in terms of disposable income, a yearly income of 1.53 million yen is at the level of relative poverty. On the other hand, the contribution burden per household under National Health Insurance is not too different from that borne by insurants in other health insurance schemes. The share of yearly income taken up by contributions to National Health Insurance thus amounts to 10.2 per cent, significantly heavier than in the case of government-managed health insurance at 6.7 per cent and society-managed health insurance at 4.6 per cent. Supposing an annual income of 2 million yen, under Local Governments' National Health Insurance the annual contribution would be 150,000 to 200,000 yen; whereas, with the same yearly income, the annual contribution for an insurant of government-managed health insurance would be 80,000 yen (Kokumin kenkō hoken chūōkai 2004).

The proportion of households in arrears on their National Health Insurance contributions rose from 16.1 per cent in 1996 to 19.0 per cent in 2006 (Yoshinaka 2007: 169). In 2008 the proportion was 20.6 per cent, corresponding to roughly 4.5 million households (Kōsei-rōdō-shō 2008). When the time comes for persons who are deemed capable of paying premiums but have not done so for a given period of time, to renew their insurance certificate, they are issued a Short-Term Health Insurance Member Certificate valid for a limited period. Those who are in arrears for over one year with no valid reason have their health insurance certificates revoked, and receive a Health Insurance Member Eligibility Certificate instead.[13] This certificate allows them to access medical facilities, but they will be required to pay treatment costs on the spot.[14] Their access to medical care is thus restricted.

According to the Health Insurance Bureau of the Ministry of Health, Labour and Welfare, in the past few years Short-Term Health Insurance Member Certificates have been issued to about 1.2 million households and Health Insurance Member Eligibility Certificates have been issued to more than 0.3 million households per years (Kōsei-rōdō-shō 2008). In a growing number of cases, municipal governments have also seized bank accounts and real estate of those in arrears (*Asahi Shinbun* 4 February 2007). As National Health Insurance has come to serve as the default destination for people excluded from Employees' Health Insurance, health insurance for all in Japan has become a mirage.

The swelling ranks of unemployed people without unemployment benefits

According to a report published by the ILO in late March 2009, in more than half of the OECD countries a majority of the unemployed are not receiving unemployment benefits. This report includes a graph showing the proportion of the unemployed not receiving unemployment benefits, according to the latest figures available for China, Japan, the US, Canada, the UK, France and Germany. The figure for Japan was the second highest among this group at 77 per cent, following China at 84 per cent. The figure for Germany, by contrast, was just 6 per cent, an order of magnitude lower than that for Japan; France was at 20 per cent, the US at 59 per cent, Canada at 56 per cent and the UK at 45 per cent. It should be noted that the latest figures available for Japan were averages from FY2006, whereas for China the total number of unemployed was inferred from statistics describing the distribution of employees in cities and in villages for the year 2005. Both of these figures therefore predate the financial and economic crisis. The statistics for the North American and European countries, on the other hand, are from December 2008, except Germany's, which is from October 2008 (ILO 2009: figure 5).

As previously noted, the recent distribution of unemployment duration in Japan is similar to patterns in Continental Western Europe and Southern Europe. However, it is clear that the proportion of the unemployed not receiving unemployment

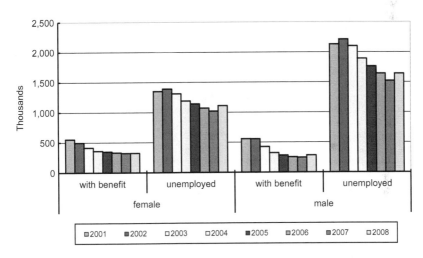

Figure 5.8 Persons receiving unemployment benefit and the number of unemployed, by gender

Source: Fiscal year average number of persons with basic allowance of general jobseekers benefit (from Kosei-rōdō-shō, *Koyō hoken jigyō nenpō*, various years) and fiscal year average number of unemployed persons (from the *Labour Force Survey*).

benefits is much higher in Japan than it is in Western Europe. According to the Ministry of Health, Labour and Welfare's *Annual Report on Employment Insurance Activities*, their percentage has hovered around 77–8 per cent since 2004 (having been around 70 per cent in 2002). In other words, this is not a recent development. Looked at the other way around, the number of unemployed persons who do receive benefits as shown in Figure 5.8 has been decreasing in recent years for both men and women, but the ratio is clearly higher for women at around 30 per cent than for men at 16 per cent (the ratios themselves are not shown in Figure 5.8, since not all unemployed are entitled to benefits to begin with).

To receive unemployment benefits, one must have been enrolled in employment insurance. The conditions for enrolment are 20 or more contracted working hours per week, and an expected term of employment of one year or more. According to the 2007 'General Survey on Diversified Types of Employment' (*Shūgyō keitai no tayōka ni kansuru sōgō jittai chōsa*), 99 per cent of regular employees have employment insurance, but only 60 per cent of non-regular employees do, and within that group only 48 per cent of part-timers and 31 per cent of temporary workers. If we take into account the gender gap in the prevalence of non-regular employment, we find that the proportion of persons with unemployment insurance among employees in recent years was above 75 per cent for men, but only around 62 to 63 per cent for women (Figures extracted from successive *Annual Reports on Unemployment Insurance Activities*).

The reason why there are many unemployed who do not receive benefits among men, whose rate of employment insurance coverage is high, can be assumed to be a marked rise in the proportion of the long-term unemployed among unemployed men as shown in figure 5.4. In the Japanese system, there are no benefits for persons who are unemployed for more than a year.[15]

As indicated above, the proportion of unemployed who do not receive unemployment benefits is comparatively low in major European countries. This can be surmised to be due to the fact that in addition to unemployment insurance, these countries have unemployment assistance or jobseeker allowance systems. These allowances are not conditional on enrolment in a contribution-based plan and are paid out to those still unemployed after the period of employment insurance benefits end, to new graduates failing to find employment, and to self-employed persons who have to close down their business. By this means, even those with little history of paying employment insurance premiums can collect an allowance often indefinitely, on condition that they are genuinely seeking jobs and based on an assessment of household income.[16]

In principle, unemployment benefits (basic daily allowances) paid by employment insurance in Japan amount to between 80 and 50 per cent of the income before loss of employment, with lower wages being replaced at a higher percentage. The object of the benefit is not to provide a minimum livelihood to avoid (relative) poverty, and receiving unemployment benefits is no guarantee for avoiding poverty. Still, not receiving unemployment benefits undoubtedly increases the probability of falling into poverty. Men in Japan face a rising danger of experiencing the twin social stigma of unemployment and impoverishment.

Legal and extra-legal evasion of insurance payments

Let us dig a little deeper into the causes behind the hollowing out of the social insurance system, and of the Employees' Pension Insurance in particular. This hollowing out reflects not only developments in the labour market such as the non-regularization of employment. It can rather be argued that the social security system itself has created conditions conducive to an increasing prevalence of part-time work. Moreover, the shrinking coverage of Employees' Pension Insurance may be attributed in substantial degree to employers' evasion of their obligations under the system by means that could be called illegal – in other words, to extra-legality, which is a form of social exclusion as noted in Chapter 2. The uneven, vertically divided design of the social insurance system creates strong incentives for employers to increase their reliance on non-regular employees and to evade enrolment in the system by extra-legal means.

As mentioned already in Chapter 3, according to the 2005 *General Survey on Working Conditions* (formerly the *General Survey on Wages and Working Hours Systems*), labour costs in 2005 (average costs per worker and month) rose by 2.8 per cent as against the results of the 2002 survey, from 449,699 yen to 462,329 yen. Cash earnings for workers, on the other hand, rose only by 1.9 per cent, and legally mandated welfare expenses rose 10.8 per cent. Between the 2002 and 2005 surveys, the premiums for employment insurance, long-term care insurance and Employees' Pension Insurance were all hiked. The rise in welfare expenses therefore comes as no surprise.

What merits special attention, however, is that even though social insurance premiums were raised, the average legally mandated welfare expense per ordinary worker per month was 46,456 yen, even less than the 46,868 yen they had been in 1998. Other social insurance contributions rose, but the average premium for the Employees' Pension Insurance scheme was 23,831 yen, more than 2,000 yen less than the 25,887 yen in 1998, despite the rise of the premium rate in the intervening period. The amount of Employees' Pension Insurance contributions was obviously kept on a tight leash. As already noted, the 'ordinary workers' referenced in the *General Survey on Working Conditions* include most part-time employees, but part-time workers who work less than three-quarters of full-time equivalent are not covered by either Employees' Health Insurance or EPI. In these cases, employers therefore also do not have to pay their share of insurance contributions. It thus seems clear that the average amount of Employees' Pension Insurance contributions was kept down by increasing the proportion of 'ordinary workers' who fall outside this scheme's coverage.

There is research showing that the share of part-timers not enrolled in any employees' social insurance schemes is close to 70 per cent (65.9 per cent lacking Employees' Health Insurance, 68.3 per cent lacking EPI and 64.5 per cent lacking employment insurance) (*Asahi Shinbun* 3 September 2004). These numbers have been confirmed by the 2006 *White Paper on Labour and Economics* (Kōsei-rōdō-shō 2006: 208–10). As mentioned above, during the debate on the pension reform bills of 2004 Prime Minister Koizumi was pressed about his enrolment in the

Employees' Pension Insurance scheme without having worked for the company in question in fact. At the time, the Prime Minister replied that 'a generous, warm-hearted company president' had helped him out. The term used for 'generous' by Koizumi in Japanese was *futoppara* (thick belly). Given the tight lid corporations have kept on their social insurance – and especially EPI – contributions in recent years, it would seem that 'generous and warm-hearted' corporations have been replaced by the slogan of a management that is 'slim and cool'. In addition to this, payment of contributions to the Employees' Pension Insurance scheme has been actively evaded by extra-legal means.

Fifty million 'floating' pension records

As related above, the pension system was reformed in June 2004, but these reforms stopped short of changing the uneven, vertically divided structure of the system. The results of an administrative evaluation and inspection of the EPI published by the Ministry of Internal Affairs and Communication on 15 September 2006 revealed that in the period examined between August and November of 2005, the number of enterprises suspected of dodging enrolment had risen from 630,000 to 700,000, amounting to approximately 30 per cent of the total number of enterprises within the mandate of EPI. The suspected number of persons failing to be enrolled rose to 2.67 million, amounting to approximately 7 per cent of those who should have been covered.[17]

Then in the early summer of 2007, the so-called 'pension records scandal' broke. It first cropped up in the form of about 50 million 'unidentified' or 'floating' pension records. Soon after, 'vanished' pension records, referring to contributions that were supposed to have been collected but for which records could not be located, came to additionally attract attention.

The 50 million floating pension records were records of contribution collections administered by the Social Insurance Agency, for which the identity of the title holder had become unclear. The majority of these 50 million records were believed to be from persons who changed jobs or married before 1997, causing them to have multiple pension accounts. From 1997 all citizens above age 20 were assigned a 'basic pension identification number', allowing integrated administration of their contribution records, even if the pension scheme under which they were enrolled changed due to job change, marriage or any other reason. At the time the basic pension identification number was introduced, people with multiple pension accounts were asked to return postcards with their names, addresses and other relevant information. The floating pension records are accounts for which no postcards were received.

Through mid-May of 2007, the Social Insurance Agency, the government and the ruling party showed little enthusiasm about investigating the 'owners' of these 'unidentified' contributions. After the Koizumi administration left office in September 2006, new Prime Minister Shinzō Abe declared in the Diet in May 2007 that 'it would be inadvisable to needlessly stir up the public's worries'. But as it became progressively clearer that in many cases this involved loss of benefits, the public's distrust and ire grew apace. Consequently it was decided on 14 June 2007 to set up an Investigative Committee for the Pension Records Problem (*Nenkin kiroku mondai kenshō iinkai* 年金記録問題検証委員会) within the Ministry of Internal Affairs and Communications, with a mandate to investigate the circumstances and causes behind the matter and determine who was responsible.[18] It was also decided to set up a Third-party Committee to Check Pension Records (*Nenken kiroku kakunin dai-sansha iinkai* 年金記録確認第三者委員会) within the Ministry to make fair and impartial judgments about how to correct the Social Insurance Agency's pension records, consisting of a central committee and 50 local committees set up throughout the country, to which pensioners and insurants could appeal.[19] However, since it was clear that the Abe administration's response was behindhand, it only exacerbated public distrust. This was one of the factors that led to the ruling party's loss in the Upper House elections of July, and thus ultimately helped to seal the fate of the Abe cabinet.

The Investigative Committee for the Pension Records Issue released its report on 31 October 2007. According to this report, the root cause of the floating pension record problem lay in the Social Insurance Agency's doctrine of 'deferred adjudication' (*saiteiji shugi* 裁定時主義). Deferred adjudication refers to the view that the pension benefit amount a person is entitled to need not be calculated until that person actually applies to receive that entitlement, at which time the person's contribution records are traced back.[20] The wording of the report returned by this committee, chaired by former public prosecutor general Kunihiro Matsui, reflects a scathing judgment on the Social Insurance Agency and on the Ministry of Health, Labour and Welfare.

However, even though the investigative committee did look into the misappropriation of collected contributions from the vanished pension records by the social insurance administration and municipal bureaucrats, it did not look into other causes of this problem. It soon became clear that the Committee's investigation of the vanished pension records had been insufficient, in light of further developments from the summer of 2008 onwards.

Erased pension registrations – Employees' Pension Insurance as a mechanism for exclusion

It should be more accurate to speak of 'erased' than of 'vanished' pension records, as it turned out that records had been falsified with significant involvement from personnel of the Social Insurance Agency. This was not a matter of simple data entry errors or embezzlement by individual staffers. It had long been surmised that it was not uncommon for employers to fail to enrol employees in EPI on the grounds that they were employed only on a trial basis, to fail to pass on pension contributions deducted from pay checks to social insurance offices, and to underreport the standard remuneration used for calculating pension contributions. These are falsifications perpetrated by employers. But Social Insurance Agency bureaucrats were complicit in such fraud not only by tacitly approving these falsifications or phony discontinuations of employment, but in many cases by also actively abetting them. As for the question of why civil servants would abet pension fraud, the answer lies in the fact that these actions reduced the denominator used in calculating the pension contribution collection ratios of each social insurance office, thus boosting the metric by which they were evaluated.

The Social Insurance Agency at long last admitted that there had been involvement by its personnel on 9 September 2008 at a special cabinet meeting called to discuss the pension registration problem. But even then only a single case in which a Tokyo businessman had confessed to altering documents was acknowledged.[21] Pension bureaucrats remained adamant that there was no institutional complicity.

On 18 September, however, Minister of Health, Labour and Welfare Yōichi Masuzoe revealed in a meeting of the Diet's Committee on Health, Labour and Welfare that there were 69,000 cases of records with a very high likelihood of being falsified, and admitted that he believed that there had been institutional complicity of Social Insurance Agency personnel. It soon became apparent that even these 69,000 cases were just the tip of an iceberg. Based on investigations by the Third-party Committee to Check Pension Records and on testimony from people involved in the process, it was found that there were three typical ways in which records were falsified: (1) reduction of the standard remuneration by five salary ranks or more; (2) reduction of the standard remuneration for the past six months or more; and (3) forfeiture of eligibility status directly after reducing the standard remuneration (so that the pension mandate was no longer applicable). The 69,000 cases reported by the Minister had been only those in which all three of these methods were applied concurrently. The total number of cases where one or more of these methods was applied was estimated at 1.44 million (*Asahi Shinbun* 17 October 2008).

In early October, Minister of Health, Labour and Welfare Masuzoe formed the Committee for the Investigation of Retroactive Adjustment of Standard Remunerations (*Hyōjun hōshū sokyū teisei jian tō ni kansuru chōsa iinkai* 標準報酬遡及訂正事案等に関する調査委員会) reporting directly to him and chaired by Shūya Nomura, a professor at Chūō University Law School. However, this committee's ambit was restricted to investigating only the 69,000 cases described above. In its report, submitted on 28 November, the committee stated that it had found 'no small number' of cases where the sum total of the retroactively reduced standard remuneration exactly equalled the total amount the employer was in arrears on contributions. This strongly suggested that the reduced standard remuneration reported was a falsification calibrated to cancel out the amount that the company was in arrears. The report therefore concluded that 'there was institutional complicity at the level of individual social insurance offices' in these falsifications (Outline of the Report of the Committee for the Determination and Rectification of Base Pay 28 November 2008).[22] In other cases that came to light insurance premiums that the employer was supposed to have paid had been embezzled in amounts not matching the reduction in the standard remuneration, meaning that even the 1.44 million erased pension records mentioned above do not tell the whole story. For records predating February 1986, it is murky even how many records have potentially been falsified (*Asahi Shinbun* 3 October 2008).

By not only quietly condoning but also abetting the erasure of pension records by employers, the Social Insurance Agency which is tasked to oversee the pension programme in fact took a leadership role in extra-legality. As a result, Japan's social insurance system has not only been hollowed out, but can be said to have been transformed into a massive instrument of exclusion from social security coverage and benefits.

Summary

The first two *honebuto* policy statements issued after the launch of the Koizumi administration promised building 'a society that is friendly to working women' and enactment of pension reform 'in accordance with the ideal of a gender-equal society'. Five women were named to the first Koizumi cabinet, the largest number in a single cabinet to date as of 2010. In addition, many more women experts committed to the cause of gender equality were appointed to participate in government advisory bodies than in the past, myself among them.

Koizumi's structural reforms promised an attempt to revamp the existing Japanese-style system root-and-branch: Japanese-style management with its so-called lifetime employment and seniority wage practices, the financial system that supported it, regulations that protected small retailers and small and medium-sized enterprises, and the use of FILP and tax allocations to local governments to channel funds to public-works projects that propped up employment in rural areas. Indeed postal privatization, Koizumi's signature issue, amounted to a reform of FILP.

Gender relations based on the 'male breadwinner' model were a cornerstone of the prevailing Japanese social system. It is therefore no wonder that there were feminists willing to cooperate with Koizumi's structural reforms. Yet political scientist Tarō Miyamoto has aptly described this intersection between gender equality and structural reform agendas as an 'uneasy alliance' (Miyamoto 2008: 159).

But in the pension reforms that were actually implemented a break with the male breadwinner model was deferred. There also was a rising backlash against gender equality in conjunction with the issue of low birth rates. The 'muscular' economic structure that the Koizumi administration boasted of was one in which corporate earnings rose while employee incomes remained static, and growth was dependent on exports. Even as the economy recovered, the income disparities widened inexorably and Japan's relative poverty rate rose to the highest level among OECD countries.

Concerning the issue of non-regularization of employment, the revision of the Worker Dispatch Law in June 2003 lifted the ban on dispatching workers to manufacturing jobs, effective 1 March 2004. Following this, the employment crisis that began toward the end of 2008 and continued into the first half of 2009 saw dispatched workers in the manufacturing sector lose jobs on a vast scale at one sweep. Still, it should not be ignored that the regulation on equal employment opportunities for men and women were strengthened along with the easing of other labour regulations. The 2006 revision of the Equal Employment Opportunity Law prohibited employment discrimination also towards men and included a ban on indirect discrimination.[23]

What reforms to the social security system were carried through in the end? Since 2000, there has been a parade of structural reforms that raised the burden of contributions while holding down benefits. As touched upon in Chapter 4, the ratio of social security premiums to GDP rose consistently and surpassed the tax burden on income and corporate profits after 2000. The primary method of raising the social security burden has been raising social insurance premium rates. In the case of Employees' Health Insurance, the range of the compensation on which the insurance premium is imposed was broadened in 2006. In particular, the pension reform of 2004 instituted an annual rise in the Employees' Pension Insurance premium rate of 0.354 per cent and in the monthly National Pension contribution of 280 yen through 2017.

Meanwhile, as shown in Figure 5.9, the rise in the ratio of social security benefit costs against national income has been rigidly held in check, particularly since FY2002. A wide variety of methods have been used to curb the costs. Let us summarize the benefit cost control policies that have been described here and in Chapter 3: (1) raising of the pension benefit eligibility age from 60 to 65 (adopted in the 1994 pension reform, with the eligibility age scheduled to reach 65 for men in 2025, and for women in 2030); (2) changing the pension amount adjustment method (in 1994, pension indexation was changed from nominal wages to net wages, and from 2008 0.9 per cent was deducted from the inflation rate as a 'macro-economic adjustment'); (3) raising of user payment rates for insurants of

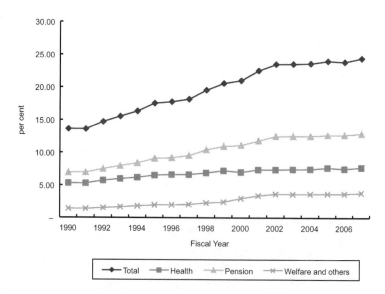

Figure 5.9 Cost of social security benefits (per cent of national income)

Source: Kokuritsu shakai hoshō jinkō mondai kenkyūsho (National Institute of Population and Social Security Research), *Shakai hoshō kyūfuhi* (The Cost of Social Security in Japan), various years.

the Employees' Health Insurance scheme (from 0 per cent to 10 per cent in 1984, to 20 per cent in 1997 and 30 per cent in 2003); (4) tightening of the approval process for long-term care needs under the long-term care insurance system (needs formerly categorized as 'requiring assistance' or Care Level 1 were moved to coverage under newly minted 'preventive-care benefits', with payouts changed to a monthly fixed fee); and (5) lowering of remuneration for medical services rendered (in FY2002 and FY2008).

Social security premiums are inherently regressive. A hike in premiums thus means a heavier burden for those with low incomes. That is to say, as seen in the case of contributions of Class 1 insured persons under the National Pension scheme or insurance premiums under the National Health Insurance scheme, there is a fixed amount equal for all subscribers regardless of income, in addition to a ceiling (standard remuneration maximum) to the income on which an employee's social insurance premium rate is imposed. Furthermore, fixed shares of the expenses (30 per cent, 10 per cent, etc.) are imposed on users as patient or user payment under the health insurance and long-term care insurance plans, again constituting a disproportionate burden on those with low incomes. The functionality of the livelihood security system for lone-mother households and elderly women who live alone in particular is thereby reduced. In view of these continued 'structural reforms' of social security, the government's *National Commission on Social Security* (*Shakai hoshō kokumin kaigi* 社会保障国民会議) expressed its view in 2008 that reinforcing the functioning of Japan's social security system was indispensible (Shakai hoshō kokumin kaigi 2008).

It is the contention of this book that prior to reinforcing the functioning of Japan's livelihood security system, attention must be called to the fact that it is currently functioning in reverse. As non-regularization of employment in particular of women and young men is progressing, the uneven, vertically divided design of Japan's social insurance system has reduced the coverage of female employees. Regressivity of the social security burden has made it even heavier, causing people to drop out of the system. Beyond that, the unevenness and vertical division of the system creates powerful incentives for employers to pursue non-regularization of their employees or evade imposition of social security mandates by extra-legal means. What is more, as in the case of the so-called 'erased pension records', the Social Insurance Agency, the very institution that administers the programme, has abetted such evasion of pension obligations under the law. This can only be described as a reverse functioning of the system.

As mentioned at the end of Chapter 4, as of the middle of the first decade of the 21st century, Japan was the only OECD country where redistribution via taxation and social security actually resulted in raising the poverty rate for considerable segments of the population. This, too, is a startling demonstration of the system functioning in reverse. Only in Japan, the relative poverty rate among households with heads of working age where all adults are employed (dual-earner households, working lone-parent households and working single-member households) is in fact higher in terms of disposable income level after redistribution than it is in terms of market income level. The same is the case for children. The relative poverty rate of one-earner couple families – i.e. male breadwinner households – on the other hand decreases, if only slightly, through redistribution. The Japanese livelihood security system's surpassing all other OECD countries in its adherence to the male breadwinner model is glaringly apparent in this.

6 Beyond exclusion – building a cohesive society

In Japan's livelihood security system since the latter half of the 1990s, young people and women have faced exclusion, while middle-aged and older male breadwinners continued to be relatively secure. What the Japanese system had 'accomplished' by the early years of the new millennium was to turn Japan into one of the worst performers among OECD countries in terms of both its relative poverty rate and income disparity. Worse still, male breadwinners, although privileged by the system, have not remained unaffected by exclusion either. Even while the annual toll of traffic accident deaths averages about 5,000 in Japan, the number of suicides has exceeded 30,000 for the 12th straight year since 1998, with males in their forties and fifties accounting for 10,000 of the total. Needless to say, not only middle-aged or older men commit suicide in Japan. Japan has the world's second highest suicide rate for women and the seventh highest for men. By contrast, Japan's birth rate is among the world's lowest, second only to the Republic of Korea.

Neither birth rate nor suicide rate are generally considered measures of social exclusion. However, the Japanese total fertility rate (TFR) has not only remained below replacement level (i.e. the level of fertility at which a population maintains its numbers in the long term) for more than 20 years. It is also much lower than the number of children people would actually wish to raise. It therefore seems safe to say that Japan's birth rate decline is also linked to 'livelihood difficulties' encountered in giving birth to and bringing up children in Japan, and that its high suicide rate is an indicator of 'livelihood difficulties' experienced in making one's way in Japanese society. In the face of these facts, there can be no denying that Japan's livelihood security system has fallen into a state of dysfunction. I would like to emphasize, at the risk of being repetitive, that Japan's livelihood security system is not simply dysfunctional, but functioning in reverse, as this book has sought to demonstrate. To turn its reverse functioning back into positive functioning, Japan's livelihood security system is in dire need of fundamental restructuring.

The framework of this chapter is as follows. Section 1 will review the recommendations by the National Commission on Social Security (NCSS), established by the Liberal Democratic Party-led coalition government in its dying days. The contents of the Commission's report suggest that the LDP-led government avoided looking squarely at the critical state of the livelihood security system, and proved unable to come to decisions regarding the called-for reforms. A reorganization of welfare government is necessary, which will root it in 'livelihood cooperation'. In Section 2, I therefore argue that welfare government should be restructured into a system of three welfare governments as a means of attaining universal provision of services and a unification of public pension programmes. In realizing universal service provision, livelihood cooperation outside the government must also be expected to play a significant role. 'Livelihood cooperation' refers to livelihood security provided on the basis of spontaneous cooperation at the meso-level of society. In the definition of the 'Common Objectives in the Fight against Poverty and Social Exclusion' adopted by the 2000 Nice European Council, this concept encompasses social economies, social partners, non-governmental organizations (NGOs) and corporate social responsibility. Section 3 will present an overview of social cooperatives in Italy as best-practice examples of livelihood cooperation. Section 4 will conclude the argument of this book by considering once more the relationship between social inclusion and market functions.

I would like to point out that, with regard to the 'social responsibility' of ordinary corporations, I find it neither realistic nor desirable to ask corporations to do anything more to assume responsibility for the functioning of the livelihood security system than cease their extra-legal practices. In Japanese society, which is far more corporate-oriented than that of other countries, what is truly required of corporations is to enable their employees to secure a livelihood sphere where they can feel a degree of independence from their workplaces and expand involvement in the public sphere in their capacity of citizens. It is fine for corporations to be 'slim and cool'. What must be hoped for in Japan is further development of the social economy, as discussed in Section 3 below.

The National Commission on Social Security's failure to face realities

Hope and reassurance impaired

Yasuo Fukuda became Prime Minister of Japan by winning the Liberal Democratic Party's presidential election in September 2007 on the policy pledge that he would make Japan a country of 'hope and reassurance, where young people have hopes for the future and elderly people have a sense of reassurance'. Another important component of his pledge was to 'make the pension, health care, nursing care, and welfare systems solid and reliable'.[1] Premier Fukuda's campaign pledge of 'hope', 'reassurance' and 'reliability' of institutional arrangements can be thought of as a response to the following social realities.

For one thing, the fact that 'young people' are having difficulty in realizing their 'hopes' has been an important factor precipitating the demographic trend of birth rate decline. As the *2008 White Paper on the Birthrate-Declining Society* points out, if people could marry and start a family as they 'wished', the total fertility rate would rise to approximately 1.75 by 2040. However, estimated on the basis of the current situation, the total fertility rate in 2040 will be only 1.25 (Naikakufu, Kyōsei shakai seisaku tōkatsukan 2008a: 29).

A survey conducted by a special working group of the Ministry of Health, Labour and Welfare's Social Security Council found that the percentage of people who are married is correlated, among men, with income level and employment status (regular or non-regular). In the case of women, it is correlated in addition to employment status with availability of parental leave and access to child care. The percentage of people who have children, on the other hand, was correlated in addition to availability of parental leave at the woman's workplace with length of working hours and the extent to which the husband shares housework and child-rearing tasks (Sakai hōshō shingikai, Jinkō kōzō no henka ni kansuru tokubetsu bukai: 3rd Meeting, Material 3).

According to the most recent statistics for each country acquired by the World Health Organization (WHO) and quoted also in Japanese government's *White Paper on Suicide Countermeasures*, the suicide rate (number of suicides per 100,000 people) in Japan in 2007 stood at 24.4 for men and women combined, the sixth highest in the world. Broken down by gender, Japan's rate for men, 35.8, and that for women, 13.7, were respectively the seventh and the second highest in the world. The six countries with higher suicide rates for men than Japan were Russia and other former Soviet Union (FSU) countries, with Belarus leading the list, and Hungary. The only country with a higher rate for women than Japan was the Republic of Korea (Naikakufu, Kyōsei shakai seisaku tōkatsukan 2008b). Japan's suicide mortality rate rose sharply between 1997 and 1998 and subsequently remained stubbornly high, only to rise still further between 2006 and 2007. The rates for the FSU countries and Hungary, by contrast, have continuously declined since 1995.[2]

The University of Tokyo's Center for International Research on the Japanese Economy is currently conducting a research project on suicide called 'Studies on Suicide' (SOS). An international comparative study undertaken by the project's members tried to identify factors leading to the decision to commit suicide with a particular focus on Japan, using comparable data from OECD countries gathered between 1980 and 2000. According to the analysis, factors strongly correlated with the suicide rate include real per capita GDP (negative correlation), per capita GDP growth rate (negative), unemployment rate, birth rate (negative), divorce rate and the Gini coefficient, and these correlations were particularly strong in Japan (Chen, Choi and Sawada 2009). These findings suggest that suicide in Japan is more likely to be caused by economic factors such as low income, unemployment and income disparities than elsewhere, and that the role social and political countermeasures should (and could) play in mitigating the high incidence of suicide is therefore large.

If we take Prime Minister Fukuda's policy pledge at the time of the LDP presidential election at its face value, he took up the helm of government reflecting on the deplorable fact that the Japanese people's hopes and sense of reassurance had been impaired, and that politics and public administration had lost their confidence. This marked a significant departure from the attitudes taken by his predecessors. Prime Minister Koizumi, for example, when asked about the burning issue of widening economic inequalities during the ordinary session of the Diet in 2006, repeated over and over again: 'Income gaps are not as serious as they are made out to be.' Prime Minister Abe, who succeeded Koizumi, answered when questioned about the problem of missing pension records as if he were an idle spectator: 'You should not stir up people's anxieties on this issue.'

Nonetheless, the Fukuda cabinet's popularity rating, which stood high at its inception, soon plummeted. In January 2008, his government established the NCSS, in the hope that this would help boost the dwindling popularity rating. All the members of the Commission, including its chairperson, Professor Hiroshi Yoshikawa of the University of Tokyo, are reported to have been handpicked by Fukuda himself. The NCSS submitted its interim report on 19 June 2008, but before the final report could be issued, Fukuda announced his resignation on 1 September. The final report subsequently was included into the Asō cabinet's 'Mid-term Program' concerning social security and public finances from tax revenues, announced on 24 December 2008.[3]

A perpetual 'It is criticized that'

How did the NCSS perceive the present state of affairs, and what countermeasures did it propose? In its interim report submitted on 19 June, the Commission spelled out its view of the present situation in a relatively straightforward manner. It asserts that the Japanese livelihood security system is faced by the following five problems: 'delay in implementing measures against the declining birth rate', 'further aging of the population', 'deterioration of systems that provide health care and long-term care services', 'a weakening of safety net functions' and 'erosion of trust in the system' (Shakai hoshō kokumin kaigi 2008a: 4–6).

Regarding the basic orientation of the social security reforms to be pursued, the interim report states that 'strengthening of social security functions' should be prioritized (Shakai hoshō kokumin kaigi 2008a: 6). Regarding the performance of the social security reforms thus far, it asserts that the implementation of the 'structural reforms' from 2000 onwards had the effect of heightening 'consistency of the social security system with economic and fiscal policies' (ibid.: 4). It is based on this perception that the NCSS recommended prioritizing 'strengthening' the system's 'functions'. The NCSS, nonetheless, did not depart from the existing structural reform policy line. What is especially striking is that in commenting on the 'weakening of safety net functions', which after all is directly relevant to the task of 'strengthening social security functions', the Commission rather strangely did not assume any responsibility of its own.

Instead, the report merely notes that, first, '*it is criticized* that polarization of the labour market and the entrenchment of disparities' (italics added) have had the effect of causing increasing numbers of non-regular workers to drop out of the employees' social insurance schemes. Second, it continues to state that '*it is also criticized* that' the trend toward polarization of the labour market and the increase in the number of non-regular workers have been 'exacerbated' by failure to implement necessary reforms of the social security system (including expansion of social insurance coverage to non-regular workers). Third, the report notes that '*it is also criticized* that' the 'livelihood security and income redistribution functions' of social security are not working effectively in the face of such problems as the increase of elderly people living alone and the working poor (Shakai hoshō kokumin kaigi 2008a: 5).

These passages clearly refer to the issue of social exclusion discussed in this book, but the NCSS does not state its own position on them here. It merely states repeatedly that there are criticisms, without stating at the same time who is making them. Its discussion of the problem is presented in a style markedly different from that adopted in its discussions of other issues. Its reference to 'the weakening of safety net functions' sounds as if it was talking about someone else's problem. It is for this reason that it stands out. On the other hand, the Commission did not offer any counterarguments to these criticisms, which in effect means that it admitted their cogency. The attitude shown by the Commission in this matter can only be described as vague and uncertain.

In fact, at the seventh meeting of the Commission on 19 June 2008, where the draft interim report was discussed, one of the commission members, Tsuyoshi Takagi, then President of Rengō (the Japanese Trade Union Confederation), pointed out that he found something odd about the style in which the passage concerning the 'weakening of safety net functions' was written. He queried whether the adoption of this style was intended to mean that the Commission itself 'did not admit that there is something like a weakening of safety net functions'. However, the Chair of the Commission, Prof. Yoshikawa, did not respond directly to any comments or questions by the Commission's members. Proposing that these points should be further discussed in preparing the final report, he asked the Commission to give its approval to the draft for the interim report 'for the time being'.[4] There is, however, no evidence to suggest that the points raised by Takagi regarding the draft interim report were discussed at any of the subsequent plenary meetings of the NCSS.[5]

As for the question of where the mentioned criticisms had been made, the Japanese edition of this book published in March 2007 was among the sources for them. There is of course nothing extraordinary about the NCSS's report not commenting on the work of individual researchers. There are, however, other sources to which the NCSS should have responded in a more straightforward manner; these include the 2005 OECD report and the OECD's *Economic Survey of Japan 2006*, both of which were used not only in this book but also debated in the Diet.

Concerns raised by the OECD and the Japanese government's response

How did the government of Japan respond to the OECD's concerns about the income distribution and labour market situation of Japan? According to the OECD's report entitled *Income Distribution and Poverty in OECD Countries in the Second Half of the 1990s*, issued in March 2005 and discussed in Chapter 2 of this book, Japan as of 2000 ranked tenth among the 27 member countries of the OECD in terms of the Gini coefficient, and third from the bottom above Mexico and the US in terms of the OECD's 'composite measure of relative poverty' (OECD 2005b: 23, 10). The Japanese government addressed this OECD report in its *Annual Report on the Japanese Economy and Public Finance* for FY2006, issued in July 2006. In its Chapter 3, the latter set aside a section on 'Economic disparity from the viewpoint of the household sector' and pointed out that the rise in income disparity in Japan since the mid-1980s was attributable to changes in demographic factors, including population aging. The Annual Report also made a rebuttal to the OECD 2005 report by pointing out that the OECD's estimate of Japan's relative poverty rate had been based on the *Comprehensive Survey of Living Conditions*, but that if calculations were made on the basis of the *National Survey of Family Income and Expenditure* instead, Japan's relative poverty rate was not particularly high (Naikakufu 2006: 262, 265–6). One point of criticism that has been raised about the *Comprehensive Survey of Living Conditions* is that elderly households are over-represented by it (Naikakufu 2007; Suzuki 2008).

In July 2006, the OECD published its *Economic Survey of Japan 2006*. According to this survey and a working paper written in 2007 using similar data (both of which were used in Chapter 4) the relative poverty rate as a percentage of the working-age population of Japan in 2000 stood at 13.5 per cent, which was the second highest after the US at 13.7 per cent (Jones 2007: 21, 27). On the question of whether income disparity had been growing wider in Japan since the mid-1980s, the OECD, perhaps out of consciousness of the debate taking place in Japan, admitted that the aging population was one factor contributing to the growing disparity among the entire population. For this reason, the OECD proceeded to compile an analysis with restricted focus on the working-age population, only to point out that an important factor underlying the increasing disparity was dualism in the labour market.

The government was questioned concerning this indication of the OECD in a meeting of the Lower House Budget Committee on 13 February 2007 by Kazuo Shii, a Lower House member and Chair of the Japanese Communist Party. In his response, Prime Minister Abe asserted that 'since some of the statistics and data referred to by the OECD's *Economic Survey of Japan 2006* are of a dubious nature, the report needs to be closely scrutinized in order to determine whether it is reliable or not'. Abe stuck fast to the official government view that had been upheld since the Koizumi cabinet. However, Kiyoshi Ōta moved quickly to make a thoroughgoing review of the OECD's *Economic Survey of Japan 2006*, including an examination of the propriety of the Survey's data sources. Ōta had priorly asserted, in his capacity as an economist working for the Economic Planning Agency, that 'the degree of disparity in Japan is not rising' (Ōta 1999). This time, however, he carried out the verification study as chief researcher of the Japan Research Institute and special researcher of the Economic and Social Research Institute of the Cabinet Office. His conclusion was that it could not be said that the OECD's estimates based on the *Comprehensive Survey of Living Conditions* and on the *Survey on the Redistribution of Income* had overestimated the extent of income disparity in Japan (Ōta 2006a: 10).[6]

As already shown in Table 4.4, the OECD's *Economic Survey of Japan 2006* also focused on the redistributive effects of taxes and social security. More specifically, even though Japan's Gini coefficient and the relative poverty rate measured at the level of market income are not exceptionally high by the standards of OECD countries, they are among the highest when measured at the level of disposable income (OECD 2006). Ōta further buttressed this contention by the OECD as follows (Ōta 2006b).

First, redistributive effects in Japan are small because social security benefits paid to the working-age population are small, and because the income redistribution effect of taxes is small. With regard to the relative poverty rate, Ōta points to the fact that the tax rate imposed on middle-income earners in Japan is not much different from that imposed on low-income earners, and is therefore relatively lower than the tax rates imposed on middle-income earners in the West. He points out that this fact has the effect of raising the poverty rate in Japan. This is because, given the definition of the relative poverty rate as the percentage of the population that lives on one half or less of the median equivalent income, a low rate of tax imposed on middle-income earners has the effect of pushing up the level of their disposable income. This in turn translates into a higher relative poverty rate. Second, Ōta argues that the fact that family allowances constitute only a small portion of social security benefits paid to the working-age population in Japan has had the effect of elevating its relative poverty rate above that of European countries especially among households with children (Ōta 2006b).

Ambiguity of the National Commission on Social Security's proposals

The NCSS said nothing about the foregoing observations made by the OECD reports, nor about the discussions they aroused inside Japan. Its interim report asserted that the social security system, through its income redistribution functions, 'has realized "social justice" in the sense of equality in benefits and fairness in tax and social security contributions' (Shakai hoshō kokumin kaigi 2008a: 7). Among the Commission's members, Tsuyoshi Takagi once again expressed his objections to this passage, asking: 'Is this indeed an accurate description of current realities?' and: 'Would it not be more accurate to say that the income redistribution function of tax payments has all but disappeared?' Committee Chair Yoshikawa did not reply to Takagi's questions this time either.[7] Page 8 of the Reference Material attached to the interim report traces how the redistributive effects of the Japanese social security system have improved over the years, while also revealing that improvement through taxation has been stagnant or on the decrease. However, the question of the tax system is not touched upon in its interpretation of the data (Shakai hoshō kokumin kaigi 2008a: Reference Material 8). What is more, the NCSS did not include any international comparisons.[8]

Why did the NCSS leave matters at talking about the 'weakening of safety net functions' as if this were someone else's problem? The style of description cannot be characterized as having resulted from careless oversight, or from evasiveness caused by excessive prudence. It can only be seen as a result of the Commission's stubborn refusal to face realities. Perhaps this also explains why the NCSS's proposal of a 'reform for function strengthening' was left ambiguous and ill-defined.

164 *Beyond exclusion – building a cohesive society*

With regard to pension reform, arguably the most urgent issue, the NCSS carried out a simulation study of several reform plans (including the option of maintaining the status quo) comparing projected insurance premiums and scope of the national treasure burden, prospective impact on individual households and corporations, and listing 'advantages and disadvantages' for each plan. Even in its final report, however, the NCSS was merely 'looking forward to discussions deepening further', and ended without specifying a recommended reform plan (Shakai hoshō kokumin kaigi 2008b: 4).[9] This is what I had in mind when I pointed out earlier that the outgoing LDP-led governments failed to look squarely at the critical state of the livelihood security system of Japan, and had rendered themselves incapable of coming to a decision about urgently called-for reforms.

Universal services and a unified pension plan

A system of three welfare governments

Since the end of the 1990s, I have been proposing with Naohiko Jinno and Masaru Kaneko that Japan's current welfare government be restructured into a 'system of three welfare governments' (Jinno and Kaneko 1999). Social policies implemented by these three welfare governments would need to shift their emphasis from income transfer to service security, returning to the basic fact that people's needs are intrinsically diverse and individual. Moreover, the services provided by social policies should be provided on a universal basis, and for income transfer itself the principle of collaborative risk sharing should be clearly defined.

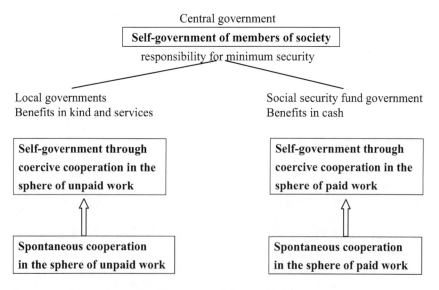

Figure 6.1 Schematic image of the system of three welfare governments
Source: Jinno 2000: 79.

Figure 6.1 presents a schematic image of the 'system of three welfare governments'. Local government guarantees to provide benefits in kind, including services, in response to the people's various livelihood needs. The social security fund government takes charge of transferring income to substitute for earnings. The central government assumes the responsibility for providing minimum security on a nationwide basis. There are several reasons for why we have focused on 'welfare governments' as opposed to the 'welfare state'. For one thing, we do not want to limit attention solely to the role of the central government as the representative of 'sovereignty', but wish to emphasize the roles local governments can be expected to play as organs of self-governance by local citizens, and the power and authority necessary for performing those roles. For another, we believe that, instead of treating the social security fund as one of the central government's special accounts, as it has been until now, the fund should be equipped with a democratic regime and given substance as a 'government' in its own right. Democratic regime here means an arrangement whereby insured persons and employers who contribute social insurance premiums elect their own representatives, and participate in the management and administration of the fund through these representatives.

Local government would be vested with primary responsibility for guaranteeing that residents be provided with goods and services on a 'universal' basis in accordance with needs. In other words, the role of local governments would be expanded vis-à-vis those of the central and social security fund governments. Tax revenue sources appropriate for and corresponding to the execution of such increased responsibility should be transferred to local governments, and the competencies of citizens for local self-determination and self-governance should be enhanced (Kimura and Miyazaki 2006).

Historically, the establishment of the social insurance system was owed to spontaneous development of forms of cooperation such as the mutual help activities of labour unions and friendly societies in work sites or occupation fields, which were subsequently given legally binding force. Social security funds in France and Germany were essentially characterized as 'governments' in the sense that they were administered by representatives elected by their subscribing members. The task of the social security fund government is to provide cash benefits to an insured person to substitute for earnings when this person's ability to earn an income is suspended or lost due to sickness, unemployment, retirement at old age or child care and nursing care needs. The 'ability-to-pay principle' is adopted, meaning that each person is required to contribute to the fund in proportion to their earnings, and entitled to receive benefits in proportion to their contribution. In Japan, it is especially urgent to resolve the regressive nature of contributions. Rescinding the flat-rate insurance premium of the Class 1 insured persons under the National Pension Plan, and similar premiums for the National Health Insurance Plan, abolishing the ceilings on the standard remuneration used to calculate the earnings-related premium for the employees' social insurance schemes, and levying social insurance premiums on a simple earnings-proportional basis will not only resolve the problem of regressive contributions, but will also improve the revenue raising capability of the social security system without raising premium rates.

The guarantee of a national minimum provided by the central government would be implemented broadly in two dimensions. On the one hand, it would guarantee a minimum market income, with macro-economic policies for the prevention of the emergence of mass unemployment, regulations on dismissals and regulations concerning working hours and minimum wages also being important. On the other hand, it would guarantee a minimum disposable income and a minimum of goods and services, provided in part to individual persons and in part to local governments. One category of individuals to whom the central government should provide disposable incomes directly is school-age children, who are prohibited from engaging in income-earning activities (child allowances). Another category of people who also need to be directly supported by the central government's public assistance scheme includes those not eligible to receive earnings-substituting cash benefits from the social security fund government, either because they have insufficient insurance premium contributions or because their specified benefit payment periods have ended. Persons with disabilities, self-employed persons, students and homemakers would be more likely than others to fail to pay sufficient insurance premiums. In addition, since these benefits are for substituting earnings and not meant to help the recipients sustain the minimum standard of living, there may be cases where social insurance benefits are insufficient to cover the minimum costs of daily life. It is the obligation of the central government to pay these people non-contributory cash benefits, namely, public assistance benefits to enable them to maintain a minimum livelihood.

The guaranteed minimum provided by the central government to local governments is for guaranteeing the national minimum of goods and services. Even if local governments are charged with the responsibility for providing goods and services to meet the needs of residents, there must be some national minimum standard for the level of goods and services guaranteed. If, for instance, the proportion of elderly people in the local population is high, placing a heavy burden on the local government, or if the local government is suffering from a deficit in financial capability, it may become impossible for the local government alone to satisfy the national minimum standard. In such a case, it would be the responsibility of the national government to guarantee that the national minimum standard be met by financially assisting local governments.

In this way, the provision of social insurance benefits by the social security fund government, the guaranteed minimum provided by the central government, and the guarantee of services by local governments would work together to provide universal services. This does not mean, however, that it is the welfare governments alone that realize the provision of universal services, as I will explain in Section 3.

Building 'sustainable communities' on the basis of universal services

What exactly are universal services? The term 'universalism', which is opposed to 'selectivism', has been used in the fields of income security and social administration to indicate that eligibility for cash and service benefits is not limited or differentiated according to occupation, place of residence, family relationship and especially income. In a slightly different context, the word 'universal' has also come to be used since the early half of the 1990s in reference to a design of products, environments and services, such that they are safe, easy to use and easily understood for everybody, regardless of age, gender and physical condition. Whereas the concept of 'barrier-free' was coined with elder persons, persons with disabilities, pregnant women and persons with infants as people with 'special needs' in mind, and is concerned with removing the 'barrier' faced by these people, universal design is oriented from the outset to satisfying the needs of all types of people in all kinds of situations (Mace 1998). At first, this term was mainly applied to industrial design, but it in recent years it has also come to be adopted for such areas as 'community development' and 'human resource development'.

In parallel with these developments, an obligation to provide 'universal services' also in network industries such as electronic communications, electricity, town gas, water, railways and postal services, has been emphasized since the latter half of the 1990s. According to a recommendation submitted by the Telecommunications Council (currently the Information and Communications Council) in 2000, a universal service has the following three defining features: (1) it is a service indispensable for the livelihood of people; (2) the conditions of its supply must be appropriate, including the condition that it must be supplied at a price affordable by everybody; and (3) it is a service of which a universal, equitable and stable supply should be secured throughout Japan (Denki tsūshin shingikai 2000).

If universal services are seen in light of this definition, child care, health care, education, nursing care and the like should naturally be included under them, but in present-day Japan universal provision of these services is not realized. They are indispensable for sustaining each and every person as they are born, grow up, learn, work, rest, nurture, support each other, attend the deathbeds of loved ones and finally conclude their own lives. Unless these services are supplied on a universal basis, it is difficult in various localities for people to strike roots and continue to live there, and to play an active role in safeguarding and developing their communities. A locality in which people can no longer hope to raise children and continue to live, cannot survive as a 'sustainable city'.

If not only the quantity but also the quality of services is considered, the distance to be traversed before services indispensable for people's livelihood are supplied on a universal basis is even greater. Also if uniform and standardized services are supplied in a mechanical fashion, without taking into consideration regional differences such as climatic conditions or individual factors in converting services into 'functionings', needs are not met in a 'universal, equitable and stable' way.

Design of products, cities and workplaces so far implicitly considered a young to middle-aged 'able-bodied' man of Japanese nationality with a sizeable income and a wife to represent the norm. Universalization means to reflect in the design of products or institutions the fact not only that people are diverse, but also that individuals change over time and every person has various needs. Such a design will also be of benefit to those who happen to represent the norm as an 'ordinary, able-bodied man in the prime of life' at a certain point in time.

168 Beyond exclusion – building a cohesive society

A unified pension scheme to enable social insurance to serve its original purpose

In contrast to the ideal of the 'three welfare governments' explained above, the welfare state in the latter half of the 20th century, as repeatedly argued in this book, reduced the livelihood needs of people, which are diverse and individual by their very nature, to the single dimension of disruption or loss of income-earning ability by a male breadwinner. Furthermore, the welfare state bureaucratically managed the social security system by defining such a person's need for income in a uniform and top-down manner. What is especially characteristic about Japan's social security system is that the payment of social security benefits is heavily concentrated on the elderly, while benefits both in kind (services) and in cash directed towards needs other than health care are meagre. This makes it necessary for cash benefits, such as those paid by public assistance programmes and pensions, to be of amounts large enough to enable beneficiaries to purchase essential goods and services on the market.

As pointed out in Chapter 4, the standard benefit level of the livelihood protection scheme, Japan's public assistance programme, is relatively high, ranking it about sixth highest among the OECD countries. This is partly due to the fact that with child allowance benefits being meagre and subject to income restrictions, and with ordinary housing benefits being virtually nonexistent, the minimum cost of living must be wholly covered by livelihood protection allowances as such. On the other hand, the principle of 'subsidiarity' (i.e. the principle that a livelihood protection benefit should be payable only after the beneficiary's own assets and support from relatives has been thoroughly mobilized) is applied so rigorously that a beneficiary is only allowed, for instance, to have savings of up to one half of the amount of the monthly minimum living cost (Shakai hoshō shingikai fukushi bukai seikatsu hogo seido ni kansuru senmonka iinkai: Material of the 17th Meeting).[10] In not a few cases, persons who judged on the basis of their income are actually in need of livelihood protection benefits, therefore have their applications turned down or choose not to file applications to begin with. It is not at all rare for the standard benefit level of livelihood protection to be higher than the income or consumption expenditures of low-income households, with the result that the beneficiaries also become the subject of a kind of reverse-discrimination envy.

With regard to Japan's pension benefits, it should be pointed out that even though their immediate purpose was not to guarantee the minimum cost of living, the reference standard for the 'model pension' was a replacement rate of at least 50 per cent of the average earning, or the average consumption expenditure of a working-age household. There is income redistribution within the pension system insofar as the replacement rate for low-income earners becomes higher. It should be pointed out once again, at the risk of being repetitive, that the 'model pension' refers to the benefit paid to a husband, who has earned the average wage as a Class 2 insured person for 40 years, and his wife, who has been Class 3 insured person for 40 years. In the UK and Sweden, as noted in Chapter 4, pension benefits barely amount to 40 per cent of the average wage. Given the fact that in these countries, particularly in Sweden, health care and welfare services are universally guaranteed, and that a housing benefit also exists, the amount that must be paid out of the pension benefit for living expenditures is not large. In Japan, however, pensioners need to have own savings in addition to public pensions, since they need to cover not only the minimum costs of living but also user payments for medical care and nursing care out of their pensions.

The proposal of this book is that by guaranteeing the provision of universal services the need for cash benefits is reduced, and that cash benefits should be made to clearly reflect the original purpose of the social insurance system of income substitution through mutual cooperation. As I have stated earlier, it is urgently necessary to restore overall progressivity in the tax and social security systems. As noted also in Chapter 4, although the revenue from taxes, especially direct taxes, of Japan's welfare government has declined, the social insurance premium burden, which is regressive, has increased. The poverty reduction and income redistribution effects of the tax and social security systems, especially the tax system, are extremely limited and dependent on social security benefits to a disproportionately large degree. It is therefore essential that the regressivity of social insurance premiums is eliminated, and progressivity mainly of individual income taxes restored. To do so, it is necessary to raise the maximum taxation rate on individual income further, and to include financial assets income (i.e. dividends, interests and capital gains), which are now subject to separate taxation at low rates, under a consolidated tax scheme.

How should the public pension system be restructured? For several years I have been proposing, together with Masaru Kaneko and Naohiko Jinno, that the public pension system should be reorganized into a unified program for the entire population (Kaneko and Jinno 1999; Kaneko 1999; Ōsawa 2000). As demonstrated in Chapter 5, it has become clear in the past several years that not only has the public pension system become hollowed out. Due to the spread of precarious employment conditions and extra-legal evasion of contribution payments by enterprises, it has also turned into a mechanism for spurring social exclusion. Unification of the public pension system is thus an urgent task. A unified pension system means, first, that the present two-tiered structure, consisting of the Basic Pension portion and the earnings-related portion, is abolished in favour of a single-tiered one. Second, unlike the current uneven, vertically divided structure of the present system under which people with different kinds of occupations or in different occupational fields, with different working hours and annual earnings, enrol in different pension schemes, a unified system would be a system in which the entire population participates under the same conditions.

Under a unified system, contributions would be made simply proportional to earnings. Under the current system, one half of the premium for an employed person is contributed by the employer, but given the prospect that employment patterns will become increasingly diverse, and employees, whether they like it or not, will become increasingly mobile, it would be rational to ask employers to pay their share of contributions to Employees' Pension Insurance premiums as a lump-sum amount calculated on the basis of the apparent size of a business, such as the total wage bill or gross sales. The employer's own pension premium would be made proportional to the income from his or her business activities. The switch to the new system would require a transition period of 30 to 40 years, during which the pension reserve fund would be drawn down, and the total amounts of premium contributions and pension benefits would gradually come into balance on the macro level as the proportion of elderly people in the population stabilizes.

Regarding pension benefits under this envisioned unified system, the following three points should be noted. First, pension benefits should be strictly proportional to contributions. More specifically, the annual pension benefit amount should be calculated as the 'current value of the total contribution divided by the anticipated number of years of pension receipt', where the 'anticipated number of years of pension receipt' is the period from the time when the beneficiary begins to receive the pension to the average life expectancy of the cohort to which the beneficiary belongs. However, an income slide would be introduced whereby the pension benefit for each year would be adjusted upward by the average rate of increase in incomes (employment income and business income) earned by the current working generation.

However, this alone would mean that pension benefits for persons with low incomes or without income for prolonged periods of time, would be exceedingly small. Under the current system, among persons with low lifetime incomes, only the dependent spouses of Class 2 insured employees are eligible to receive Basic Pension benefits to the full amount as Class 3 insured persons, without having paid insurance premiums. If spouses of self-employed persons and unmarried persons, on the other hand, are exempted from the payment of premiums on account of low income, their pension benefits will also be small. Exempting a person from pension premium payments on account of low income accords with the ability-to-pay principle, but receipt of benefits by persons who did not pay contributions is out of joint with the basic purpose of social insurance benefits, namely to substitute for lost earnings.

Benefits under the unified system should therefore, second, include a price-indexed minimum pension as a means of guaranteeing the minimum income. The amount of this minimum pension benefit would be made loosely proportional to the total contribution made by each person. The gradient of proportionality of the minimum pension benefit to the contribution would be more relaxed than that of regular pension benefits, but introducing a certain gradient would preserve an incentive for low-income earners to contribute. The minimum pension benefits would be financed by the general account budget upon completion of the tax system reform, including the adoption of consolidated taxation on asset incomes. (In other words, instead of relying on a special-purpose indirect tax as the only tax revenue source, tax revenues from the progressive income tax and corporate tax would also be tapped). Among the systems that are actually at work in the world at present, the arrangement described above is similar to the Swedish pension system.

Third, pension benefits should be divided between spouses according to the income-splitting method. Under this rule, the contributions paid by a married couple in each year or month are aggregated and divided by two, the resulting amount being regarded as the contribution of each. This is to prevent a situation where spouses of husbands with substantial economic means, who have spent many years as homemakers, end up relying on the minimum pension. Regarding the question of whether the married couple or the individual should be the unit of the system, this proposal for making the married couple the unit may be considered a transitional one. In the current situation in Japan, the disparity in financial means between women and men (reflecting the large gender gap in wage levels and in employment opportunities) is one of the largest among advanced industrial countries. It is not that there is simply disparity between husband and wife. Rather, income-earning ability is being transferred from the wife to the husband through the wife's 'supportive contributions' in the form of household duties and child care. My proposal is an interim measure that takes this fact into consideration. However, a couple may be exempted from the application of this rule by mutual agreement.

If pension splitting between spouses is adopted, survivor's pension for spouses will no longer be necessary, since regardless of whether a married couple part ways by divorce or death, their total contributions during the period when they were married, that is the basis for calculation of their future pension benefits, are split in two. Figure 6.2 schematically illustrates how the pension benefit amount received under the earnings-related unified pension scheme changes with the amount of contributions made.

One advantage of a unified pension system such as this is that it embodies the spirit of social solidarity in addition to safeguarding the incentive to contribute by maintaining the ability-to-pay principle. The ability-to-pay principle at work on the benefit-payment side means that for members of each age-cohort, the total amount of pension benefits receivable by a certain individual is, on average, equivalent to the total contributions made by the person concerned (excluding the minimum pension portion). The expression 'on average' means that a person who lives beyond the average life expectancy of the cohort would end up receiving in excess of the average amount, but a person who passes away before that age would end up receiving less than the average amount. Aside from the minimum pension, the pension system would not contain in itself any factor of vertical redistribution from high-income to low-income earners. At the same time, through its mechanism of adjusting the pension benefits to the earnings of the working-age generation, the system would institutionalize the spirit of inter-generational solidarity. Furthermore, it would include a mechanism to encourage elderly persons to continue working, if they are willing to do so, and to continue to pay contributions. Such a mechanism would enable elderly persons to postpone their retirement and to start receiving pension benefits at advanced ages, which means that by reducing the anticipated years of pension receipt, they would be able to increase the amount of pension benefits receivable per year.

Another advantage of the unified pension system is its 'portability'. Given the fact that under this system, everybody would continue subscribing to the same system under the same conditions, even in the case of change of occupation or workplace, perfect 'portability' in the literal sense of this word would be achieved. Effectively breaking with the male breadwinner model, it would be neutral to

172 *Beyond exclusion – building a cohesive society*

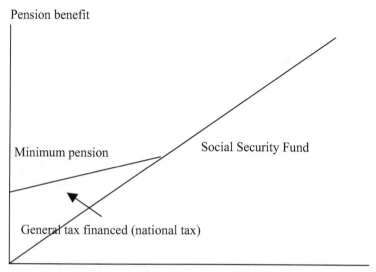

Figure 6.2 Pension benefit formula
Source: Jinno and Kaneko 1999: 28.

choice of occupation and lifestyle, and able to guarantee the individual's right to self-determination to the maximum possible degree.

Participation of the concerned parties in realizing universal services

With regard to universal services, the following questions may well be raised. Is it really possible for designers, who are not omnipotent, to design universal services with such superb and exquisite functions at a reasonable cost? And is it not possible for a design created with people with specific needs in mind to be more difficult to use than standard designs for people with different needs? If people with certain types of needs or under certain conditions are regarded simply as end-users of a design, the designers must indeed be omnipotent, and the realization of a universal service will be nothing more than a utopian dream. The indispensable key to turning this dream into reality is for people with various needs to play a leading role in the design process themselves. To make it possible for such persons to recognize and voice their own needs, 'cooperation' at a level close to the bearers of needs is indispensible.

Local governments, as welfare governments, must be organs of self-governance for and by their residents. It must be ensured in a thoroughgoing manner that diverse types of people, as the subjects and main actors, have ample opportunities to participate in the planning and implementation of services, and in the overall administration of community affairs. Even if a local government is expected to guarantee the provision of a universal service, the service workers who take care of the service need not be full-time employees of the local government. So long as the local government properly performs the regulatory work of maintaining the quality and quantity of services and the work of procuring financial resources, the concrete tasks of delivering and supplying the services may be performed by family members or friends. If a family member or friend who is employed takes leave of absence to carry out child care or nursing care, his or her substitution for earned income during the absence from work would be paid by the social security fund government. If an unemployed family member or friend serves as a caregiver, providing child care or nursing care, he or she will be guaranteed vacations from the caring work (which will be taken over temporarily by a replacement caregiver dispatched by the local government), and all caregivers involved would be supported by counselling and other services. Needless to say, the caregiver may also be a not-for-profit cooperative organization or a commercial enterprise. This is why I stated above that it is not the welfare governments alone that would realize the provision of universal services.

Once universal services are guaranteed, things will begin to move in a virtuous cycle, with more diverse residents being able to participate to a higher degree, and the design of services becoming more universal in turn. In the existing welfare services, persons on the receiving end of services have been regarded merely as objects for whose sake the provision of services should be 'arranged'. But under a system of universal services these same persons will participate in the design and operation of services as main actors, enabled to do so by community-based 'livelihood cooperation'. Naturally, the geographical extent of the 'community' in which particular needs are to be met varies according to the type of needs, modes of transportation and communications networks, and other factors. 'Community' here should therefore not be equated with the area of a currently existing municipality. As best-practice examples of community-based 'livelihood cooperation', the social cooperatives of Italy warrant a closer look.

Learning from 'livelihood cooperation' practices in Italy

The 1991 Italian Law on Social Cooperatives: an overview of the cooperatives as of 2001

According to Carlo Borzaga, who coordinated a joint study in 15 European countries on the means of combating social exclusion, it was Italy where the most concentrated development of the third sector (social economy) in the ten-year period from 1995 to 2004 exceeding all expectations took place (Borzaga 2004: 45). According to Natsuko Tanaka's assiduous research on the social economy, especially cooperatives, in Italy and Japan, the turning point in the growth of the social economy in Italy was the enactment of the Law on Social Cooperatives (Law 381) in 1991. This legislation was the culmination of a ten-year long movement (Tanaka 2004b: Chapter 3).

Let us first take a brief overview of the current situation of the social economies in Europe based on a 2006 report by the International Centre of Research and

Information on the Public, Social and Cooperative Economy (CIRIEC) entitled *Social Economy in the European Union*. Compiled as a comprehensive survey report for the European Economic and Social Committee, its Chapter 6 presents various statistical data. Cross-national comparisons of the estimated scale of paid employment in the social economies in 2002–3 show that its ratio to total paid employment averaged 7.0 per cent for the 15 older member countries of the EU, and 4.3 per cent for the 10 new member countries. Broken down by country, the ratios in Western Europe were 7.0 per cent in the UK, 5.8 per cent in Germany and 8.7 per cent in France. By contrast, those in Northern and Southern Europe were 5.0 per cent in Sweden, 6.2 per cent in Denmark, 8.5 per cent in Finland, 5.9 per cent in Spain, 7.5 per cent in Italy, 5.5 per cent in Portugal and 2.9 per cent in Greece (CIRIEC 2006: 46). As already pointed out in Chapter 1, in their discussion of the scale of non-profit organizations (NPOs), which do not distribute profits, L.M. Salamon and other researchers at Johns Hopkins University point out that NPOs in the UK and Continental Western European countries are relatively large in size, but those in Northern and Southern Europe tend to be small. However, compared in terms of the share of total employment occupied by the social economy, including cooperatives and mutual aid organizations, the ratios in the UK and the Continental Western European countries were not significantly higher than in the Northern and Southern European countries (except for Greece).

In the table describing the social economy by country, the enterprises in the social economy are broken down into the three categories of cooperatives, mutual societies (companies) and associations or foundations, indicating the number of (full-time equivalent) jobs provided, the number of enterprises in each category and so on. Since the survey dates vary widely, accurate comparisons cannot be made, but countries where cooperatives accounted for more than a half of the jobs provided by the social economy were Italy, Finland, Sweden and Spain. By contrast, in countries such as France, Denmark, Germany, the Netherlands and the UK, associations and foundations accounted for a majority of the jobs provided in the social economy. In the case of Italy, the social economy provided a total of 1,336,000 jobs, of which 837,000 were in cooperatives, and 499,000 in associations and foundations. The employment shares of worker cooperatives and social cooperatives in the total number of jobs provided by cooperatives were 364,000 and 190,000, respectively (CIRIEC 2006: 48–66).

What exactly are social cooperatives? As Natsuko Tanaka recounts in her work (Tanaka 2004b: Chapter 3), the 1991 Law on Social Cooperative Societies states in Article 1 that the purpose of social cooperative societies is to 'pursue the general interest of the community for human advancement and social integration of citizens'. Ordinary cooperatives established in accordance with the Civil Code are recognized as entities that 'operate for the collective interest of their members', and are prohibited from supplying services to non-members. By contrast, the purpose of social cooperatives is to pursue the 'public interest' defined as the 'general interests of the community'. As regards surplus earnings, the Civil Code's provisions on mutual societies apply. Social cooperatives are therefore not obliged to remain 'non-profit' in the sense of 'not distributing surpluses'. Article 2, which concerns volunteer members who work without payment, prescribes that such workers must comprise less than 50 per cent of the workers, and that their work should be complementary to that of paid professional workers, but not 'substitute' for the work of professionals. In other words, social cooperatives are not allowed to use unpaid, non-professional volunteer workers for the purpose of providing services at reduced costs. In addition, 'public or private corporate bodies ... may be admitted as members of social cooperative societies' (Article 11).

Article 1 also defines two types of social cooperatives. Type A cooperatives manage and provide services in sectors such as social welfare, health care, education. Type B cooperatives engage in agricultural, manufacturing, commercial, service and other activities with the objective of integrating 'socially disadvantaged people' into the labour market. Article 4 provides that in Type B social cooperatives, at least 30 per cent of the workers must be socially disadvantaged people, namely, people with physical, mental and sensory disabilities, former patients of psychiatric hospitals, people undergoing psychiatric treatments, drug addicts, alcoholics, prisoners and former prisoners, and juvenile delinquents. According to Article 5, public bodies may be exempted from the application of regulations concerning public works contracts and can contract with cooperatives, if such contracts are made with the objective of creating job opportunities for disadvantaged people. In other words, in such cases public bodies are allowed to conclude contracts with these cooperatives at their own discretion, instead of granting contracts to the lowest bidders. Furthermore, social cooperatives are exempt from paying mandatory contributions for social security programmes in the case of employment of a socially disadvantaged person (Borzaga 2004: 55). Since taxes and contributions to social insurance programmes account for 45 per cent of the labour expenses of Italian corporations (Table 4.1 of this volume), this indeed amounts to very favourable treatment.

The Italian National Statistical Institute (ISTAT) conducted a fact-finding survey of social cooperatives and their federations towards the end of 2001, and announced its findings in 2003. The survey found that the number of social cooperatives increased rapidly following the enactment of the 1991 Law. Of the 5,515 cooperatives that existed across the country at the time of the survey, 61.7 per cent were established in 1992 and after, and 35.4 per cent in the period between 1997 and 2001. The combined membership was 211,800, made up of 208,000 individual members (natural persons) and 4,214 corporate members including municipalities. This means that 36 persons per 10,000 Italians were members of social cooperatives in 2001. The average number of members per cooperative was 45 for Type A cooperatives, and 31 for Type B cooperatives, but the majority of cooperatives were small in size, those with less than 20 members accounting for more than 50 per cent of Type A cooperatives (ISTAT 2004).

There are four categories of individual members: members working as paid employees; service users (i.e. users of the services and their families); volunteer members (unpaid but covered by workers' accident compensation insurance); and supporting members who give financial support to the cooperatives without being directly involved in service provision. Cooperatives having members in two or more categories account for 82.3 per cent of the total. In the case of Type

B cooperatives the percentage was as high as 95.4 per cent; cooperatives having members in all four categories accounted for up to 22.3 per cent of the total, and in the case of Type B cooperatives the percentage stood at 38.8 per cent. Clearly, the multi-stakeholder approach predominates in their governance (ISTAT 2004).

A total of 201,422 persons were engaged in paid and unpaid activities, and of these paid working members numbered 147,000, non-member employees 26,000, voluntary workers 24,000, and conscientious objectors and members of religious organizations 4,000. Broken down by gender, women accounted for 74.4 per cent of the paid working members, 70.3 per cent of the non-member employees and 51.7 per cent of the volunteer workers (ISTAT 2004). The fact that the ratio of women among the paid workers is considerably higher than that of volunteer workers is significantly different from the situation in cooperatives, such as consumer cooperatives, in Japan.

The percentage breakdown of Type A cooperatives by services provided in 2001 (multiple answers allowed) was as follows: support for social education (provided by 44.8 per cent of the cooperatives); housing support (36.3 per cent); recreation, diversion and vitality enhancement (34.3 per cent); and socialization with like-minded people and social participation (19.7 per cent). The services were used by more than two million people, who were comprised of young people (37.2 per cent); persons experiencing *disagio* (living difficulties) (14.6 per cent); 'ordinary users' (14.0 per cent); non-independent elderly persons (8.9 per cent); and independent elderly persons (7.6 per cent). Persons experiencing *disagio* include a wide spectrum of people such as unemployed persons, victims of violence, the poor, lone mothers and families of these people (ISTAT 2004).

Type B cooperatives had a total of 37,000 paid workers, of whom 'socially disadvantaged people' numbered 18,700, or 50.5 per cent, this ratio being well above the legally prescribed minimum of 30 per cent. The breakdown of the disadvantaged people was: people with disabilities (50.3 per cent); drug addicts (18.2 per cent); patients undergoing psychiatric treatment (14.5 per cent); and prisoners and former prisoners (7.4 per cent).

Lega, CGM and Type B cooperative Pulisoft

In September 2005 I visited the headquarters of the Lombardia Regional Federation of Lega, a national association of left-leaning cooperatives, in Milan. Lega, having approximately 1,400 social cooperatives under its umbrella, ranks with Consorzio Gino Mattarelli (CGM), the national association of Catholic-affiliated social cooperatives (note that approximately half the social cooperatives are not affiliated with any national associations). Lega is basically an organization engaged in lobbying activities mainly on behalf of consumer cooperatives, housing cooperatives and production workers' cooperatives. Varelio Di Iorio, whom I interviewed, had been in charge of the production workers' section of the Lombardian Regional Federation of Lega for 30 years. His keyword was 'efficiency'.

For approximately five years following the establishment of the 1991 law, the social cooperatives affiliated with Lega had taken on contracts from municipalities to carry out child care, nursing care, visiting care and similar services, but since the contracts were available only on a yearly basis, the cooperatives were not able to make sufficient investments in facilities. Large sums of investment money are necessary to build day centres for children, youths and the elderly, and caring houses for the elderly. Constituting part of the cooperative scene in Italy are also cooperative banks and Unipol, a mutual association. Taken together, cooperatives have the fourth largest share in the financial sector of the country. Just as cooperatives have become leading enterprises in the retail and construction industries, it is possible for social cooperatives to become leading enterprises in the field of welfare services. With regard to the size of social cooperatives, Varelio Di Iorio is of the opinion that the larger the size the more democratic it will be, and the greater will be its investment and personnel recruitment opportunities. He was critical of the generally small size of enterprises in Italy, which he believed was responsible for their inefficiency. Traditional welfare services in Italy were dictated by *assistantialismo*, a salvationist attitude, and were 'like pockets with huge holes in them', but Type B social cooperatives would be able to work for the inclusion of disadvantaged people into society by integrating them into the labour market.

Consorzio Gino Mattarelli is the national federation of Catholic-affiliated social cooperatives. Established in 1987, CGM was named after Gino Mattarelli, member of the Chamber of Deputies (Lower House), who played a leading role in the enactment of the Law on Social Cooperatives. I visited the headquarters of CGM in the City of Brescia, a suburb of Milan, in September 2005, and interviewed its president, Johnny Dotti. According to Dotti, CGM as a business entity, employing 30,000 paid workers and aided by the cooperation of 5,000 volunteers, is already larger than Alitalia, and is closing in on Fiat. He affirmed that this is large enough to enable CGM to work for social development and reform.

Dotti adds, however, that having experienced this remarkable quantitative growth, CGM is now faced with the need to transform itself qualitatively. He repeats time and again that 'qualitative improvement' is an urgent necessity, and that the key to accomplishing this task was to 'enter deeply into a limited area, and become firmly entrenched there'. The idea of a limited geographical area means that for an area with a population of 50,000 to 100,000, one business consortium would be established under which would be organized 15 or so social cooperatives and enterprises. These would pursue their specialized activities while working together to develop relationships and build confidence with the local residents.

Social cooperatives need to 'become firmly rooted in the local area' because, explains Dotti, the economy having developed to its present state, people's needs for welfare services and the needs of unemployed people are not uniform. The needs of individuals, who may for example be adults disabled from birth or elderly people suffering from dementia, are highly diverse. Moreover, there is now more diversity among the unemployed, since it is not unusual now for managerial workers in their forties to be fired, which means that it is no longer possible to implement a standardized method for reintegration into the labour market. In other words, the needs of these people can no longer be met by a narrow range of ready-made solutions, and different solutions must be devised for different clients. To do this, not only municipal offices and professionals, but also families, communities and volunteers need to finely interact in multilayered, overlapping networks. In order for social cooperatives to maintain autonomy from municipalities, energize volunteer workers, lure investments and help socially disadvantaged people find jobs, it is essential that they are rooted in specific communities. Another feature of CGM is that it limits the president's tenure of office to a maximum of two terms of three years each, and that the great majority of its officials are unpaid to prevent their work from turning into professional careers.

With an introduction from CGM, I also visited the Type B social cooperative Pulisoft in the City of Cremona, in the southern part of the Lombardia region, and interviewed Vice-President Federica. Established in 1992, the mission of the cooperative is to integrate persons with mental disorders into the labour market. Specifically, it performs the cleaning of public schools, parks, sport facilities and ordinary houses on a contractual basis.

Pulisoft had 40 members at its inception. Its present workforce of paid workers consists of eight persons with mental disorders and five mentally healthy persons. Cleaning work contracted out by the city authority is awarded for one year based on competitive bidding. Provided the work is priced below a certain level, the city may award contracts on a discretionary basis, but the City of Cremona does not give preferential treatment to social cooperatives. If the contractor fails to make a successful bid the following year, the successful bidder is obliged to guarantee jobs for half the employees of the former contractor. Since, however, it is not appropriate to leave disabled workers in the care of another enterprise, the cooperative is performing cleaning work for ordinary homes and offices in addition to undertaking contract work for the city.

Persons with mental disabilities are first introduced to Pulisoft by social assistants, certified clinical psychologists, psychiatrists and so on. Pulisoft staff members interview the persons concerned, noting down their personal history, and determining whether they are capable of make a living on their own. Federica then interviews each person, informing them of the conditions of affiliation with the social cooperative, and assessing each person's communicative competence and work ability. Based on monthly interviews, assessments of each person's ability to take care of himself or herself, sociability, work ability, communicative ability, ability to manage money and so on are recorded in individual files. Interviews with specialist doctors are also held each month. Newly employed disabled persons are treated as 'trainees' who receive 'incentive salaries' from the city for two years, but for the first two months after they start working, it is necessary for them to be accompanied by workers with no disability. Moreover, the cooperative routinely includes at least two mentally healthy workers in each work team.

The productivity and efficiency of cooperative living

Should these efforts to attain the social inclusion of 'socially disadvantaged people' through pecuniary and non-pecuniary means be regarded as 'protection'? The answer is no. Gøsta Esping-Andersen points out that in the post-industrial knowledge economy, substantial equality of opportunity is an essential condition for ensuring 'efficiency', realization of gender equality in particular being a lynchpin in this (Esping-Andersen 2002: 3, 10; Esping-Andersen 2009). This insight constitutes an integral part of the strategy of the European Union, which, unlike the US, strives to survive harsh global competition by establishing a capitalism that incorporates the principles of social inclusion and cohesiveness, and thus seeks to become a main actor in building a better world order (Walby 2002).

Pulisoft's Federica points out that although for-profit enterprises sometimes perform work sloppily in trying to finish tasks in as little time as possible, social cooperatives are additionally generating social profits. Borzaga argues, as Natsuko Tanaka relates, that only accurately assessing the 'productivity' of people with disabilities, and providing an environment in which it can easily be brought to bear, will lead to a normal functioning of the labour market. In other words, Borzaga contends that for-profit enterprises, through their simplistic worker selection practices based on gender, educational background and the presence or absence of disability (i.e. 'statistical discrimination'), and by economizing on investments in education and training for developing human resources, are causing the labour market to fail (Tanaka 2004b: 248–9).

Another form of livelihood cooperation is the 'Time Dollars' system (or the 'Time Bank' system in the UK), a time-based currency system that allows people to deposit the hours they have spent on providing welfare or social services. Pivotal for the system are the notions of the 'core economy' and 'co-production'. According to the descriptions on the TimeBanks USA website, the core economy is an 'invisible economy' that exists in the family, neighbourhood and community. Unlike the monetary economy of corporations and governments, in which exchanges are governed by the principles of contract, specialization and agreement, the working of the core economy is governed by the principles of sharing, loyalty, love and pitching in. Exchanges built on a sense of mutuality and reciprocity, not on contractual obligations, are the source of vitality of the core economy.[11] The term 'core economy' reflects the belief that this should be the core feature of an economy tailored to human beings.

The term 'core economy' was originally coined by environmental economist Neva Goodwin. Edgar Cahn, Professor Emeritus of Yale University Law School and the inventor of the Time Dollar system, adopted it from her. According to Goodwin, feminist discussions about caring labour and the non-monetized economies of the household and community have formed the basis of the notion of the core economy. The Marxist emphasis on 'social reproduction' is also said to have proved useful in conceptualizing the core economy (Goodwin and Harris 2001: 6). The concept of 'co-production', on the other hand, emphasizes the idea that welfare services and social services work most effectively when they are jointly produced by professionals and beneficiaries, that is to say, when the beneficiaries themselves make the most of their own talents, abilities and energy.[12]

Focusing attention on a 'new public commons'

The Japanese government has not been entirely unconcerned about the notion and practice of 'livelihood cooperation' characterized by voluntary cooperation among citizens at the meso-level of society. For example, the *White Paper on the National Lifestyle* for FY2004, which carried the subtitle 'Connections between Individuals to Improve Life and Local Communities: The Path to a New "Public Commons"', asserts that it is possible for voluntary 'community activities' by individuals to satisfy the 'livelihood needs that both individuals and "government bodies" are finding increasingly difficult to deal with', and it supports this assertion by giving a large number of examples taken from across the country. The *White Paper* also makes a brief reference to the activities of social cooperatives in Italy in a subsection titled 'Community-based Activities are of Great Significance both Socially and Economically' (Naikakufu 2004).

The problem is that the examples offered are mostly limited to so-called 'specified non-profit corporations' under the jurisdiction of the Cabinet Office. As pointed out repeatedly throughout this book, concrete examples of 'livelihood cooperation' should include within their scope the 'social economy', which encompasses the economic activities of foundations, cooperatives, mutual aid societies, as well as associations, social partners (trade unions and representative organizations of employers), non-governmental organizations (NGOs) and corporate social responsibility (CSR). Interestingly, in his policy speech of 26 October 2009, at the first Diet session after the September 2009 change of government, Prime Minister Yukio Hatoyama brought up the 'concept of a "new public commons" [*atarashii kōkyō* 新しい公共], in which people support each other and are of service to each other'. This led to the establishment within the Cabinet Office of a 'New Public Commons Roundtable' (*Atarashii kōkyō entaku kaigi* 新しい公共円卓会議) chaired by Professor Ikuyō Kaneko of Keio University, which held its first meeting on 27 January 2010. Although the list of members of the Roundtable includes executive officers of large and small corporations, it includes no representatives of trade unions, cooperatives or mutual aid societies. The Roundtable proposes to carry out case studies on cutting-edge approaches taken by NPOs, social enterprises, community businesses and CSR projects carried out in cooperation with NPOs (Material 3 for the First Meeting: 'Proposed Procedure for Conducting Meetings of the Roundtable on the "New Public Commons"').[13] None of the activities of cooperatives seem to have caught the attention of the Roundtable as being worthy of inclusion in its case studies.

Needless to say, not all consumer cooperatives, which comprise a dominant proportion of cooperatives, are part of the social economy. As noted in Chapter 4, consumer cooperatives in Finland and Sweden, for example, are a big presence in the retail industry, and it has been argued that these large-scale purchasing cooperatives are not very deeply committed to upholding social solidarity and cooperation, and are thus not much different from large-scale chain stores (Kawaguchi 2006: 265). These cooperatives, though having the legal status of consumer cooperatives, may be regarded as actors in the ordinary market economy, not the social economy.

By contrast, consumer cooperatives in Japan have long put into practice the principle of cooperation, with several members living close to each other forming a *han* 班 (group) as the basic unit, which then divides up the goods received in bulk among its member, and serves as a channel for feeding back information or complaints on defective or missing goods (even though the practice of delivering goods directly to member's doorsteps has been on the increase lately). Members are not simply the end points of the distribution channel, but have also been participating in the decision-making process, through mutually elected representatives, from the *han* meetings at the most basic decision-making level up to the representative general assembly (*sōdaikai* 総代会) at the highest level. On account of this member participation, consumer cooperatives in Japan have long played a pioneering role in consumer movements calling for reduced pesticide applications on food crops, additive-free foods and working for waste reduction, and their activities have had a significant influence on large chain stores. Consumer cooperatives in Japan have also been involved in social movements, in particular, the peace movement (Kurimoto 2004: 51). These features should prove valuable and positive assets as consumer cooperatives come to provide a foundation for livelihood cooperation.[14] The fact that not a few consumer cooperatives in Japan have established offshoot workers' cooperatives or workers' collectives carries significant implications for Japanese-style consumer cooperatives in the 21st century (Kasuya 2006: 190–4).

Social inclusion as key to market viability

The market as a bundle of institutions

The foregoing notions of the social economy have come to be reflected even in economic analyses that emphasize growth in monetary terms. The failure of the Russian 'transition' (price liberalization and privatization) following the collapse of the Soviet Union, the poor performance of market-oriented reforms in Latin America and the turmoil in Asian currency markets in 1997 have lent persuasiveness to economic growth theories emphasizing social factors and institutions (Ishii 2003). According to development economist Dani Rodrik, for example, the functions of the market mechanism require the support of non-market institutions, of which the following five are especially worthy of attention (Rodrik 2000): (1) private property rights, which are necessary for securing returns on investment; (2) market regulatory institutions, such as regulations concerning fair trade, the deposit insurance system, regulations concerning securities trading and environmental regulations; (3) institutions for macro-economic stabilization, such as the central bank system and the public finance system; (4) institutions for social insurance in a broad sense (including corporate practices such as lifelong employment, regulated sectors and relaxation of the pace of external liberalization); and (5) institutions for arbitrating social divisions and managing conflicts, including the rule of law, the representational party system, free elections, independent unions, social partners, institutionalization of the representation of minority groups, the social insurance system and so on.

In other words, it is ultimately social inclusion by social security and social insurance in the broader senses of these terms that sustains the market mechanism. Naoko Ishii, who has served in important posts at the Japanese Ministry of Finance, the International Monetary Fund and the World Bank, and is strongly critical of the neoclassical growth theory, has presented a penetrating analysis of the institutional arrangements that sustain the mechanism of long-term economic development. Ishii speaks of social institutions belonging into the fifth group enumerated by Rodrik as institutions for building 'social cohesion'. 'Social cohesion' as a concept was introduced by Jo Ritzen *et al.* in an effort to overcome limitations inherent in the concept of 'social capital'. It is meant to refer to a 'state of affairs in which a group of people ... demonstrate an aptitude for collaboration that produces a climate for change'. The degree of 'social cohesion' in this sense can be assessed by a number of measures, such as: (a) membership rates of organizations and participation in organization; (b) 'trust'; (c) degree of equality of income distribution (Gini coefficient and the share of income taken up by the middle class 60 per cent of the population); and (d) degree of ethnic heterogeneity ('ethnolinguistic fractionalization'; however, divisions due to gender, education, class, and disability also require attention) (Ishii 2003: 82; Ritzen, Easterly and Woolcock 2000).

Government regulations are not the only matters required for the development of market economies. No less important is 'cooperation' among people, who participate in various organizations, are linked by mutual trust, and enjoy a more or less equitable distribution of income. Ishii raises gender-based disparities in education and health care as one of the 'cleavages' that impair social cohesion (Ishii 2003: 84). Put another way, it is social inclusion that underpins economic growth.

Masaru Kaneko has questioned the dichotomy of market and institutions. As already noted in Chapter 2, he traces the emergence of social institutions, regulations and rules, to the existence of limits on the commoditization of the primary factors of production, that is, labour, capital and land (Kaneko 1987). Subsequently he went on to propose a very thought-provoking argument in *Gyaku shisutemu gaku* (Reverse Systematology), a collaborative work with a life scientist shortly after the human genome was deciphered in 2000 (Kaneko and Kodama 2004). Institutions and rules with regard to post-World War II 'advanced industrialized countries' here refers to central bank functions and the deposit insurance system in the financial markets; the social institutionalization of skills and the various institutions of the welfare state in the labour market; and protection of farmland and land lease rights, land and housing policies, and city planning and environmental policies in the land market – in other words: 'social safety nets'. 'Social institutionalization of skills and various institutions of the welfare state' includes official recognition of labour unions and the system of industrial relations, as well as regulation of labour standards, official vocational education and training programmes, formal qualifications, job placement services and the social security system.

In short, what Kaneko calls institutions and rules coincides with what Rodrik calls institutions. Kaneko's scholarship shows itself at its best when he, instead of opposing the market to institutions, persuasively argues that a market economy consists of a bundle of institutions whose foundation is the safety nets. To put this in the terminology of this book, what is bundling are forms of social inclusion.

Approximately 40 per cent of the economic growth in the US during the period of the Bush administration was owed to growth in the housing sector (Kaneko and Dewitt 2008: 9). As the housing demand by the middle and upper classes became saturated and the housing bubble began to show cracks, subprime lending spread. Needless to add, subprime loans are made out to high-risk borrowers with imperfect credit histories. Incentives such as low initial mortgage payments – as in the case of 'balloon mortgages' that give borrowers a low interest rate for a certain period of time after which the repayment amount drastically increases, or of 'interest-only mortgages' that initially require the payment of interest only – were offered. Taking advantage of these attractive features, real estate brokers lent heavily to their clients. Subprime mortgages accounted for only 5 per cent of all mortgages in 1994, but by 2006 their share reached approximately 20 per cent. Non-whites and women constitute a disproportionally large proportion of the borrowers of subprime loans. If housing prices continue to rise, the surety value of the mortgaged house would also rise, and borrowers would be able to refinance by taking out new subprime loans before their repayments shot up. In reality, however, as house prices stopped rising or even weakened, the practice of paying loans by taking out new loans became untenable. Subprime loans turned out to be 'predatory lending' (Fukumitsu 2005; Fishbein and Woodall 2006; Toyofuku 2009).

However, it is necessary to also keep in mind that 'overconsumption' in the US consists for a very considerable part of medical expenses (including contributions to employee health insurance premiums by corporations). The NLI Research Institute's 2006 report reveals that, according to the statistics on National Income and Product Accounts (NIPA) for 2004, medical expenditures took up the largest portion (20.4 per cent) of consumption expenditures, followed by rent and expenses for food, which accounted for 14.9 per cent each (Doihara 2006). The livelihood security system of the US is unique in that it lacks universal health care coverage. This not only results in a large population of uninsured people and rising medical costs, but also became a factor in triggering the global economic crisis. This is the context in which President Barack Obama's health insurance reforms must be understood.

As mentioned in Chapter 2, Japan for years had the largest current account surplus in the world up until 2004, when it was surpassed by the oil-producing countries of the Middle East due to a steep rise in the oil price. Since 2006, the world's largest current account surplus is China's, but Japan's surplus has continued to grow during this time (Naikakufu, Seisaku tōkatsukan shitsu 2008b). But, as also discussed in Chapter 2, Japan's economic recovery since 2002 was a 'jobless/joyless' one in the sense that, even though real-term corporate earnings increased more than during the bubble period in the latter half of the 1980s, employment showed little growth and employees' real incomes remained stagnant.

As to investment and savings on the macro-level, Japan is exceptional among the advanced industrialized countries in having oversavings. In the course of the latest economic recovery, the savings rate slightly increased while the investment rate remained unchanged, leading to an even greater savings surplus. In China, on the other hand, both the saving rate and the investment rate have increased significantly during the 2000s, with the saving rate remaining above the investment rate. It has been argued that given the deficient state of its social security system, households in China are so eager to save money in defence against rainy days that they are pushing the economy into a state of underconsumption (Naikakufu, Seisaku tōkatsukan shitsu 2008a).

The 2008 report of the National Institute for Research and Advancement (NIRA) has clearly shown that as wage incomes have remained stagnant, disparities in income and outstanding savings have expanded at the household level, and the saving ability of low-income earners and elderly households has declined. 'Excess savings' are only maintained in the two highest income quintiles. The report speculates that these relatively well-to-do people, driven by their anxiety about the future and distrust of the public pension system, built up excess savings by suppressing consumption expenditures over and above the decrease in their disposable incomes (NIRA 2008). The government's *Annual Report on the Japanese Economy and Public Finance* for FY2009 compares the relationship between people's confidence in the future of the public pension system and the saving rate for Japan and 11 European countries. The data used for the comparison are, in the case of Europe, drawn from the findings of *Special Eurobarometer 273*, a study on people's confidence in the future of pension systems conducted by the European Commission in 2006, and in the case of Japan from the findings of the *Special Public Opinion Survey on the Social Security System* conducted by the Cabinet Office in 2008. The *Annual Report*'s comparative study found that in countries where people's confidence in the future of the pension system was low (Germany, France and Japan), the average household saving rate tended to be high, but in countries where people's confidence is high (Denmark and Finland), the average household saving rate was negative (Naikakufu 2009: Figure 3.3–17).

The growing monetary surplus in countries with trade surpluses has boosted the demand for AAA-rated financial assets in the US particularly from private institutional investors seeking high returns from their investments, with the effect of swelling demand for securitized financial instruments, including subprime loans (Ikeo 2009). Since widening income disparities and inadequate social security systems, or strong anxiety about their future, have caused underconsumption and oversavings in China and Japan, the way the livelihood security systems of these two countries are configured can be said to have been one factor in triggering the global economic crisis. Thus, building a fairer livelihood security system that will make the disadvantaged feel more at ease, is indispensable not only for making Japanese society sustainable, but also for bringing stability to the global economy. Furthermore, it should not be overlooked that a majority of the disadvantaged anywhere are women.

Notes

1 From welfare regimes to livelihood security systems

1 Tarō Miyamoto defines 'welfare politics' as 'politics concerned with livelihood security'. Indentifying social security (social insurance, welfare/public assistance and social services) and employment policy (policies aimed at the creation and enlargement of employment opportunities) as the two pillars of livelihood security, he remarks that the defining feature of livelihood security in its present form in Japan is that 'attention has been focused on employment but not on social security' (Miyamoto 2008: 2–3).
2 Japan's de-commodification score of 27.1, recorded by Esping-Andersen in his Table 2.2, is different from the simple sum of 22.3 of the three scores (pensions, sickness, and unemployment) listed by him in his Table 2.1.
3 Miura proposes six indices that measure the degree and scope of social protection for workers against volatile market forces: (1) protection of permanent workers against dismissal; (2) regulation on atypical workers; (3) safety net toward the unemployed; (4) active labour market policies; (5) minimum wages; and (6) coverage of collective bargaining, while identifying the following six criteria to indicate employment performance: (1) unemployment rates (both standardized and long-term); (2) youth unemployment rates; (3) male employment rates (age 55–9); (4) female employment rates (age 25–54); (5) earnings dispersions among male workers; and (6) ratios of part-timers as a percentage of total employment (Miura 2001).
4 Salamon *et al* incidentally refer to their own approach as 'social origins' theory of the non-profit sector. The social origins indicated to differentiate their models are particular constellations of social forces at the time of the formation of the modern nation-state. These social forces include political elites since the establishment of monarchic absolutism, traditional landed elites as well as religious organizations and guilds, in addition to small landholders, the rising urban middle classes and working class movements (Salamon and Anheier 1998; Salamon, Sokolowski and Anheier 2000: 15–17). Needless to add, Esping-Andersen emphasized the mobilization of power resources through an alliance between the organized working class and its political representatives (the social-democratic parties) on the one hand, and the agricultural stratum on the other. Salamon *et al* look back even further into history. These debates resemble the 'Controversy on Japanese Capitalism' conducted in pre-war Japan, and the analyses of 'the transition from feudalism to capitalism' conducted by the Ōtsuka school in post-war economic historiography.
5 Evers and Laville do not specify the point in time on which their distinction of three types is based. But since the referenced literature is mainly from the early 1990s, it seems safe to assume that they are referring to the situation prevailing in the 1980s.

186 *Notes*

2 The livelihood security systems approach

1 In the diction of the World Bank, '(social) safety net' refers mainly to relief programs targeting those below the poverty line. Jinno and Kaneko, however, use this concept in a broader sense (Jinno and Kaneko 1999).
2 http://europa.eu/legislation_summaries/employment_and_social_policy/social_protection/c10119_en.htm
3 The indicators are, among others, the at-risk-of-poverty rate (share of persons with an equivalised disposable income below the at-risk-of-poverty line set at 60 per cent of the national equivalised median income), the poverty risk gap, income inequality (S80/S20, which is the ratio of total income received by the top quintile to that received by the lowest quintile), the long-term unemployment rate and the percentage of NEETS. In 2006, the in-work at-risk-of-poverty rate and low reading literacy performance at 15 years of age were added. In 2008, a further list of indicators regarding unmet needs for medical care and relating to nursing care was agreed upon.
4 http://www1.mhlw.go.jp/shingi/s0007/s0731-1_16.html
5 http://www.mhlw.go.jp/topics/bukyoku/syakai/c-fukushi/index.html
6 http://www.sia.go.jp/e/ehi.html
7 http://www.sia.go.jp/e_old/np.html
8 http://stats.oecd.org/Index.aspx?datasetcode=SOCX_AGG
9 Korpi ranked countries according to levels of general family support and dual-earner support for 1985–90, and grouped Japan as 'market-oriented' in its gender policy model.

3 The 1990s – Japan's lost decade

1 Esping-Andersen does not use the term 'male breadwinner model' himself, describing this type as 'conservative' or 'familialistic' instead. He prefers the term 'familialism' to 'male breadwinner' since his intent is to examine the degree to which families absorb social risks rather than to focus on gender relations. At the same time, he appreciates the analytical attraction of the latter approach as making the link to welfare state attributes easier to trace (Esping-Andersen 1999: 50–1).
2 In the 1996 volume edited by Esping-Andersen, the concept of 'social exclusion/inclusion' is not used.
3 http://www.gender.go.jp/toshin-e/part1.html
4 Ibid.
5 It should be noted that this was a quite pioneering recognition of the issue of 'net total social expenditure' (public and private social expenditure after social security contributions on cash transfers and direct as well as indirect taxes), which did not begin to be considered by the OECD until the mid-1990s (Adema *et al.* 1996).
6 For persons directly insured by Employees' Health Insurance schemes, user payment, which originally used to be zero, had been set at 10 per cent of the entire cost after co-payment since 1984. Those who were covered as dependent family members of the insured had to pay 30 per cent.
7 Although conducted somewhat later, a 2004 survey by the Japan Institute of Labour Policy and Training showed that 55.8 per cent of companies introduced a system in which wages would reflect work performance (*Survey on Employee Motivation Toward Work and Human Resource Management* for white-collar employees at firms employing 100+ workers). In addition, the Economic and Social Research Institute of the Cabinet Office's 2004 *Annual Survey of Corporate Behaviour* addressed to listed companies in the First and Second Sections of the Tokyo, Osaka and Nagoya stock exchanges, reported that as of January 2005, 79.8 per cent of companies had adopted performance-based employment practices for managerial employees; 76.6 per cent for general business employees; 75.0 per cent for specialist and technical employees; 73.2 per cent for sales

employees; 71.0 per cent for administrative employees; and 64.5 per cent for production workers. (http://www.esri.cao.go.jp/jp/stat/h16ank/main.html)
8 Yūji Genda calculated a breakdown of the net increase in employment by age bracket for full-time and part-time work, and found a net decline in full-time employment opportunities of 16.03 per cent for those in the 20–4 age bracket, with growth only in part-time opportunities. Unfortunately, he did not provide a breakdown by gender (Genda 2001: 191–2; Genda 2004).
9 According to the Detailed Tabulation of the Labour Force Survey, during the five-year period from 2002 to 2007 there was in fact a decrease of 480,000 regular employees, against a 1.04 million increase in part-time employees, and a 2.8 million increase in non-regular employees overall.
10 The *General Survey on Working Conditions* covers all ordinary workers in establishing labour costs throughout the companies surveyed. Ordinary workers are defined as those who meet one the following criteria: (1) workers who are hired for an indefinite period; (2) workers who are hired for longer than one month; and (3) workers who are hired for less than one month or by the day, if hired for 18 days or more in each of the two preceding months (November and December).

4 Japan in international comparison at the turn of the century

1 http://www.soumu.go.jp/gyoukan/kanri/pdf/satei_02_05.pdf
2 Naikakufu keizai seisaku sōgō kenkyūsho 2006: kenkyūkai hōkokusho (Study Group Reports): 21. (http://www.esri.go.jp/jp/archive/hou/hou030/hou021.html)
3 http://www.mof.go.jp/jouhou/soken/kenkyu/zk059/zk059dl.htm
4 http://www.stat.go.jp/english/data/shakai/2006/pdf/kaisetua.pdf
5 http://jccu.coop/info/announcement/2006/05/2005612.html.
6 http://www.eesc.europa.eu/?i=portal.en.social-economy-category-documents.3167
7 http://www.ica.coop/gender/statistics.html
8 http://www.ilo.org/public/english/protection/secsoc/downloads/stat/ses/docs/summary.pdf
9 www.oecd.org/employment/protection
10 The OECD's measure of the overall strictness of protection of regular workers is based on quantifications of: (1) 'procedural inconveniences' an employer must go through to terminate employment 'for cause' such as notification procedures and the issuing of pre-termination warnings; (2) procedures for 'no-fault' terminations such as minimum prior notification periods and severance pay; and (3) 'difficulty of dismissal', which refers to legislative provisions setting conditions under which a dismissal is seen as 'justified' or 'fair'. Strictness of employment protection legislation for temporary and fixed-term contract workers is calculated based on legal restrictions on the types of work eligible for the use of fixed-term workers, upper limits on the number or cumulative duration of fixed-term contracts, and limits on the use of temporary placement agencies (Venn 2009: 42).
11 Data from the US exclude agricultural workers. Japan's data include regular workers (full-time and part-time) in firms with five or more employees. France's data exclude construction workers.
12 In Japan, as in the US, social security contributions are not assessed on income above a certain level. As a result, high-income earners contribute at a lower rate than those earning less.
13 In Japan, the burden rate for dual-income earners in households with lower than average incomes (one-third of average income) and exactly average income is slightly higher. For higher-income households (those earning 1.33 to 1.67 times the average income), the burden rate is slightly higher for single-earner couples.
14 The fact that the public pension rate for single men is higher in Japan than in Germany is not surprising given that the OECD's estimate of the average gross pension rate (before

taxes and social security contributions) for all men in Japan, 50.3 per cent, is higher than its 45.8 per cent estimate for all men in Germany (OECD 2005c: 49).
15 This rate was estimated by the Pension Bureau, which assumed that Sweden's 1999 pension reforms would be fully implemented.
16 Of the 12 nations discussed here, all but Germany and Japan had introduced a comprehensive system prior to 1990. Germany's system was first implemented in 1995. Generally speaking, the other ten nations' long-term care insurance programmes were developed incrementally, but relatively large-scale changes were implemented in Australia in 1997, the Netherlands in 1989, Spain in 1995, Sweden in 1992 and the UK in 1993 (OECD 2005e).
17 http://www.mhlw.go.jp/topics/kaigo/osirase/jigyo/05/dl/02.pdf
18 http://www.mhlw.go.jp/topics/kaigo/osirase/jigyo/05/dl/02.pdf
19 http://www.mhlw.go.jp/topics/kaigo/osirase/jigyo/05/dl/02.pdf
20 http://www.mhlw.go.jp/toukei/saikin/hw/kaigo/service05/kekka3.html
21 Child care services data for Japan is from 1998. US data is from 1995 and Norway data from 1997. Data from all other nations is from 1998–2000. Maternity leave and child care leave data for all nations is from 1999–2001. Flexi-time data for the US is from 1997 and from 1995–6 for all other nations. The data is concerned with formal child care arrangements, including: group-care in child care centres (nurseries, kindergarten, playschools), residential care including specialist services such as care for disabled children, child minders based in their own home and carers who are not a family member but frequently live in with the family (OECD 2001: 143, Tables 4.7 and 4.8).
22 http://stats.oecd.org/Index.aspx?datasetcode=SOCX_AGG
23 http://www.ipss.go.jp/s-info/j/seiho/seiho.asp

5 Taking stock of the Koizumi reforms

1 http://www.kantei.go.jp/jp/kakugikettei/2001/honebuto/0626keizaizaisei-ho.html
2 http://www5.cao.go.jp/keizai-shimon/explain/pamphlet/2001.pdf
3 In the case marital splitting of EPI pensions at the time of divorce, there is both compulsory splitting and splitting based on consent. Compulsory splitting applies to the period of enrolment as a Class 3 insured person after April 2008, and consensual splitting applies to divorces effective after 1 April 2007. In this case, the entire amount contributed by husband and wife during the time of their marriage can be split into half. (If there is no consensus, the case will be decided in court.)
4 Surviving spouse EPI pension benefits for a surviving spouse under 30 with no children were made to expire after five years. The age of eligibility for the supplemental benefit for widows of middle age and older was raised from over 35 to over 40 at the time of the husband's death.
5 http://www.mhlw.go.jp/topics/kaigo/topics/0603/dl/data.pdf
6 http://www5.cao.go.jp/keizai-shimon/cabinet/2006/decision0707.html
7 http://www.jil.go.jp/kokunai/statistics/databook/2008/04/4–6.xls
8 http://www.mhlw.go.jp/kaiken/daijin/2009/10/k1020.html
9 The material cautions that results vary by statistic used. If the *National Survey of Family Income and Expenditure* is used as opposed to the *Comprehensive Survey of Living Conditions* relied upon by the OECD, Japan's relative poverty rate is 9.5 per cent, placing it just in the middle position among all OECD countries.
10 http://www.gpif.go.jp/kanri/kanri03.html
11 http://www.sia.go.jp/infom/tokei/index.htm
12 http://www.sia.go.jp/infom/tokei/index.htm
13 http://www.kokuho.or.jp/english/kokuho/e_nonpayment/index.htm
14 If one applies at the municipal insurance office, these medical treatment fees minus 30 per cent patient payment will be reimbursed. However, the amount of premium payments in arrears may be deduced.

15 The period for which unemployment benefits under Japanese employment insurance are paid varies by reason for the discontinuation of employment, age and length of insurance enrolment between 90 and 330 days. In the case of bankruptcy or lay-offs the benefit period is longest, in all other ordinary cases of dismissal it extends to up to 150 days. Also, the majority of non-regular employees are employed for a fixed period of time, 'cessation of employment' in their case is not recognized as 'bankruptcy, dismissal, etc.', regardless of whether the employees would have wished to renew their contract or not. In these cases, the hurdle for eligibility to receive benefits is high, and benefit periods are short.
16 In 2005, the following 12 out of 29 OECD countries possessed an unemployment assistance system in addition to unemployment insurance: Australia, Austria, Finland, France, Germany, Greece, Ireland, New Zealand, Portugal, Spain, Sweden and the UK (OECD 2009a: unemployment assistance benefits).
17 http://www.soumu.go.jp/s-news/2006/060915_1.html
18 http://www.soumu.go.jp/hyouka/nenkinmondai.html
19 http://www.soumu.go.jp/hyouka/nenkindaisansha.html
20 http://www.soumu.go.jp/s-news/2007/pdf/071031_3_02.pdf
21 http://www.kantei.go.jp/jp/singi/nenkin/dai7/sankou1.pdf
22 http://www.mhlw.go.jp/topics/2008/12/dl/tp1201-4a.pdf
23 Indirect discrimination refers to norms that do not appear immediately linked to gender, yet disproportionally disadvantage one sex, without need or relation to assigned tasks. The following three practices were prohibited by an ordinance of the Ministry of Health, Labour and Welfare: (1) conditions on height, weight or bodily strength at the time of recruitment; (2) demanding willingness to relocate within Japan in the case of career-track positions at the time of recruitment; and (3) prior relocation as a condition for career advancement.

6 Beyond exclusion – building a cohesive society

1 http://www.news.janjan.jp/election/0709/0709170492/1.php
2 http://www.who.int/mental_health/prevention/suicide/suicideprevent/en/index.html
3 http://www.kantei.go.jp/jp/kakugikettei/2008/1224tyuuki.pdf
4 http://www.kantei.go.jp/jp/singi/syakaihosyoukokuminkaigi/kaisai/dai07/07gijiyousi.pdf: 8, 15
5 http://www.kantei.go.jp/jp/singi/syakaihosyoukokuminkaigi/kaisai/index.html
6 Ōta also found that estimates of the relative poverty rate and the Gini coefficient derived on the basis of the *Employment Status Survey* and the *Housing and Land Survey* are more or less the same as those derived on the basis of the *Comprehensive Survey of Living Conditions* and the *Survey on the Redistribution of Income*.
7 http://www.kantei.go.jp/jp/singi/syakaihosyoukokuminkaigi/kaisai/dai07/07gijiyousi.pdf: 8
8 As already mentioned in Chapter 5, among the high-level organizations of the former government, the Council on Economic and Fiscal Policy published a document entitled *On the Current Situation of Income Inequality* on 22 April 2009, comparing Japan's relative poverty rate with that of other countries. The *Annual Report on the Japanese Economy and Public Finance* for FY2009, published in July the same year, dealt squarely with the relative poverty rate, the Gini coefficient and redistributive effects of the taxation and social security systems – all issues that the OECD had been raising since 2005.
9 With regard to reforms of the health care, long-term care and welfare services, the NCSS emphasized the need to take steps that would enhance these services while at the same time making them more efficient (Shakai hoshō kokumin kaigi 2008a: 12–15; Shakai hoshō kokumin kaigi 2008b: 7–9, 12). With regard to countermeasures for reversing the falling birth rate and measures for supporting the raising of the next generation, the NCSS asserts that these are 'investments in the future' and that 'the necessary funds

need to be injected into them promptly and intensively', but when it comes to the concrete amounts of funding, the NCSS made the rather modest proposal that the current budget of 4.3 trillion yen should be increased by 1.5 to 2.4 trillion yen (Shakai hoshō kokumin kaigi 2008a: 15, 18; Shakai hoshō kokumin kaigi 2008b: 10–11). The NCSS also underlined the need to expand the coverage of the Employees' Pension scheme and the employment insurance scheme to include eligibility for non-regular workers. Also included in the NCSS's proposals were: a raise in the minimum wage rate; more intensive use of the arrangements for insurance premium payment exemption; reinforcement of the minimum security functions of the Basic Pension; and the introduction of a social security number and social security card as a means of preventing the emergence of people not covered by any pension plan (Shakai hoshō kokumin kaigi 2008b).

10 http://www.mhlw.go.jp/shingi/2004/10/s1027-3a.html#3-2
11 http://www.timebanks.org/core-economy.htm
12 http://www.timebanks.org/co-production.htm
13 http://www5.cao.go.jp/entaku/shiryou/22n1kai/pdf/100127_susumekata.pdf
14 For further details on examples of livelihood cooperation in practice in Japan, see Ōsawa (2007).

Bibliography

Japanese government statistics

The National Fertility Survey *Shusshō dōkō kihon chōsa* 出生動向基本調査
Comprehensive Survey of Living Conditions *Kokumin seikatsu kiso chōsa* 国民生活基礎調査
Employment Status Survey *Shūgyō kōzō kihon chōsa* 就業構造基本調査
Family Income and Expenditure Survey *Kakei chōsa* 家計調査
Family Savings Survey (Savings and Liabilities in Family Income and Expenditure Survey since 2002) *Chochiku dōkō chōsa* 貯蓄動向調査
General Survey on Working Conditions *Shūrō jōken sōgō chōsa* 就労条件総合調査
General Survey on Wages and Working Hours Systems *Chingin rōdō jikan seido tō sōgō chōsa* 賃金労働時間制度等総合調査
Housing and Land Survey *Jūtaku/tochi tōkei chōsa* 住宅・土地統計調査
Japanese Panel Survey of Consumers *Shōhi seikatsu ni kansuru paneru chōsa* 消費生活に関するパネル調査
Labour Force Survey *Rōdōryoku chōsa* 労働力調査 (Detailed Tabulation *Shōsai shūkei* 詳細集計)
National Survey of Family Income and Expenditure *Zenkoku shōhi jittai chōsa* 全国消費実態調査
Population Census of Japan *Kokusei chōsa* 国勢調査
Population Projections for Japan *Shōrai suikei jinkō* 将来推計人口
Research into the State of Young People (Cabinet Office 2003) *Jakunensō no ishiki jittai chōsa* 若年層の意識実態調査
Special Public Opinion Survey on the Social Security System (Cabinet Office) *Shakai hoshō seido ni kansuru tokubetsu seron chōsa* 社会保障制度に関する特別世論調査
Summary of the Survey of Institutions and Establishments for Long-term Care *Kaigo sābisu shisetsu – jigyōsho chōsa kekka no gaikyō* 介護サービス施設・事業所調査結果の概況
Survey on the Redistribution of Income *Shotoku saibunpai chōsa* 所得再分配調査
Survey on Time Use and Leisure Activities *Shakai seikatsu kihon chōsa* 社会生活基本調査
Vital Statistics of Japan *Jinkō tōtai tōkei* 人口動態統計

Works in English

Adema, W., Eklind, B., Lotz, J., Einerhand, M. and Pearson, M. (1996), 'Net Public Social Expenditure', Labour Market and Social Policy Occasional Papers, No. 19, Paris: OECD.

Adema, W. and Ladaique, M. (2009), 'How Expensive is the Welfare State?: Gross and Net Indicators in the OECD Social Expenditure Database (SOCX)', OECD Social, Employment and Migration Working Papers, No. 92, OECD Publishing.

Apospori, E. and Millar, J. (eds) (2003), *The Dynamics of Social Exclusion in Europe, Comparing Austria, Germany, Greece, Portugal and the UK*, Cheltenham, UK and Northampton, USA: Edward Elgar.

Barnes, M. *et al.* (2002), *Poverty and Social Exclusion in Europe*, Cheltenham, UK and Northampton, USA: Edward Elgar.

Becker, G. S. (1965), 'A Theory of the Allocation of Time', *Economic Journal*, 75(299), 493–517.

Becker, G. S. and Ghez, G. R. (1975), *Allocation of Time and Goods over the Life Cycle*, New York: Columbia University Press.

Beveridge, Sir William (1942), *Social Insurance and Allied Services*, Reported by William Beveridge, 1942, rep. 1958.

Bhalla, Ajit S. and Lapeyre, F. (2004), *Poverty and Exclusion in a Global World*. Hampshire and New York: Palgrave (2nd revised edn).

Bonoli, G. (2003a), 'Social Policy through Labour Markets: Understanding National Differences in the Provision of Economic Security to Wage Earners', *Comparative Political Studies*, 36 (9), 1007–31.

Bonoli, G. (2003b), 'The Politics of the New Social Policies, Providing Coverage against New Social Risks in Mature Welfare States', Paper presented at the conference 'The Politics of New Social Risks', Lugano, Switzerland, 25–27 September 2003.

Bordo, M., Eichengreen, B., Klingebiel, D. and Martinez-Peria, M.S. (2001), 'Is the Crisis Problem Growing More Severe?' *Economic Policy*, 16 (32), 51–82.

Borzaga, C. (2004), 'From Suffocation to Re-emergence: the Evolution of the Italian Third Sector', A. Evers and J. L. Laville (eds) *The Third Sector in Europe*, Cheltenham and Northampton: Edward Elgar.

Borzaga, C. and Defourny, J. (eds) (2001), *The Emergence of Social Enterprise*, London: Routledge.

Bruce, M. (1968), *The Coming of the Welfare State*, 4th edn, London: B.T. Batsford.

Campbell, J.C. (2002), 'Japanese Social Policy in Comparative Perspective', World Bank Institute Working Papers Stock No. 37197.

Castles, F. and Mitchell, D. (1993), 'Worlds of Welfare and Families of Nations', in F. Castles (ed.) *Families of Nations*, Dartmouth: Aldershot, 93–129.

Chen, J., Choi, Y.J. and Sawada, Y. (2009), 'How Is Suicide Different in Japan?' *Japan and the World Economy*, Elsevier, Vol. 21(2), 140–50.

CIRIEC (International Centre of Research and Information on the Public, Social and Cooperative Economy) (2006), *The Social Economy in the European Union* (the Report drawn up for the European Economic and Social Committee by CIRIEC) http://www.eesc.europa.eu/groups/3/index_en.asp?id=1405GR03EN

Council for Gender Equality of Japan (1996), *Vision of Gender Equality: Creating New Values for the 21st Century*, http://www.gender.go.jp/english_contents/toshin-e/index.html

Department of Social Security (DSS) (1996), *Social Assistance in OECD Countries*, Vol. 1, London: DSS.

Duncan, R. (2003), *The Dollar Crisis, Causes, Consequences, Cures*, Clementi Loop: John Wiley & Sons (Asia).

Dwyer, D. and Bruce, J. (eds) (1988), *A Home Divided: Women and Income in the Third World*, Stanford: Stanford University Press.

Elson, D. (1994), 'Micro, Meso, Macro: Gender and Economic Analysis in the Context of Policy Reforms', in I. Bakker (ed.) *The Strategic Silence: Gender and Economic Policy*, London and Ottawa: Zed Press and North-South Institute, 33–45.

Esping-Andersen, G. (1990), *The Three Worlds of Welfare Capitalism*, Cambridge: Polity Press.

Esping-Andersen, G. (ed.) (1996), *Welfare States in Transition National Adaptations in Global Economies*, London: SAGE.

Esping-Andersen, G. (1999), *Social Foundations of Postindustrial Economies*, Oxford: Oxford University Press.

Esping-Andersen, G. (2009), *The Incomplete Revolution: Adapting Welfare States to Women's New Roles*, Cambridge: Polity Press.

Esping-Andersen, G. with Gallie, D., Hemerijck, A. and Myles, J. (2002) *Why We Need a New Welfare State*, Oxford: Oxford University Press.

Estévez-Abe, M. (2008), *Welfare and Capitalism in Postwar Japan*, Cambridge: Cambridge University Press.

European Council (2000), *Fight against poverty and social exclusion – definition of appropriate objectives*, http://ec.europa.eu/employment_social/social_inclusion/docs/approb_en.pdf

Evers, A. and Laville, J.L. (eds) (2004), *The Third Sector in Europe*, Cheltenham, UK and Northampton, USA: Edward Elgar.

Ferrera, M. (1996), 'The "Southern Model" of Welfare in Social Europe', *Journal of European Social Policy*, 6 (1), 17–37.

Fishbein, A. and Woodall, P. (2006), *Women are Prime Targets for Subprime Lending: Women are Disproportionately Represented in High-Cost Mortgage Market*, Consumers Federation of America.

Folbre, N. (1986), 'Cleaning House: New Perspectives on Households and Economic Development', *Journal of Development Economics*, 22(1), 5–40.

Fukasaku, K., Masahiro, K., Plummer, M.G. and Alexandra, T-D. (eds) (2005), *Policy coherence toward East Asia: Development challenges for OECD countries*; Paris: OECD.

Goodwin, N.R. and Harris, J.M. (2001) 'Better Principles: New Approaches to Teaching Introductory Economics', Global Development and Environment Institute Working Paper No. 01–05, Tufts University.

Harrison, A. (1993), 'National Assets and National Accounting', in E. Lutz (ed.) *Toward Improving Accounting for the Environment*, Washington: World Bank, 22–45.

Hill, T.P. (1979), 'Do-It-Yourself and GDP', *The Review of Income and Wealth*, 25 (1), 31–39.

Honohan, P. and Klingebiel, D. (2000), 'Controlling the Fiscal Costs of Banking Crises', World Bank Policy Research Working Paper No. 2441.

ILO (2004), *Economic Security for a Better World*, Socio-Economic Security Programme. Geneva: International Labour Office.

Johnson, A. (2005), *European Welfare States and Supranational Governance of Social Policy*, Basingstoke and New York: Palgrave Macmillan.

Jones, C. (1993), 'The Pacific Challenge', in C. Jones (ed.) *New Perspectives on the Welfare State in Europe*, London: Routledge, 198–217.

Bibliography

Jones, R.S. (2007), 'Income Inequality, Poverty and Social Spending in Japan', Economic Department Working Papers No. 556, Paris: OECD.

Katrougalos, G. and Lazaridis, G. (2003), *Southern European Welfare States, Problems, Challenges and Prospects*, New York: Palgrave Macmillan.

Kilkey, M. (2000), *Lone Mothers Between Paid Work and Care: The Policy Regime in Twenty Countries*, Aldershot: Ashgate.

Korpi, W. (2000), 'Faces of Inequality: Gender, Class, and Patterns of Inequalities in Different Types of Welfare States', *Social Politics*, 7 (2), 127–91.

Lewis, J. (1992), 'Gender and the Development of Welfare Regimes', *Journal of European Social Policy*, 2 (3), 159–73.

Lewis, J. (2004), 'The State and the Third Sector in Modern Welfare States: Independence, Instrumentality, Partnership', in A. Evers and J.L. Laville (eds) (2004) *The Third Sector in Europe*, Cheltenham, UK and Northampton, USA: Edward Elgar, 169–187.

Mace, R. (1998), 'Last Speech A Perspective on Universal Design', an edited excerpt of a presentation made by Ronald L. Mace, FAIA, at 'Designing for the 21st Century: An International Conference on Universal Design' on 19 June 1998, http://www.design.ncsu.edu/cud/about_us/usronmacespeech.htm.

Ministry of Economy, Industry and Trade (METI) of Japan (2008), *White Paper on Economy, Industry and Trade 2008*, http://www.meti.go.jp/english/report/data/gWT2008fe.html.

Ministry of Internal Affairs and Communications of Japan, Statistics Bureau (2006), *2006 Survey on Time Use and Leisure Activities, Summary of Results (Questionnaire B)*, http://www.stat.go.jp/english/data/shakai/2006/pdf/gaiyo-b.pdf

Mitchell, D. (1991), *Income Transfers in Ten Welfare States*, Aldershot: Avebury.

Miura, M.(2001), 'Globalization and Reforms of Labor Market Institutions: Japan and Major OECD Countries,' Discussion Paper F-94, Institute of Social Science, University of Tokyo.

National Institute for Population and Social Security Research (2001), *The Cost of Social Security in Japan: FY 2000*, Tokyo: NIPSSR.

National Institute for Population and Social Security Research (2002), *The Cost of Social Security in Japan: FY 2001*, Tokyo: NIPSSR.

OECD (1976), *The 1974–5 Recession and the Employment of Women*, Paris: OECD.

OECD (1999a), *Employment Outlook*, Paris: OECD.

OECD (1999b), *Taxing Wages*, Paris: OECD.

OECD (2000), *Employment Outlook*, Paris: OECD.

OECD (2001), *Employment Outlook*, Paris: OECD.

OECD (2004a), *Employment Outlook*, Paris: OECD.

OECD (2004b), Benefits and Wages, Paris: OECD.

OECD (2005a), *Employment Outlook*, Paris: OECD.

OECD (2005b), 'Income Distribution and Poverty in OECD Countries in the Second Half of the 1990s,' OECD Social, Employment and Migration Working Papers No. 22 by Foerster, M. and d'Ercole, M., http://www.oecd.org/dataoecd/48/9/34483698.pdf

OECD (2005c), *Pensions at a Glance, Public Policies across OECD Countries*, Paris: OECD.

OECD (2005d), *Taxing Wages*, Paris: OECD.

OECD (2005e), Health Project, *Long-term Care for Older People*, Paris: OECD.

OECD (2007), *Revenue Statistics 1965–2006*, Paris: OECD.

OECD (2009a), *Benefits and Wages 2007: OECD Indicators*. http://www.oecd.org/document/3/0,3343,en_2649_34637_39617987_1_1_1_1,00.html

OECD (2009b), *Employment Outlook 2009, Tackling the Jobs Crisis*, Paris: OECD.

Orloff, A.S. (1993), 'Gender and the Social Rights of Citizenship: State Policies and Gender Relations in Comparative research,' *American Sociological Review*, 58 (3), 303–28.

Osawa, M. (1992), 'Corporate-Centered Society and Women's Labor in Japan Today', *U.S.-Japan Women's Journal*, English Supplement, No. 3, September 1992, 3–35.

Osawa, M. (1993), 'Feminization of Employment in Japan', *Annals of the Institute of Social Science*, No. 34, March 1993, 47–70.

Osawa, M. (1994), 'Bye-bye Corporate Warriors: the Formation of a Corporate-Centered Society and Gender-Biased Social Policies in Japan', *Annals of the Institute of Social Science*, No. 35, March 1994, 157–94.

Osawa, M. (1996), 'Will the Japanese Style System Change? Employment, Gender and the Welfare State', *The Journal of Pacific Asia*, Vol. 3, 69–94.

Osawa, M. (1998), 'The Feminization of the Labour Market', in Junji Banno ed., *The Political Economy of Japanese Society*, Vol. 2, Oxford University Press, 144–74.

Osawa, M. (2000), 'Government Approaches to Gender Equality in the mid-1990s', *Social Science Japan Journal*, Vol. 3, No. 1, Oxford University Press, 2000, 3–19.

Osawa, M. (2001), 'People in Irregular Modes of Employment: Are They Really Not Subject to Discrimination?' *Social Science Japan Journal*, Vol.4 No.2, October 2001, 183–99.

Osawa, M. (2002) 'Gendering Labor in the Context of Japan's Labor and Social Policy Studies', in Sung-Jo Park, Arne Holzhausen and Benjamin Lunau (eds.) *Social Science-Centered Studies on Modern Japan*, Berlin: Institute for East Asia Studies, Freie Universität Berlin, 113–31.

Osawa, M. (2002), 'Twelve Million Full-time Housewives: The Gender Consequences of Japan's Postwar Social Contract', in Oliver Zunz, Leonard Schoppa, and Nobuhiro Hiwatari (eds.), *Social Contracts under Stress, The Middle Classes of America, Europe and Japan at the Turn of the Century*, New York: Russell Sage Foundation, 255–77.

Osawa, M. (2003), 'How has the Lost Decade Started? Issues of the "Corporate-Centered Society" and its Reforms in the Early 1990s', in Carl le Grand and Toshiko Tsukaguchi-le Grand (eds.), *Women in Japan and Sweden, Work and Family in Two Welfare Regimes*, Stockholm: Almqvist & Wiksell International, 45–62.

Osawa, M. (2005), 'Koizumi's 'robust policy': governance, the Japanese welfare employment regime and comparative gender studies', in Glenn D. Hook (ed.) *Contested Governance in Japan, Sites and issues*, London and New York: RoutledgeCurzon, 111–29.

Osawa, M. (2007), 'Comparative Livelihood Security Systems from a Gender Perspective, with a Focus on Japan', in Sylvia Walby, Heidi Gottfried, Karin Gottschall and Mari Osawa (eds.), *Gendering the Knowledge Economy, Comparative Perspectives,* Basingstoke and New York: Palgrave Macmillan, 2007, 81–108.

Osawa, M. (2007), 'The Livelihood Security System and Social Exclusion: the 'Male Breadwinner' Model Revisited', in Ilse Lenz, Charlotte Ullrich and Barbara Fersch (eds.) *Gender Orders Unbound? Globalisation, Restructuring and Reciprocity*, Opladen and Farmington Hills: Barbara Budrich Publishers, 277–301.

Osawa, M. (2010), 'Challenges to the Livelihood Security System in Japan from a Gender Perspective', in Miyoko Tsujimura and Mari Osawa (eds.) *Gender Equality in Multicultural Societies: Gender, Diversity, and Conviviality in the Age of Globalization*, Sendai: Tohoku University Press, 73–96.

Oxley, H., Burniaux, J.M., Dang, T.T. and d'Ercole, M.M. (1999), 'Income Distribution and Poverty in 13 OECD Countries', *OECD Economic Studies*, 29, 55–94.

Peng, I. (2004), 'Postindustrial Pressure, Political Regime Shifts, and Social Policy Reform in Japan and South Korea,' *Journal of East Asian Studies* 4, 389–425.

Ritzen, J., Easterly, W. and Woolcock, M. (2000), 'On "Good" Politicians and "Bad"

Policies: Social Cohesion, Institutions, and Growth', Papers 2448, World Bank – Country Economics Department.
Rodrik, D. (1999), 'Institutions for High-Quality Growth: What They Are and How to Acquire Them', Paper prepared for an IMF conference on Second Generation Reforms.
Sainsbury, D. (ed.) (1994), *Gendering Welfare States*, London: SAGE.
Sainsbury, D. (1996), *Gender, Equality and Welfare State*, Cambridge: Cambridge University Press.
Salamon, L.M. and Anheier, H.K. (1996), 'Social Origins of Civil Society: Explaining the Nonprofit Sector Cross-nationally', *Working Papers of the Johns Hopkins Comparative Nonprofit Sector Project*, No. 22.
Salamon, L.M. and Anheier, H.K. (1998), 'Social Origins of Civil Society: Explaining the Nonprofit Sector Cross-nationally', *Voluntas*, 9 (3), 213–48.
Salamon, L.M., Sokolowski, S.W. and Anheier. H.K. (2000), 'Social Origins of Civil Society: An Overview', Working Paper of the Johns Hopkins Comparative Nonprofit Sector Project, No. 38, Baltimore: The Johns Hopkins Center for Civil Society Studies.
Sen, A. (1990), 'Gender and Cooperative Conflicts', in I. Tinker (ed.) *Persistent Inequalities: Women and World Development*, New York and Oxford: Oxford University Press, 123–49.
Sen, A. (1992), *Inequality Reexamined*, Oxford: Oxford University Press.
Sen, A. (2000), 'Social Exclusion: Concept, Application and Security, Social Development Papers', No. 1, Office of Environment and Social Development. Asian Development Bank, June 2000.
Shirahase, S. (2003), 'Wives' Economic Contribution to the Household Income in Japan with Cross National Perspective', Luxembourg Income Study Working Paper Series, No. 349.
Social Protection Committee (2001), *Report on Indicators in the Field of Poverty and Social Exclusion*.
Spear, R., Thirty, B. and Vivet, D. (2000), *Report on Third System and Employment*, Liège: CIRIEC International.
Stiglitz, J. (2002), *Globalization and its Discontents*, New York: W.W. Norton & Company.
Taylor-Gooby, P. (2004), 'New Social Risks in Postindustrial Society: Some Evidence on Responses to Active Labour Market Policies from Eurobarometer', *International Social Security Review*, 57 (3), 45–64.
Thane, P. (1996), *The Foundations of the Welfare State*, 2nd edn, London: Addison Wesley Longman.
Venn, D. (2009), 'Legislation, collective bargaining and enforcement: Updating the OECD employment protection indicators', www.oecd.org/els/workingpapers.
Wade, R. (2002), 'Globalization, Poverty and Income Distribution: Does the Liberal Argument Hold?', LSE DESTIN Working Paper Series 02–33.
Walby, S. (2001), 'Globalization and Regulation: the New Economy and Gender in the UK', Paper presented to the conference of the American Sociological Association, Anaheim, August 2001.
White, G. and Goodman, R. (1998), 'Welfare Orientalism and the Search for an East Asian Welfare Model', in R. Goodman, G. White and H. Kwon (eds) *The East Asian Welfare Model: Welfare Orientalism and the State*, London: Routledge, 3–24.
Whiteford, P. and Adema, W. (2007), 'What Works Best in Reducing Child Poverty: A Benefit or Work Strategy?', OECD Social, Employment and Migration Working Papers 51, Paris: OECD.

Works in Japanese

Abe, A. 阿部彩 (2005), 'Kodomo no hinkon—kokusai hikaku no shiten kara' 子どもの貧困－国際比較の視点から [Child poverty in international comparison], in Kokuritsu Shakai Hoshō – Jinkō Mondai Kenkyūsho 国立社会保障・人口問題研究所 [National Institute of Population and Social Security Research] (ed) *Kosodate setai no shakai hoshō* 子育て世帯の社会保障 [Social security for households with children], Tokyo: University of Tokyo Press, 119–42.

Abe, A. 阿部彩 (2006), 'Sōtaiteki hakudatsu no jittai to bunseki – Nihon no maikurodēta o mochiita jisshō kenkyū' 相対的剥奪の実態と分析－日本のマイクロデータを用いた実証研究 [Empirical Analysis of Relative Deprivation in Japan using Japanese Microdata], in Shakai Seisaku Gakkai 社会政策学会 [Society for the Study of Social Policy] (ed) *Shakai seisaku ni okeru fukushi to shūrō* 社会政策における福祉と就労 [Linking Welfare and Work: New Trends in Social Policy], Shakai Seisaku Gakkaishi 社会政策学会誌 [Journal of Social Policy and Labor Studies], No. 16: 251–75. Kyoto: Houritsu Bunka Sha.

Abe, A. 阿部彩 (2008), 'Nihon ni okeru kosodate setai no hinkon – sōtaiteki hakudatsu to shakai seisaku' 日本における子育て世帯の貧困・相対的剥奪と社会政策 [Child Poverty and Deprivation in Japan], in *Shakai Seisaku Gakkai* 社会政策学会 [Society for the Study of Social Policy] (ed.) *Kosodate o meguru shakai seisaku: sono kinō to gyaku kinō* 子育てをめぐる社会政策: その機能と逆機能 [Social Policies on Raising Children: Functions and Reverse Functions], Shakai Seisaku Gakkaishi 社会政策学会誌 [Journal of Social Policy and Labor Studies], No. 19: 21–40. Kyoto: Houritsu Bunka Sha.

Bhalla, A.S. and Lapeyre, F. (2005), *Gurōbaruka to shakaiteki haijo – hinkon to shakaiteki mondai e no atarashii apurōchi* グローバル化と社会的排除－貧困と社会問題への新しいアプローチ trans. ed. by H. Fukuhara and K. Nakamura 福原宏幸・中村健吾監訳 [Japanese translation of *Poverty and Exclusion in a Global World*, 2nd revised edn] Kyoto: Shōwadō.

Campbell, J.C. (2008), 'Japan's long-term care in cross-national comparison', trans. Mari Ōsawa, in Ch. Ueno 上野千鶴子, Y. Ōkuma 大熊由紀子, M. Ōsawa 大沢真理, N. Jinno 神野直彦, and Y. Soeda 副田義也 (eds) *Kea o sasaeru shikumi* ケアを支えるしくみ [The foundations of long-term care], Kea sono shisō to jissen ケアその思想と実践 [Long-term care: Theory and practice series], No. 5, Tokyo: Iwanami Shoten, 169–88.

Danjo kyōdō sankaku kaigi, Eikyō chōsa senmon chōsakai 男女共同参画会議影響調査専門調査会 Council for Gender Equality, Specialist Committee on Gender Impact Evaluation (2002a), '*Raifusutairu no sentaku to zeisei, shakai hoshō seido, koyō shisutemu' ni kansuru chūkan hōkoku* 「ライフスタイルの選択と税制・社会保障制度・雇用システム」に関する中間報告 [An interim report on 'Lifestyle choices and tax, social security and employment systems'].

Danjo kyōdō sankaku kaigi, Eikyō chōsa senmon chōsakai 男女共同参画会議影響調査専門調査会 Council for Gender Equality, Specialist Committee on Gender Impact Evaluation (2002b), '*Raifusutairu no sentaku to zeisei, shakai hoshō seido, koyō shisutemu' ni kansuru hōkoku* 「ライフスタイルの選択と税制・社会保障制度・雇用システム」に関する報告 [A report on 'Lifestyle choices and tax, social security and employment systems'].

Danjo kyōdō sankaku kaigi, Eikyō chōsa senmon chōsakai 男女共同参画会議影響調査専門調査会 Council for Gender Equality, Specialist Committee on Gender Impact Evaluation (2004), '*Raifusutairu no sentaku to koyō, shūgyō ni kansuru seido, kankō ni tsuite no hōkoku. 「ライフスタイルの選択と雇用・就業に関する制度・慣行」について の報告 [A report on 'Lifestyle choices and institutions and practices of employment'].

Denki tsūshin shingi kai 電気通信審議会 Telecommunications Council (2000) 'IT kakumei o suishin suru tame no denki tsūshin jigyō ni okeru kyōsō seisaku no arikata ni tsuite no ichiji tōshin' IT 革命を推進するための電気通信事業における競争政策の在り方についての一次答申 [First report on competition policies in the telecommunications industry to further the IT revolution].

Doihara, S. 土肥原晋 (2006), 'Beikoku "kajō shōhi" no kōzō' 米国「過剰消費」の構造 [The structure of over-consumption in the US], *Nissei Kisoken Report* ニッセイ基礎研 REPORT [NLI Research Institute Report] 113: 16–25.

Esping-Andersen, G. (2001), *Fukushi shihon shugi no mittsu no sekai: Hikaku fukushi kokka no riron to dōtai* 福祉資本主義の三つの世界―比較福祉国家の理論と動態 trans. N. Okazawa 岡沢憲芙 and T. Miyamoto 宮本太郎 [Japanese translation of *The Three Worlds of Welfare Capitalism*], Kyoto: Minerva Shobō.

Fujiwara, Ch. 藤原千沙 (2004), 'Josei no shotoku hoshō to kōteki fujo' 女性の所得保障と公的扶助 [Women's income security and public assistance], in M. Ōsawa 大沢真理 (ed.) *Fukushi kokka to jendā* 福祉国家とジェンダー [Welfare states and gender], Sōsho gendai no keizai shakai to jendā 叢書現代の経済・社会とジェンダー [Economy, society and gender today series], No. 4. Tokyo: Akashi Shoten, 199–232.

Fukazawa, K. 深澤和子 (2002), 'Fukushi kokka to jendā poritikkusu – Jendā kankei no senryakuteki tenkan e no michi' 福祉国家とジェンダー・ポリティックス―ジェンダー関係の戦略的転換への途 [Welfare states and gender politics: The path to strategically transforming gender relations], in T. Miyamoto 宮本太郎 (ed.) *Fukushi kokka saihen no seiji* 福祉国家再編の政治 [The politics of welfare state restructuring]. Kōza – Fukushi kokka no yukue 講座・福祉国家のゆくえ [Course in the future of the welfare state series], No. 1. Kyoto: Minerva Shobō.

Fukumitsu, H. 福光寛 (2005), 'Amerika no jūtaku kin'yū ni taisuru arata na shiten – Shōkenka no shinten no naka de no sabupuraimu sō ni taisuru ryakudatsuteki kashitsuke' アメリカの住宅金融に対する新たな視点―証券化の進展の中でのサブプライム層に対する略奪的貸付 [A new perspective of US mortgage financing: Predatory lending to subprime borrowers during mortgage securitization], *Seijo University Economic Papers* 成城大学経済研究 170: 57–88.

Fukushima, M. 福島瑞穂 (1995), *Kekkon wa bakuchi de aru* 結婚はバクチである [Marriage is a gamble], Tokyo: Daiwa Shobō.

Genda, Y. 玄田有史 (2001), 'Kekkyoku, wakamono no shigoto ga nakunatta – kōreika shakai no jakunen koyō' 結局、若者の仕事がなくなった―高齢社会の若年雇用 [In the end, the jobs for young people disappeared: Youth employment in an aging society], in T. Tachibanaki 橘木俊詔 and D. Wise (eds) *'Nichibei hikaku' – Kigyō kōdō to rōdō shijō* ＜日米比較＞企業行動と労働市場 [Japan-US comparison: Corporate behaviours and labour markets], Tokyo: Nihon Keizai Shinbunsha, 173–202.

Genda, Y. 玄田有史 (2003), 'Rekka suru jakunen to jieigyō no shotoku kōzō' 劣化する若年と自営業の所得構造 [Deterioration of the income structure of youth and the self-employed], in Y. Higuchi 樋口美雄 and Ministry of Finance, Policy Research Institute 財務省財務総合政策研究所 (eds) *Nihon no shotoku kakusa to shakai kaisō* 日本の所得格差と社会階層 [Income gaps and social classes in Japan], Tokyo: Nihon Hyōronsha, 145–68.

Genda, Y. 玄田有史 (2004), *Jobu kurieishon* ジョブ・クリエイション [Job creation], Tokyo: Nihon Keizai Shinbunsha.

Hattori, R. 服部良太 and Maeda, E. 前田栄治 (2000) 'Nihon no koyō shisutemu ni tsuite'

日本の雇用システムについて [Japan's employment system], *Nippon Ginkō chōsa geppō* 日本銀行調査月報 [Bank of Japan monthly report], January. http://www.boj.or.jp/type/ronbun/ron/research/data/ron0001b.pdf (accessed 31 January 2011).

Hamada, K. 浜田浩児 (2006), 'Mushō rōdō no kahei hyōka – Shūnyū kaisōbetsu no mushō rōdōgaku to shotoku bunpai' 無償労働の貨幣評価－収入階層別の無償労働額と所得分配 [The monetary assessment of unpaid work: The amount of unpaid work by household income group and income distribution], *Tōkei* 日本統計協会月刊誌「統計」[*Monthly Statistics* (Japan Statistical Association)] 57(7): 7–13.

Higuchi, Y. 樋口美雄, Ōta, K. 太田清 and the Institute for Research on Household Economics 家計経済研究所 (eds) (2004), *Joseitachi no Heisei fukyō – Defure de hatarakikata, kurashi wa dō kawattaka* 女性たちの平成不況－デフレで働き方・暮らしはどう変わったか [Women in the Heisei recession: How deflation has changed ways of working and living], Tokyo: Nihon Keizai Shinbunsha.

Hirowatari, S. 広渡清吾 (1990), *Futatsu no sengo shakai to hō no aida – Nihon to Doitsu* 二つの戦後社会と法の間－日本とドイツ [Between two postwar societies and law: Japan and Germany], Tokyo: Ministry of Finance, Printing Bureau.

Igami, K. 居神浩 (2003), 'Fukushi kokka dōtairon e no tenkai – jendā no shiten kara' 福祉国家動態論への展開－ジェンダーの視点から [Developing a dynamic theory of the welfare state from a gender perspective], in T. Uzuhashi 埋橋孝文 (ed.) *Hikaku no naka no fukushi kokka* 比較のなかの福祉国家 [Welfare states in comparison]. Kōza – Fukushi kokka no yukue 講座・福祉国家のゆくえ [Course in the future of the welfare state series], No. 2. Kyoto: Minerva Shobō, 43–67.

Igarashi, J. 五十嵐仁 (2008), 'Shinjiyūshugika ni okeru rōdō no kisei kanwa – sono tenkai to hanten no kōzu' 新自由主義下における労働の規制緩和その展開と反転の構図 [Labour deregulation under neo-liberalism: The structure of developments and reversals]. In *Shakai Seisaku Gakkai dai-116 kai taikai kyōtsū rondai hōkoku* 社会政策学会第116回大会共通論題報告 [Plenary session presentation of the 116th Annual Conference of the Society for the Study of Social Policy].

Ikeo, K. 池尾和人 (2009), *Kin'yū, keizai kiki to kongo no kisei kantoku taisei* 金融・経済危機と今後の規制監督体制 [The financial and economic crisis and the future of regulatory oversight], Tokyo: Tōkyō Zaidan Seisaku Kenkyū 東京財団政策研究 [Tokyo Foundation Policy Research].

Ishii, N. 石井菜穂子 (2003), *Chōki keizai hatten no jisshō bunseki* 長期経済発展の実証分析 [Long-term economic development: An empirical analysis], Tokyo: Nihon Keizai Shinbunsha.

Irokawa, T. 色川卓男 (2003), 'Kinrōsha kakei kōzō no kokusai hikaku- Nichi-Bei-Kan-Doku no hikaku' 勤労者家計構造の国際比較－日・米・韓・独の比較 [International comparison of worker household economic structures: Japan, the US, Korea and Germany], in T. Uzuhashi 埋橋孝文編 (ed.) *Hikaku no naka no fukushi kokka* 比較のなかの福祉国家 [Welfare states in comparison]. Kōza – Fukushi kokka no yukue 講座・福祉国家のゆくえ [Course in the future of the welfare state series], No. 2. Kyoto: Minerva Shobō, 135–65.

Istituto nazionale di statistica (ISTAT) (2001), *Le cooperative sociali in Italia*; trans. Okayasu Kisaburō 岡安喜三郎 (2004) *Kyōdo no hakken* 協同の発見 [The discovery of cooperation], supplemental issue (*Itaria shakaiteki kyōdō kumiai chōsa hōkoku* イタリア社会的協同組合調査報告 [Report on social cooperatives in Italy]): 46–61.

Iryō keizai kenkyū kikō 医療経済研究機構 [Institute for Health Economics and Policy] (2005), *Iryō to fukushi no sangyō renkan ni kansuru bunseki kenkyū, sōgō hōkokusho* 医療と福祉の産業連関に関する分析研究　総合報告書 [Analytic research on industrial

Iwata, M. 岩田正美 (2006), 'Basu ni kagi wa kakatte shimatta ka? Gendai Nihon no hinkon to fukushi seisaku no mujun' バスに鍵はかかってしまったか?―現代日本の貧困と福祉政策の矛盾 [Is the Bus Locked? Poverty and Social Policy in Contemporary Japan], *Shisō* 思想, 983: 135–52.

Iwami, T. 石見徹 (2007), *Gurōbaru shihon shugi o kangaeru* グローバル資本主義を考える [Reflecting on global capitalism], Kyoto: Minerva Shobō.

Jinkō Mondai Shingikai 人口問題審議会 [Population problem advisory council] (1997), *Shōshika ni kansuru kihonteki kangaekata ni tsuite – Jinkō genshō shakai, mirai e no sekinin to sentaku* 少子化に関する基本的考え方について―人口減少社会、未来への責任と選択 [Basic implications of the declining birthrate and depopulating society: Responsibilities and choices for the future].

Jinno, N. 神野直彦 (2000), 'Shakaihoshō o jūjitsu saseru "mittsu no seifu taikei" to iu kangaekata' 社会保障を充実させる「三つの政府体系」という考え方 [The concept of "the system of three governments" to strengthen social security], *Ekonomisuto* エコノミスト [Weekly Economist], 8 February, 78–82.

Jinno, N. 神野直彦 and Ōsawa, M. 大沢真理 (2004), 'Zaisei to nenkin seido – Jendā e no zaisei shakaigakuteki apurōchi' 財政と年金制度―ジェンダーへの財政社会学的アプローチー [Public finance and the pension system: A sociological public finance approach to gender], in M. Ōsawa (ed.) *Fukushi kokka to jendā* 福祉国家とジェンダー [Welfare states and gender], Sōsho Gendai no Keizai, Shakai to Jendā 叢書現代の経済・社会とジェンダー [Economy, society and gender today series], No. 4. Tokyo: Akashi Shoten, 41–64.

Jinno, N. 神野直彦 and Kaneko, M. 金子勝 (1999), '*Fukushi seifu' e no teigen – Shakai hoshō no shintaikei o kōsō suru* 「福祉政府」への提言 社会保障の新体系を構想する [Proposal for a 'welfare government': Planning a new system of social security], Tokyo: Iwanami Shoten.

Josei no raifustairu no henka tō ni taioushita nenkin no arikata ni kansuru kentōkai 女性のライフスタイルの変化等に対応した年金の在り方に関する検討会 Study Group on Pension Systems That Would Suit the Changing Lifestyles of Women (2002), *Josei to nenkin – Josei no raifustairu no henka tō ni taioushita nenkin no arikata ni kansuru kentōkai hōkokusho* 女性と年金―女性のライフスタイルの変化等に対応した年金の在り方に関する検討会 報告書 [Women and pensions: Report from the Study Group on Pension Systems That Would Suit the Changing Lifestyles of Women], Tokyo: Shakai Hoken Kenkyūsho.

Kanai, K. 金井郁 (2010), 'Koyō hoken seido ni okeru hōkatsusei – hiseiki rōdōsha no sēfuti netto' 雇用保険制度における包括性―非正規労働者のセーフティネット [The comprehensiveness of unemployment insurance: Non-regular workers' safety net], in K. Komamura 駒村康平 (ed.) *Saitei shotoku hoshō* 最低所得保障 [Minimum income guarantee], Tokyo: Iwanami Shoten.

Kaneko, M. 金子勝 (1997), *Shijō to seido no seiji keizaigaku* 市場と制度の政治経済学 [The political economy of markets and institutions], Tokyo: University of Tokyo Press.

Kaneko, M. 金子勝 (1999), 'Kyoshutsuzei-hōshiki no shotoku hirei nenkin o' 拠出税方式の所得比例年金を [Proposing an income-related pension system financed by payroll tax], in N. Jinno 神野直彦 and M. Kaneko 金子勝 (eds) *Fukushi seifu e no teigen – shakai hoshō no shintaikei o kōsō suru* 福祉政府への提言―社会保障の新体系を構想する [A proposal for the welfare government: Planning a new system of social security], Tokyo: Iwanami Shoten, 15–45.

Kaneko, M. 金子勝 and Jinno, N. 神野直彦 (1999), 'Kyōryoku shakai no nenkin o tsukuru' 協力社会の年金を創る [Establishing a pension system for a cooperative society], *Sekai* 世界 659: 98–110.

Kaneko, M. 金子勝 and Kodama, T. 児玉龍彦 (2004), *Gyaku shisutemugaku: shijō to seimei no shikumi o tokiakasu* 逆システム学―市場と生命のしくみを解き明かす ['Reverse Systemology': Clarifying the mechanism of market and life], Tokyo: Iwanami Shoten.

Kaneko, M. 金子勝and DeWit, A. (2008), *Sekai kin'yū kiki* 世界金融危機 [The global financial crisis], Iwanami Booklet series, No. 740. Tokyo: Iwanami Shoten.

Kasuya, N. 粕谷信次 (2006), 'Naze T. Jante-shi o shōsei shite, shinpojiumu o kaisai suru ka' なぜ、T・ジャンテ氏を招請して、シンポジウムを開催するか [Why invite Thierry Jeantet and hold a symposium?], *Bokkō suru shakaiteki kigyō to shakaiteki keizai: Tieri Jante-shi shōhei [Tokyo, Osaka, Kumamoto] Shimin Kokusai Fōramu no kiroku* 勃興する社会的企業と社会的経済: ティエリ・ジャンテ氏招聘「東京・大阪・熊本」市民国際フォーラムの記録 [The rise of social enterprise and the social economy: Thierry Jeantet, guest speaker. (Tokyo, Osaka and Kumamoto) Citizens' International Forum Report], Tokyo: Dōji Daisha.

Katsumata, Y. 勝又幸子 (2005), 'Kosodate setai ni taisuru shakai hoshō kyūfu no genjō to kokusai hikaku' 子育て世帯に対する社会保障給付の現状と国際比較 [Social security benefits for households with children: Current conditions in international comparison', in National Institute of Population and Social Security Research (ed.) *Kosodate setai no shakai hoshō* 子育て世帯の社会保障 [Social security for households with children], Tokyo: University of Tokyo Press, 53–81.

Katsumata, Y. 勝又幸子 and Yamada, A. 山田篤裕 (1998), 'Kenkyū shiryō – shakai hoshōhi kokusai hikaku kiso dēta' 研究資料・社会保障費 国際比較基礎データ [Research material on social security costs: Basic data for cross-national comparisons], *Kaigai shakai hoshō jōhō* 海外社会保障情報 [Databook of Overseas Social Security (National Institute of Population and Social Security Research)], 123: 101–12.

Kawaguchi, A. 川口章 (2004), 'Josei no shūgyō to shusshōritsu no dōkō' 女性の就業と出生率の動向 [Trends in women's employment and birthrates]. In *Shakai seisaku gakkai 109-kai taikai kyōtsū rondai hōkoku* 社会政策学会109回大会共通論題報告 [Plenary session presentation at the 109th Annual Conference of the Society for the Study of Social Policy].

Kawaguchi, K. 川口清史 (2006), 'Shakaiteki keizairon to seikyō' 社会的経済論と生協 [Theories of the social economy and co-operative associations], in Gendai Seikyōron Henshū Iinkai 現代生協論編集委員会 (ed.) *Gendai seikyōron no tankyū (rironhen)* 現代生協論の探求＜理論編＞ [Current theories of co-operative associations], Tokyo: Kōpu Shuppan, 259–75.

Keizai-kikaku-chō 経済企画庁 Economic Planning Agency, Quality-of-Life Policy Bureau (ed.) (1991), *Kojin seikatsu yūsen shakai o mezashite* 個人生活優先社会をめざして [Working towards a society that places individuals first]. In Dai-13 ji Kokumin Seikatsu Shingikai Sōgō Seisaku Bukai, Kihon Seisaku Iinkai chūkan hōkoku 第13次国民生活審議会総合政策部会・基本政策委員会中間報告 [Interim report of the Basic Policy Subcommittee under the Comprehensive Policy Group, in the 13th Quality-of-Life Council].

Keizai-kikaku-chō 経済企画庁 Economic Planning Agency (1992), *Seikatsu taikoku 5-ka nen keikaku – chikyū shakai to no kyōzon o mezashite* 生活大国5か年計画―地球社会との共存をめざして [The five-year plan for building a lifestyle superpower: A scenario for Japan's coexistence with the global community].

Keizai-kikaku-chō 経済企画庁 Economic Planning Agency (1997), *Anata no kaji no nedan* wa oikura desu ka? Muhōshū rōdō no kahei hyōka あなたの家事の値段はおいくらですか？－無報酬労働の貨幣評価についての研究 [How much is your housework worth? Research on monetary assessments of unpaid work].

Keizai-kikaku-chō 経済企画庁 Economic Planning Agency (1998), *1996-nen no mushō rōdō no kahei kachi* 1996年の無償労働の貨幣価値 [Monetary value of unpaid labour in 1996].http://www5.cao.go.jp/98/g/19981105g-unpaid.html (accessed 29 January 2006).

Keizai-sangyō-shō 経済産業省 Ministry of Economy, Trade and Industry (2004), *Tsūshō hakusho Heisei 16-nen ban* 通商白書平成16年版 (2004 White Paper on international trade).

Keizai-sangyō-shō 経済産業省 Ministry of Economy, Trade and Industry (2008), *Tsūshō hakusho Heisei 20-nen ban* 通商白書平成20年版 (2008 White Paper on international trade).

Kim, S. 金成恒 (2006), 'Hikakuronteki shiten kara mita Kankoku fukushi kokka no keisei to hatten – "okureta fukushi kokkaka" to "okureta minshuka" no tōgō kyokumen' 比較論的視点からみた韓国福祉国家の形成と発展－「遅れた福祉国家化」と「遅れた民主化」の統合局面 [The formation and development of the Korean welfare state in comparative theoretical perspective: The integration of 'delayed welfare state formation' and 'delayed democratization']. In Shakai Seisaku Gakkai dai-112 kai taikai kyōtsū rondai hōkoku 社会政策学会第112回大会報告 [Panel session presentation at the 112th Annual Conference of the Society for the Study of Social Policy].

Kimura, Y. 木村佳弘 and Miyazaki, M. 宮崎雅人 (2006), 'Chihō bunken kaikaku e no michinori' 地方分権改革への道程 [The path to decentralization reform], in N. Jinno 神野直彦 and E. Ide 井手英策 (eds) *Kibō no kōsō – bunken, shakai hoshō, zaisei kaikaku no tōtaru puran* 希望の構想─分権・社会保障・財政改革のトータルプラン [An agenda of hope: A total plan for decentralization, social security, and financial reform], Tokyo: Iwanami Shoten, 41–94.

Kita, A. 北明美 (2004), 'Jidō teate seido ni okeru jendā mondai' 児童手当制度におけるジェンダー問題 [Gender problems in the child allowance system], in M. Ōsawa 大沢真理 (ed.) *Fukushi kokka to jendā* 福祉国家とジェンダー [Welfare states and gender]. Sōsho gendai no keizai shakai to jendā 叢書現代の経済・社会とジェンダー [Economy, society and gender today series], No. 4. Tokyo: Akashi Shoten, 159–98.

Kokumin kenkō hoken chūōkai 国民健康保険中央会 All-Japan Federation of National Health Insurance Organizations (2004), *Kokumin kenkō hoken no antei o motomete – Iryō hoken seido no kaikaku* 国民健康保険の安定を求めて－医療保険制度の改革 [Stabilizing national health insurance: Reforming the medical insurance system].

Kokuritsu shakai hoshō jinkō mondai kenkyūsho 国立社会保障・人口問題研究所 National Institute for Population and Social Security Research (various years), *Shakai hoshō kyūfuhi* 社会保障給付費 [The Cost of Social Security].

Kokuritsu shakai hoshō jinkō mondai kenkyūsho 国立社会保障・人口問題研究所 National Institute for Population and Social Security Research (various years), *Shakai hoshō tōkei nenpō* 社会保障統計年報 [Annual Social Security Statistics].

Komamura, K. 駒村康平 (2003), 'Teishotoku setai no suikei to seikatsu hogo 低所得世帯の推計と生活保護 [Estimated data on low income households and livelihood protection], *Mita Shōgaku Kenkyū* 三田商学研究 [Mita Business Review] 46(3): 107–26.

Kōrei shakai o yokusuru josei no kai 高齢社会をよくする女性の会 Women's Association for a Better Aging Society (1995), 'Arata na kōteki kaigo shisutemu ni kansuru yōbō あらたな公的介護システムに関する要望 [Requirements for a new public care system], *Chingin to shakai hoshō* 賃金と社会保障 [Wages and social security] 1164: 20–2.

Kōsei-rōdō-shō 厚生労働省 Ministry of Health, Labour and Welfare (2002a), *Heisei 14-nen* ban kōsei rōdō hakusho 平成14年版厚生労働白書 [2002 White Paper on health, labour and welfare], Tokyo: Gyōsei.

Kōsei-rōdō-shō 厚生労働省 Ministry of Health, Labour and Welfare (2002b), *Nenkin kaikaku no kokkaku ni kansuru hōkōsei to ronten ni tsuite* 年金改革の骨格に関する方向性と論点について [Directions and issues regarding the framework for pension reform].

Kōsei-rōdō-shō 厚生労働省 Ministry of Health, Labour and Welfare, Equal Employment, Children and Families Bureau (2002c), *Heisei 14-nen ban josei rōdō hakusho – Hataraku josei no jitsujō* 平成14年版女性労働白書 – 働く女性の実情 [2002 White Paper on working women: Actual conditions of working women], Tokyo: Japan Institute of Workers' Evolution (21世紀職業財団).

Kōsei-rōdō-shō 厚生労働省 Ministry of Health, Labour and Welfare (2004), *Heisei 16-nen ban rōdō keizai hakusho* 平成16年版労働経済白書 [2004 White Paper on labour economics].

Kōsei-rōdō-shō 厚生労働省 Ministry of Health, Labour and Welfare (2006a), *Heisei 18-nen ban rōdō keizai hakusho* 平成18年版労働経済白書 [2006 White Paper on labour economics].

Kōsei-rōdō-shō 厚生労働省 Ministry of Health, Labour and Welfare, Equal Employment, Children and Families Bureau (2006b), *Heisei 18-nen ban josei rōdō hakusho: Hataraku josei no jitsujō* 平成18年版女性労働白書 – 働く女性の実情 [2006 White Paper on working women: Facts on working women], Tokyo: Japan Institute of Workers' Evolution (21世紀職業財団).

Kōsei-rōdō-shō 厚生労働省Ministry of Health, Labour and Welfare (2006c), *Kaigo kyūfuhi jittai chōsa kekka no gaikyō Heisei 18 nen ban* 介護給付費実態調査結果の概況平成18年版 [Survey of Long-term Care Benefit Expenditure: Summary of findings 2006].

Kōsei-rōdō-shō 厚生労働省 Ministry of Health and Labour and Welfare (2008), *Heisei 20-nendo kokumin hoken (shichōson) no zaisei jōkyō ni tsuite – sokuhō* 平成20年度国民健康保険（市町村）の財政状況について＝速報 [Update on the financial state of municipality-managed national health insurance schemes 2008

Kōsei-rōdō-shō, Tōkei jōhōbu 厚生労働省大臣官房統計情報部 Ministry of Health, Labour and Welfare, Statistics and Information Dept. (2002), *Heisei 14-nen ban shūrō jōken sōgō chōsa* 平成14年版就労条件総合調査 [2002 General survey of working conditions], http://www.mhlw.go.jp/toukei/list/11–22.html.

Kōsei-rōdō-shō, Tōkei jōhōbu 厚生労働省大臣官房統計情報部 Ministry of Health, Labour and Welfare, Statistics and Information Dept. (2006), *Heisei 18-nen ban shūrō jōken sōgō chōsa* 平成18年版就労条件総合調査 [2006 General survey of working conditions], http://www.mhlw.go.jp/toukei/list/11–22.html

Kōseishō 厚生省 Ministry of Health and Welfare (1985), *Kōsei hakusho Shōwa 60-nen ban* 厚生白書昭和60年版 [White Paper on health and welfare 1985]. http://wwwhakusyo.mhlw.go.jp/wp/index.htm.

Kōseishō 厚生省 Ministry of Health and Welfare, Minister's Secretariat, Policy Division (ed.) (1994), *21 seiki fukushi bijon – Shōshi, kōrei shakai ni mukete* 21世紀福祉ビジョン—少子・高齢社会に向けて [21st century welfare vision: Towards an aging society with fewer children], Tokyo: Dai-Ichi Hoki.

Kōseishō 厚生省 Ministry of Health and Welfare (1998), *Heisei 10-nen ban kōsei hakusho: Shōshi shakai o kangaeru – kodomo o umisodateru koto ni 'yume' o moteru shakai o* 平成10年版厚生白書 少子社会を考える—子どもを産み育てることに「夢」を持てる社会を [1998 White Paper on health and welfare: Thinking about birthrate decline: Creating a society were people can cherish the dream of raising children], Tokyo: Gyōsei.

Kurimoto, A. 栗本昭 (2004), 'Kaigai hikaku no naka de no 21 seikigata seikyōron' 海外比較のなかでの21世紀型生協論 [Studies on 21st century type cooperative associations in international comparison], in Y. Nakamura 中村陽一 and 21-Seiki Kōpu Kenkyū Sentā 21世紀コープ研究センター (eds) *21 seikigata seikyōron* 21世紀型生協論 [Studies on the 21st century type cooperative associations], Tokyo: Nihon Hyōronsha, 45–77.

Kurimoto, A. 栗本昭 (manuscript), 'Nihon no shakaiteki keizai no tōkeiteki haaku ni mukete' 日本の社会的経済の統計的把握に向けて [Towards a statistical evaluation of the social economy in Japan].

Matsubara, R. 松原隆一郎 (2005), *Bundan sareru keizai – Baburu to fukyō ga kyōson suru jidai* 分断される経済 –バブルと不況が共存する時代 [The fragmented economy: The age when an economic bubble and a recession co-exist], Tokyo: NHK Books.

Matsumoto, A. 松本淳 and Takahashi, M. 高端正幸 (2006), 'Taikeiteki na shakai hoshō seido kaikaku – Nenkin, iryō kaikaku de shakai no kizuna o kyōka suru' 体系的な社会保障制度改革―年金・医療改革で社会の絆を強化する [Systematic reform of the social security system: Strengthening social bonds through pension and health care reforms], in N. Jinno 神野直彦 and E. Ide 井手栄策 (eds) *Kibō no kōsō: Bunken, shakai hoshō, zaisei kaikaku no tōtaru puran* 希望の構想―分権・社会保障・財政改革のトータルプラン [An agenda of hope: A total plan for decentralization, social security, and financial reform], Tokyo: Iwanami Shoten, 95–146.

Mifune, M. 御船美智子 (2006), 'Seikatsu sōzōron kara mita seikyō' 生活創造論からみた生協 [Cooperative associations from the perspective of life creation studies], in Gendai Seikyōron Henshū Iinkai 現代生協論編集委員会 (ed.) *Gendai seikyōron no tankyū (rironhen)* 現代生協論の探求＜理論編＞ [Current theories of co-operative associations], Tokyo: Kōpo Shuppan, 59–82.

Mitsubishi sōgō kenkyūsho, Sangyō seisaku kenkyūbu 三菱総合研究所 産業政策研究部 Mitsubishi Research Institute, Industrial Policy Research Group (2002), *Pāto taimu chingin kakusa shukushō no rōdō juyō oyobi rōdō hiyō e no eikyō bunseki – Chingin kaksusa shukushō wa kigyō no kosuto futanzō nashi ni koyōsha no zōka o motarasu* パートタイム賃金格差縮小の労働需要および労働費用への影響分析―賃金格差縮小は企業のコスト負担増なしに雇用者の増加をもたらす [Impact analysis: How reduction of the wage gap between part-time and full-time workers affects labour demand and labour costs: Increasing the number of employees without raising the cost burden of firms]. Research Report: Mitsubishi Research Institute; July 2002, www.mri.co.jp/NEWS/2002/pr02080100.html.

Miura, M. 三浦まり (2003), 'Rōdō shijō kisei to fukushi kokka – Kokusai hikaku to Nihon no ichizuke' 労働市場規制と福祉国家―国際比較と日本の位置づけ [Labor market regulations and welfare states: International comparisions and Japan's ranking] in T. Uzuhashi 埋橋孝文 (ed.) *Hikaku no naka no fukushi kokka* 比較のなかの福祉国家 [Welfare states in comparison]. Kōza – Fukushi kokka no yukue 講座・福祉国家のゆくえ [Course in the future of the welfare state series], No. 2. Kyoto: Minerva Shobō, 109–33.

Miyamoto, T. 宮本太郎 (1997), 'Hikaku fukushi kokka no riron to genjitsu' 比較福祉国家の理論と現実 [Theories and evidences in the international comparison of welfare states], in N. Okazawa 岡沢憲芙 and T. Miyamoto 宮本太郎 (eds) *Hikaku fukushi kokkaron – Yuragi to orutanatibu* 比較福祉国家論―ゆらぎとオルタナティブ [Comparative studies of welfare states: Fluctuations and alternatives], Kyoto: Houritsu Bunka Sha, 12–43.

Miyamoto, T. 宮本太郎 (2002), 'Gurōbaruka to fukushi kokka no seiji – Atarashii fukushi seiji no bunmyaku' グローバル化と福祉国家の政治―新しい福祉政治の文脈 [Globalization and welfare state politics: The new context of welfare politics], in T. Miyamoto 宮本太郎

(ed.) *Fukushi kokka saihen no seiji* 福祉国家再編の政治 [The politics of welfare state restructuring]. Kōza – fukushi kokka no yukue 講座・福祉国家のゆくえ [Course in the future of the welfare state series], No. 1. Kyoto: Minerva Shobō, 1–35.

Miyamoto, T. 宮本太郎 (2003), 'Fukushi rejiimuron no tenkai to kadai – Esupin-Anderusen o koete?' 福祉レジーム論の展開と課題—エスピン・アンデルセンを越えて? [Issues and developments in studies of welfare regimes: Can we go beyond Esping-Andersen?], in T. Uzuhashi 埋橋孝文 (ed.) *Hikaku no naka no fukushi kokka* 比較のなかの福祉国家 [Welfare states in comparison]. Kōza – fukushi kokka no yukue 講座・福祉国家のゆくえ [Course in the future of the welfare state series], No. 2. Kyoto: Minerva Shobō, 11–41.

Miyamoto, T. 宮本太郎 (2006), 'Posuto fukushi kokka no gabananasu – Atarashii seiji taikō' ポスト福祉国家のガバナンス – 新しい政治対抗 [Post-welfare state governance: New political contestation], *Shisō* 思想, 983: 27–47.

Miyamoto, T. 宮本太郎 (2008), *Fukushi seiji – Nihon no seikatsu hoshō to demokurashii* 福祉政治 – 日本の生活保障とデモクラシー [Welfare politics: Livelihood security and democracy in Japan], Tokyo: Yūhikaku Publishing.

Mizushima, J. 水島治郎 (2002), 'Tairikugata fukushi kokka – Oranda ni okeru fukushi kokka no hatten to hen'yō' 大陸型福祉国家—オランダにおける福祉国家の発展と変容 [Continental European welfare states – The development and transformation of the Netherlands' welfare state], in T. Miyamoto 宮本太郎 (ed.) *Fukushi kokka saihen no seiji* 福祉国家再編の政治 [The politics of welfare state restructuring]. Kōza – fukushi kokka no yukue 講座・福祉国家のゆくえ [Course in the future of the welfare state series], No. 1. Kyoto: Minerva Shobō: 117–48.

Mizushima, J. 水島治郎 (2006), 'Oranda ni okeru arata na koyō, fukushi kokka moderu' オランダにおける新たな雇用・福祉国家モデル [The Netherlands' new model of employment and welfare state] *Shisō* 思想 983: 167–84.

Muramatsu, Y. 村松安子 (2005), *Jendā to kaihatsu'ron no keisei to tenkai – Keizaigaku no jendāka e no kokoromi* 「ジェンダーと開発」論の形成と展開—経済学のジェンダー化への試み [The formation and development of 'gender and development' studies: An attempt at gendering economics], Tokyo: Miraisha.

Murata, K.村田啓子 (2003), *Mikurodēta ni yoru kakei kōdō bunseki – Shōrai fuan to yobi chochiku* ミクロデータによる家計行動分析—将来不安と予備貯蓄 [Microdata analysis of households' financial behavior: Future anxiety and anticipatory saving]. Discussion Paper: Nippon Ginkō Kin'yū Kenkyūsho 日本銀行金融研究所 [Bank of Japan Institute for Monetary and Economic Studies]; 2003-J-9.

Murozumi, M. 室住眞麻子 (2006), *Nihon no hinkon – Kakei to jendā kara no kosatsu* 日本の貧困 – 家計とジェンダーからの考察 [Poverty in Japan: A look through the lens of household budgets and gender], Kyoto: Houritsu Bunka Sha.

Naikakufu 内閣府 Cabinet Office (2003a), *Heisei 15-nen ban kokumin seikatsu hakusho* 平成15年版国民生活白書 [2003 White Paper on the national lifestyle].

Naikakufu 内閣府 Cabinet Office (2003b), *Danjo kyōdō sankaku hakusho* Heisei 15-nen ban男女共同参画白書 平成15年版 [2003 White Paper on gender equality].

Naikakufu 内閣府 Cabinet Office (2004a), *Heisei 16-nen ban kokumin seikatsu hakusho* 平成16年版国民生活白書 [2004 White Paper on the national lifestyle].

Naikakufu 内閣府 Cabinet Office (2004b), *Shōshika shakai hakusho Heisei 16-nen ban* 少子化社会白書　平成16年版 [2004 White Paper on the birthrate-declining society].

Naikakufu 内閣府 Cabinet Office (2006), *Heisei 18-nendo nenji keizai zaisei hōkoku* 平成18年度年次経済財政報告 [2006 Annual report on the Japanese economy and public finance].

Naikakufu 内閣府 Cabinet Office (2007), 'Shotoku saibunpai chōsa to zenkoku shōhi jittai chōsa no Gini keisū no chigai ni tsuite' 所得再分配調査と全国消費実態調査のジニ係数の違いについて [On the difference between Gini coefficients in the Income Redistribution Survey and the National Survey of Family Income and Expenditure], *Konshū no Shihyō* 今週の指標 [Topics of Economic Indicators], No. 834.

Naikakufu 内閣府 Cabinet Office (2008), *Heisei 20-nendo nenji keizai zaisei hōkoku* 平成20年度年次経済財政報告 [2008 Annual report on the Japanese economy and public finance].

Naikakufu 内閣府 Cabinet Office (2009)、*Heisei 21-nendo nenji keizai zaisei hōkoku* 平成21年度年次経済財政報告 [2009 Annual report on the Japanese economy and public finance].

Naikakufu, Kyōsei shakai seisaku tōkatsukan 内閣府共生社会政策統括官 Cabinet Office, Director General for Policies on Cohesive Society (2008a), *Heisei 20-nen ban shōshika shakai hakusho* 平成20年版少子化社会白書 [2008 White Paper on the birthrate-declining society], http://www8.cao.go.jp/shoushi/whitePaper/w2008/20pdfhonpen/20honpen.html.

Naikakufu, Kyōsei shakai seisaku tōkatsukan 内閣府共生社会政策統括官 Cabinet Office, Director General for Policies on Cohesive Society (2008b), *Heisei 20-nen ban jisatsu taisaku hakusho* 平成20年版自殺対策白書 [2008 White Paper on suicide countermeasures], http://www8.cao.go.jp/jisatsutaisaku/whitepaper/index-w.html.

Naikakufu, Keisai shakai sōgō kenkyūsho 内閣府経済社会総合研究所 Cabinet Office, Economic and Social Research Institute (ESRI) (2006), 'Kōmuinsū no kokusai hikaku ni kansuru chōsa' 公務員数の国際比較に関する調査 [Studies on the number of public employees in international comparison], *Naikakufu Keizai Shakai Sōgō Kenkyūsho Kenkyūkai Hōkoku* 内閣府経済社会総合研究所研究会報告 [ESRI research group report], No. 21.

Naikakufu, Seisaku tōkatsukan shitsu 内閣府政策統括官室 Cabinet Office, Office of the Director-General for Policy Planning (2008a), *Sekai keizai no chōryū* 世界経済の潮流 [World economic trends], Vol. 1.

Naikakufu, Seisaku tōkatsukan shitsu 内閣府政策統括官室 Cabinet Office, Office of the Director-General for Policy Planning (2008b), *Sekai keizai no chōryū* 世界経済の潮流 [World economic trends], Vol. 2.

Nakamura, K. 中村圭介 (2004), 'Ōsugiru no ka, soretomo kōritsuteki ka – Nihon no kōmuin' 多すぎるのか、それとも効率的か－日本の公務員 [Excessive or efficient? Japan's civil servants], *Nihon Rōdō Kenkyū Zasshi* 日本労働研究雑誌 [Japan labour research journal], April: 18–21.

Nakamura, K. 中村圭介 (2006), *Seika shugi no shinjitsu* 成果主義の真実 [The truth about performance-based pay], Tokyo: Tōyō Keizai Shinpōsha.

Nakano, M. 中野麻美 (2006), *Rōdō danpingu* 労働ダンピング [Labour dumping], Tokyo: Iwanami Shoten.

Nakashima, T. 中嶋哲夫, Matsushige, H. 松繁寿和 and Umezaki, O. 梅崎修 (2004), 'Chingin to satei ni mirareru seikashugi dōnyū no kōka – Kigyōnai maikurodēta ni yoru bunseki' 賃金と査定に見られる成果主義導入の効果－企業内マイクロデータによる分析 [Impact of the introduction of performance-based pay on wages and evaluations: An analysis based on corporate microdata], *Nihon Keizai Kenkyū* 日本経済研究 [Japan economic research] 48: 18–33.

Nihon keieisha dantai renmei, Shin Nihonteki Keiei Shisutemu tō Kenkyū Purojekuto 日本経営者団体連盟、新・日本的経営システム等研究プロジェクト (ed.) (1994) *Shin Nihonteki keiei shisutem tō kenkyū purojekuto (chūkan hōkoku)* 新・日本的経営システ

ム等研究プロジェクト(中間報告) [The research project on the new Japanese style management (interim report)], Tokyo: Nikkeiren 日本経営者団体連盟 [Japan Federation of Employers' Associations].

Nihon keieisha dantai renmei, Shin Nihonteki Keiei Shisutemutou Kenkyū Purojekuto 日本経営者団体連盟、新・日本的経営システム等研究プロジェクト (ed.) (1995), *Shinjidai no 'Nihonteki keiei' chōsen subeki hōkō to sono gutai saku* 新時代の「日本的経営」挑戦すべき方向とその具体策 [Adapating Japanese style management to the new era: Critical challenges and concrete strategies], Tokyo: Nikkeiren 日本経営者団体連盟 [Japan Federation of Employers' Associations].

Nihon sōgō kenkyūsho, Chōsabu 日本総合研究所調査部 Japan Research Institute, Research Division (2004) *'04-nen nenkin kaikaku no hyōka to kadai* 04年年金改革の評価と課題 [2004 pension reform assessment and issues].

NIRA kenkyū sōsho NIRA 研究叢書 (2008), *Kakei ni nemuru 'kajō chochiku' – Kokumin seikatsu no shitsu no kōjō ni wa 'chochiku kara shōhi e' to iu hassō ga fukaketsu* 家計に眠る「過剰貯蓄」—国民生活の質の向上には「貯蓄から消費へ」という発想が不可欠 [Excessive saving lying dormant in household accounts: Changing preferences from saving to consumption is necessary to raise the nation's quality of life], Tokyo: NIRA.

Noble, G.W. (2006), 'Seijiteki riidāshippu to zaisei tōyūshi kaikaku – Seika to genkai' 政治的リーダーシップと財政投融資改革 – 成果と限界 [Political leadership and the reform of the Fiscal Investment and Loan Program: Outcomes and limitations], trans. M. Toyofuku 豊福実紀, in University of Tokyo, Institute of Social Science (ed.) *Koizumi kaikaku e no jidai* 小泉改革への時代 [Prelude to the Koizumi reform]. 'Ushinawareta 10 nen' o koete 「失われた10年」を超えて [Overcoming the 'lost decade' series], No. 2, Tokyo: University of Tokyo Press, 191–218.

Noda, S. 野田昌吾 (2006), 'Posuto shinhoshu shugi jidai no hoshu seiji', ポスト新保守主義時代の保守政治 [Conservative politics after the era of neo-conservatism], in T. Miyamoto 宮本太郎 (ed.) *Hikaku fukushi seiji – Seido tenkan no akutā to senryaku* 比較福祉政治 – 制度転換のアクターと戦略 [Comparative welfare politics: Actors and strategies in institutional change]. Hikaku seiji sōsho 比較政治叢書2 [Comparative politics series], No. 2. Tokyo: Waseda University Press, 26–43.

Okada, T. 岡田与好 (1981), 'Shakai seisaku to wa nani ka' 社会政策とは何か [What is social policy?] *Shakai Kagaku Kenkyū* 社会科学研究 [Journal of social science] (University of Tokyo), 32(5): 261–75.

Ōkōchi, K. 大河内一男 (1963), *Shakai seisaku (sōron) kaiteiban* 社会政策(総論)改訂版 [A theory of social policy (rev. edn.)], Tokyo: Yuhikaku Publishing.

Ōsawa, M. 大沢真理 (1986), *Igirisu shakai seisakushi – kyūhinhō to fukushi kokka* イギリス社会政策史 – 救貧法と福祉国家 [A history of British social policy: Poor laws and the welfare state], Tokyo: University of Tokyo Press.

Ōsawa, M. 大沢真理 (1993), *Kigyō chūshin shakai o koete – Gendai Nihon o 'jendā' de yomu* 企業中心社会を超えて—現代日本を<ジェンダー>で読む [Moving beyond the corporate-centred society: Reading contemporary Japan through 'gender'], Tokyo: Jiji Tsūshinsha.

Ōsawa, M. 大沢真理 (1996a), 'Shakai seisaku no jendā baiasu – Nikkan hikaku no kokoromi' 社会政策のジェンダー・バイアス—日韓比較のこころみ [Gender bias in social policy: A preliminary comparison of Japan and Korea], in H. Hara 原ひろ子, M. Maeda 前田瑞枝, and M. Ōsawa 大沢真理 (eds) *Ajia, Taiheiyō chiiki no josei seisaku to joseigaku* アジア・太平洋地域の女性政策と女性学 [Women's policies and women's studies in the Asia-Pacific region], Tokyo: Shin-yo-sha: 25–96.

Ōsawa, M. 大沢真理 (1996b), 'Shakai seisaku sōron e no jendā apurōchi – Kigyō chūshin shakai wa kōritsuteki ka' 社会政策総論へのジェンダー・アプローチ―企業中心社会は効率的か [A gende approach toward a comprehensive theory of social policy: Are corporate-centred societies efficient?], in H. Nishimura 西村豁通, Y. Nakanishi 中西洋, and E. Takenaka 竹中恵美子 (eds) *Kojin to kyōdōtai no shakai kagaku – Kindai ni okeru shakai to ningen* 個人と共同体の社会科学―近代における社会と人間 [The social science of the individual and the community: Modern society and people], Kyoto: Minerva Shobō, 123–42.

Ōsawa, M. 大沢真理 (1999a), 'Shakai hoshō seisaku – jendā bunseki no kokoromi' 社会保障政策―ジェンダー分析の試み [Social security policy: A preliminary gender analysis], in K. Mōri 毛利健三 (ed.) *Gendai Igirisu shakai seisakushi 1945–1990* 現代イギリス社会政策史1945－1990 [Social policy in Contemporary Britain, 1945–1990], Tokyo: Minerva Shobō, 89–153.

Ōsawa, M. 大沢真理 (1999b), 'Kaihatsu seisaku no hikaku jendā bunseki no moderu' 開発政策の比較ジェンダー分析のモデル [A model of comparative gender analysis in development policy], National Women's Education Center 国立婦人教育会館 (1999) *Jōsei no enpawāmento to kaihatsu – Tai, Neparu chōsa kara – Heisei 6 nendo – Heisei 10 nendo kaihatsu to jōsei ni kansuru bunka ōdanteki chōsa kenkyū hōkokusho* 女性のエンパワーメントと開発―タイ・ネパール調査から平成6年度－平成10年度開発と女性に関する文化横断的調査研究報告書 [Women's empowerment and development: A cross-cultural survey study of Nepal and Thailand from 1994 to 1998], 245–70.

Ōsawa, M.大沢真理 (1999c), 'Kōkyō kūkan o sasaeru shakai seisaku – seifuti netto o harikaeru' 公共空間を支える社会政策―セイフティネットを張り替える [Social policies to support public space: Mending the safety net], in N. Jinno 神野直彦 and M. Kaneko 金子勝 (eds) *Fukushi seifu e no teigen – Shakai hoshō no shintai kei o kōsō suru*「福祉政府」への提言－社会保障の新体系を構想する [A proposal for the welfare government: Planning a new system of social security], Tokyo: Iwanami Shoten, 186–223.

Ōsawa, M. 大沢真理 (2000),'Kōkyō kūkan o sasaeru seifuti netto' 公共空間を支えるセーフティ・ネット [The safety net supporting public space], in Y. Yamaguchi 山口定 and N. Jinno神野直彦 (eds) *2025 nen Nihon no kōsō* 2025年日本の構想 [A plan for Japan in 2025], Tokyo: Iwanami Shoten, 278–305.

Ōsawa, M. 大沢真理 (2002), *Danjo kyōdō sankaku shakai o tsukuru* 男女共同参画社会をつくる [Building a gender-equal society], Tokyo: NHK Books.

Ōsawa, M. 大沢真理 (2003), '"Dansei kaseginushi"-gata kara dakkyaku dekiru ka – Towareru zei, nenkin kaikaku no hōkō'「男性稼ぎ主」型から脱却できるか―問われる税・年金改革の方向 [Can we break free of the male breadwinner model? A critical look at the direction of tax and pension reforms], *Sekai* 世界, 711: 94–101.

Ōsawa, M. 大沢真理 (2004), 'Kore de wa kūdōka wa kuitomerarenai – Nenkin kaikaku kanrenhō no nakami to wa' これでは空洞化はくいとめられない―年金改革関連法の中身とは [This won't stop the hollowing out of the system: What is in the *Pension Reform Law*?], *Sekai* 世界, 729: 86–93.

Ōsawa, M. 大沢真理 (ed.) (2007), *Seikatsu no kyōdō – Haijo o koete tomo ni ikiru shakai e* 生活の協同―排除を超えてともに生きる社会へ [Livelihood cooperation: Overcoming exclusion to create a cohesive society], Tokyo: Nihon Hyōronsha.

Ōta, K. 太田清 (1999), 'Nihon no fubyōdōdo wa kakudai shite inai' 日本の不平等度は拡大していない [Inequality in Japan is not increasing], *Ronsō Tōyō Keizai* 論争東洋経済, 20: 172–7.

Ōta, K. 太田清 (2006a), 'Nihon no shotoku kakusa – OECD no "Tai-Nichi keizai shinsa hōkoku" ga shimesu mono' 日本の所得格差―OECDの「対日経済審査報告」が示すもの

[Income gaps in Japan: What the OECD's 'Economic Survey of Japan' tells us], *Business & Economic Review*, 16(10): 11–27.

Ōta, K. 太田清 (2006b), *Nihon no shotoku saibunpai – Kokusai hikaku de mita sono tokuchō* 日本の所得再分配―国際比較でみたその特徴 [Redistribution of personal income in Japan: A cross-country comparison], ESRI Discussion Paper series, No. 171.

Rōdōshō, Seisaku chōsabu 労働省政策調査部 Ministry of Labour, Policy Planning and Research Dept. (ed.) (1996), *Heisei 8-nen ban chingin rōdō jikan seido tō chōsa* 平成8年版賃金労働時間制度等総合調査 [1996 General survey on wages and working hours systems] Tokyo: Institute of Labour Administration 労務行政研究所.

Rōdōshō, Seisaku chōsabu 労働省政策調査部 Ministry of Labour, Policy Planning and Research Dept. (ed.) (1997), *Heisei 9-nen ban chingin rōdō jikan seido tō chōsa* 平成9年版賃金労働時間制度等総合調査 [1997 General survey on wages and working hours systems] Tokyo: Institute of Labour Administration 労務行政研究所.

Rōdōshō, Seisaku chōsabu 労働省政策調査部 Ministry of Labour, Policy Planning and Research Dept (ed.) (1998), *Heisei 10-nen ban chingin rōdō jikan seido tō chōsa* 平成10年版賃金労働時間制度等総合調査 [1998 General survey on wages and working hours systems] Tokyo: Institute of Labour Administration 労務行政研究所.

Rōdōshō, Seisaku chōsabu 労働省政策調査部 Ministry of Labour, Policy Planning and Research Dept (ed.) (1999), *Heisei 11-nen ban chingin rōdō jikan seido tō chōsa* 平成11年版賃金労働時間制度等総合調査 [1999 General survey on wages and working hours systems] Tokyo: Institute of Labour Administration 労務行政研究所.

Rōdōshō, Seisaku chōsabu 労働省政策調査部 Ministry of Labour, Policy Planning and Research Dept (ed.) (2000), *Heisei 12-nen ban chingin rōdō jikan seido tō chōsa* 平成12年版賃金労働時間制度等総合調査 [1996 General survey on wages and working hours systems] Tokyo: Institute of Labour Administration 労務行政研究所.

Scharpf, F.W. (2005), 'Gurōbaru keizaika no kokusai kyōsōryoku to fukushi kokka – Shakai hoshō, koyō, zeisei no ruikei bunseki' グローバル経済化の国際競争力と福祉国家―社会保障・雇用・税制の類型分析 [International competitiveness and welfare states under economic globalization: Typological analysis of social security, employment and tax systems], in J. Yamaguchi 山口二郎, T. Miyamoto 宮本太郎, and M. Tsubogō 坪郷實 (eds) *Posuto fukushi kokka to sōsharu gabanansu* ポスト福祉国家とソーシャル・ガバナンス [Post-welfare states and social governance], Kyoto: Minerva Shobō, 131–62.

Seikatsu keizai seisaku kenkyūsho 生活経済政策研究所 Economic Policy Institute for Quality Life (2007), *Zeisei kaikaku ni mukete – Kōhei de zeishū chōtatsuryoku ga takai zeisei o mezashite* 税制改革に向けて―公平で税収調達力が高い税制をめざして [Reforming the tax system to achieve fairness and high revenues], Seikatsuken Books series, No. 25. Tokyo: Economic Policy Institute for Quality Life.

Shakai-hoken-chō 社会保険庁 Social Insurance Agency (2006), *Heisei 17-nen no kokumin nenkin no kanyū, nōfu jōkyō* 平成17年の国民年金の加入・納付状況 [2006 Report on National Pension enrollment and payments].

Shakai-hoken-chō 社会保険庁 Social Insurance Agency (2007), *Heisei 18-nen no kokumin nenkin no kanyū, nōfu jōkyō* 平成18年の国民年金の加入・納付状況 [2007 Report on national pension enrollment and payments].

Shakai hoshō kenkyūsho 社会保障研究所 Social Security Research Institute (ed.) (1987), *Suēden no shakai hoshō* スウェーデンの社会保障 [Social security in Sweden], Tokyo: University of Tokyo Press.

Shakai hoshō kenkyūsho 社会保障研究所 Social Security Research Institute (ed.) (1989),

Nishi Doitsu no shakai hoshō 西ドイツの社会保障 [Social security in West Germany], Tokyo: University of Tokyo Press.

Shakai hoshō kokumin kaigi 社会保障国民会議 National Commission on Social Security (2008a), *Chūkan hōkoku* 中間報告 [Interim Report]. Available at http://www.kantei.go.jp/jp/singi/syakaihosyoukokuminkaigi.

Shakai hoshō kokumin kaigi 社会保障国民会議 National Commission on Social Security (2008b), *Saishū hōkoku* 最終報告 [Final Report], Available at http://www.kantei.go.jp/jp/singi/syakaihosyoukokuminkaigi.

Shakai hoshō shingikai, Nenkin bukai 社会保障審議会年金部会 Social Security Council, Pension Group (2003), *Nenkin seido kaisei ni kansuru iken* 年金制度改正に関する意見 [Opinions on revising the pension system].

Shakai hoshō seido shingikai 社会保障制度審議会 Social Security System Advisory Council (1994), *Shakai hoshō shōraizō iinkai dai-2 ji hōkoku* 社会保障将来像委員会第2次報告 [2nd report of the Committee on Envisioning the Future of the Social Security System].

Shakai hoshō seido shingikai 社会保障制度審議会 Social Security System Advisory Council (1995), *Shakai hoshō taisei no saikōchiku – Anshin shite kuraseru 21 seiki no shakai o mezashite* 社会保障体制の再構築－安心して暮らせる21世紀の社会を目指して [Restructuring the social security system to enable living with peace of mind].

Shakaiteki na engo o yōsuru hitobito ni taisuru shakai fukushi no arikata ni kansuru kentōkai 社会的な援護を要する人々に対する社会福祉のあり方に関する検討会 Investigative Committee for the Shape of Social Welfare for the Socially Vulnerable (2000), *Shakaiteki na engo o yōsuru hitobito ni taisuru shakai fukushi no arikata ni kansuru kentōkai hōkokusho* 社会的な援護を要する人々に対する社会福祉のあり方に関する検討会報告書 [Report of the Investigative Committee for the Shape of Social Welfare for the Socially Vulnerable], http://www1.mhlw.go.jp/shingi/s0012/s1208-2_16.html.

Shibagaki, K. 柴垣和夫 (1985), 'Nihon no fukushi kin'yū: Hikazei chochiku seido to jūtaku kin'yū o chūshin ni' 日本の福祉金融：非課税貯蓄制度と住宅金融を中心に [Welfare financing in Japan: The tax-exempt savings system and housing finance], in University of Tokyo Institute of Social Science (ed.) *Fukushi kokka* 福祉国家 [Welfare state series], No. 5. Tokyo: University of Tokyo Press: 109–69.

Shinkawa, T. 新川敏光 (2005), *Nihongata fukushi rejiimu no hatten to hen'yō* 日本型福祉レジームの発展と変容 [Development and transformation of the Japanese-style welfare regime], Kyoto: Minerva Shobō.

Shirai, K. 白井邦彦 (2005), 'Kinnen ni okeru Nihon no koyō hogo seido kaikaku no kokusaiteki ichi 2 – mō hitotsu no "hō to keizaigaku"' 近年における日本の雇用保護制度改革の国際的位置(下)－もうひとつの「法と経済学」[International ranking of recent reforms in Japan's employment protection system, part 2: Another form of 'law and economics'], *Aoyama Keizai Ronshū* 青山経済論集 [The Aoyama Journal of Economics], 57(3): 103–31.

Shirahase, S. 白波瀬佐和子 (2006), 'Fubyōdōka Nihon no nakami – Setai to jendā ni chakumoku shite' 不平等化日本の中身 – 世帯とジェンダーに着目して [Inside Japan's growing inequality: A closer look at households and gender], in S. Shirahase (ed.) *Henka suru shakai no fubyōdō – Shōshi kōreika ni hisomu kakusa* 変化する社会の不平等 – 少子高齢化にひそむ格差 [Inequality in a changing society: Hidden disparities in the aging society], Tokyo: University of Tokyo Press, 47–78.

Shirahase, S. 白波瀬佐和子 (2008), 'Kodomo no iru setai no keizai kakusa ni kansuru kokusai hikaku' 子どものいる世帯の経済格差に関する国際比較 [A cross-national study of income inequality among households with small children], in Shakai Seisaku

Gakkai 社会政策学会 [Society for the Study of Social Policy] (ed.) *Kosodate o meguru shakai seisaku: Sono kinō to gyaku kinō* 子育てをめぐる社会政策: その機能と逆機能 [Social Policies on Raising Children: Functions and Reverse Functions], Shakai Seisaku Gakkaishi 社会政策学会誌 [Journal of Social Policy and Labor Studies], No. 19: 3–20. Kyoto: Houritsu Bunka Sha.

Shirahase, S. 白波瀬佐和子 (2009), *Nihon no fubyōdō o kangaeru: Shōshi kōrei shakai no kokusai hikaku* 日本の不平等を考える – 少子高齢社会の国際比較 [Inequality in Japan: The declining birthrate/aging society in international comparison], Tokyo: University of Tokyo Press.

Sōmushō, Tōkeikyoku 総務省統計局 Ministry of Internal Affairs and Communication, Statistics Bureau (2002), *Heisei 13-nen shakai seikatsu kihon chōsa – Chōsa kekka* 平成13年社会生活基本調査 – 調査結果 [2002 Survey on time use and leisure activities – Survey results].

Sōmushō, Tōkeikyoku 総務省統計局 Ministry of Internal Affairs and Communication, Statistics Bureau (2006), *Heisei 17-nen shakai seikatsu kihon chōsa – Chōsa kekka* 平成13年社会生活基本調査 – 調査結果 [2006 Survey on time use and leisure activities – Survey results].

Sōrifu, Danjo kyōdō sankaku shitsu 総理府男女共同参画室 Prime Minister's Office, Office for Gender Equality (ed.) (1997), *Danjo kyōdō sankaku 2000 nen puran & bijon* 男女共同参画2000年プラン&ビジョン [Plan and vision for gender equality in 2000], Tokyo: Ministry of Finance, Printing Bureau.

Suehiro, A. 末廣昭 (ed.) (2006), *Higashi Ajia no fukushi shisutemu no yukue – Kigyōnai fukushi to kokka no shakai hoshō seido – Ronten no seiri to dētashū* 東アジアの福祉システムの行方－企業内福祉と国家の社会保障制度－論点の整理とデータ集 [Outlook for East Asian welfare systems – Corporate welfare programs and social security systems—Issues and data compilation], 平成17－19年度科学研究費補助金 (基盤(B) 研究成果報告書 Final Report for FY2005–2007 Grant-in-aid for scientific research (B).

Suzuki, H. 鈴木準 (2005), 'Kōmuin jinkenhi no kokusai hikaku' 公務員人件費の国際比較 [Personnel costs of public employees in international comparison], *Current Issue on Fiscal Policy* DIR資本市場調査部情報, No. 70. Tokyo: Daiwa Institute of Research.

Sumitani, S. 炭谷茂, Ōyama, H. 大山博, and Hosouchi, N. 細内信孝 (eds) (2004), *Sōsharu inkurūjon to shakai kigyō no yakuwari – Chiiki fukushi keikaku suishin no tame ni* ソーシャルインクルージョンと社会企業の役割 地域福祉計画推進のために [Social inclusion and the role of social enterprises: Working to implement local welfare programs], Tokyo: Gyōsei.

Suzuki, W. 鈴木亘 (2008), 'Shakai hoshō kankei no tōkei ni okeru kadai' 社会保障関係の統計における課題 [Issues regarding statistics relating to social security], *Tokei kaikaku e no teigen – 'Senmon-chi to keiken-chi no kyōyūka' o mezashite* 統計改革への提言「専門知と経験知の共有化」を目指して [Prospects for statistical reform: Towards the sharing of expert knowledge and experience knowledge], NIRA Report, October 2008.

Tabata, H. 田端博邦 (1989), 'Shakai hoshō no rekishi' 社会保障の歴史 [A history of social security], in Social Security Research Institute 社会保障研究所 (ed.) *Furansu no shakai hoshō* フランスの社会保障 [Social security in France], Tokyo: University of Tokyo Press, 85–101.

Takanashi, A. 高梨昌 (ed.) (1994), *Kawaru Nihongata koyō* 変わる日本型雇用 [Japan's changing employment system], Tokyo: Nihon Keizai Shinbunsha.

Taguchi, S. 田口さつき (2004), 'Chingin to bukka geraku – Kigyō no jinkenhi yokusei no dōkō', 賃金と物価下落　企業の人件費抑制の動向 [Falling wages and prices: Outlook for companies' labour cost reductions], *Nōrin Kin'yū* 農林金融 57(8): 16–22.

Takegawa, S. 武川正吾 (1985), 'Rōdō keizai kara shakai seisaku e – Shakai seisakuron no saisei no tame ni 労働経済から社会政策へ–社会政策論の再生のために [From labour economics to social policy: Reviving the debate on social policy], in Social Security Research Institute社会保障研究所 (ed.) *Fukushi seisaku no kihon mondai* 福祉政策の基本問題 [Fundamental problems in welfare policy], Tokyo: University of Tokyo Press, 3–32.

Takegawa, S. 武川正吾 (ed.) (2006), *Fukushi shakai no kachi ishiki – Shakai seisaku to shakai ishiki no keiryō bunseiki* 福祉社会の価値意識 – 社会政策と社会意識の計量分析 [Value consciousness in welfare societies: A quantitative analysis of social policy and social consciousness], Tokyo: University of Tokyo Press.

Takegawa, S. 武川正吾 (2006), 'Nenkin shakaigaku no kōso – Nihon no 2004 nen nenkin kaikaku', 年金社会学の構想- 日本の2004年年金改革 [Conceiving the sociology of pensions: Japan's 2004 pension reforms], in S. Takegawa 武川正吾 and I. Hegyon イ・ヘギョン (eds) (2006) *Fukushi rejiimu no Nikkan hikaku – Shakai hoshō, jendā, rōdō shijō* 福祉レジームの日韓比較 – 社会保障・ジェンダー・労働市場 [Welfare regimes in Japan and Korea: Social security, gender and labour markets], Tokyo: University of Tokyo Press: 73–96.

Tachibanaki, T. 橘木俊詔 (2005), *Kigyō fukushi no shūen – Kakusa no jidai ni dō taiō subeki ka* 企業福祉の終焉 – 格差の時代にどう対応すべきか [The demise of corporate welfare: What must be done in the age of disparity], Tokyo: Chūkōshinsho.

Tachibanaki, T. 橘木俊詔 (2006), *Kakusa shakai – Nani ga mondai na no ka* 格差社会 – 何が問題なのか [What is the downside to a differentiatial society?], Tokyo: Iwanami Shinsho.

Tachibanaki, T. 橘木俊詔 and Urakawa, Kunio 浦川邦夫 (2006), *Nihon no hinkon kenkyū* 日本の貧困研究 [Research on poverty in Japan], Tokyo: University of Tokyo Press.

Tamiya, Y. 田宮遊子 (2003), 'Kōteki nenkin seido no hensen – Jendā shiten kara no saikō' 公的年金制度の変遷－ジェンダー視点からの再考 [The transformation of the public pension system in Japan: Reconsideration from a gender perspective], *Kokuritsu Josei Kyōiku Kaikan Kenkyū Kiyō* 国立女性教育会館研究紀要 [Journal of the National Women's Education Centre of Japan], 7: 57–68.

Tanaka, T. 田中拓道 (2005), 'Furansu ni okeru shakaiteki hōsetsuron no keifu' フランスにおける社会的包摂論の系譜 [The lineage of discourses of social inclusion in France]. In Shakai Seisaku Gakkai dai-111 kai taikai hōkoku 社会政策学会第111回大会報告 [Panel session presentation at the 111th Annual Conference of the Society for the Study of Social Policy].

Tanaka, N. 田中夏子 (2004a), 'Itaria shakaiteki kyōdō kumiai no keisei katei to genkyō, kadai – Shijō no saikōchiku no ninaite to naru kyōdōgawa no torikumi to wa' イタリア社会的協同組合の形成過程と現況、課題－市場の再構築の担い手となる協同側の取り組みとは [Origins, current status and issues of social cooperatives in Italy: responses of cooperative sector as an agent for reconstructing markets], *Kyōdo no hakken* 協同の発見 [The discovery of cooperation], supplemental issue (*Itaria shakaiteki kyōdō kumiai chōsa hōkoku* イタリア社会的協同組合調査報告 [Report on social cooperatives in Italy]): 4–23.

Tanaka, N. 田中夏子 (2004b), *Itaria shakaiteki keizai no chiiki tenkai* イタリア社会的経済の地域展開 [Regional development of social economy in Italy], Tokyo: Nihon Keizai Hyoronsha.

Tokoro, M. 所道彦 (2003), 'Hikaku no naka no kazoku seisaku – Kazoku no tayōka to fukushi kokka' 比較のなかの家族政策－家族の多様化と福祉国家 [A comparison of family policies: Family diversification and welfare states], in T. Uzuhashi 埋橋孝文 (ed.) *Hikaku no naka no fukushi kokka* 比較のなかの福祉国家 [Welfare states in comparison]. Kōza – Fukushi kokka no yukue 講座・福祉国家のゆくえ [Course in the future of the welfare state series], No. 2. Kyoto: Minerva Shobō, 267–96.

Tōkyō daigaku, Shakai kagaku kenkyūsho 東京大学社会科学研究所 University of Tokyo Institute of Social Science (ed.) (1984–5), *Fukushi kokka* 福祉国家 [Welfare states series], No. 1–6. Tokyo: University of Tokyo Press.

Toyofuku, Y. 豊福裕二 (2009), 'Beikoku sabupuraimu rōn no yūshi jittai' 米国サブプライムローンの融資実態 [The truth about subprime lending in the US], *Gakujutsu no Dōkō* 学術の動向 [Trends in the Sciences] August, 60–5.

Tsumura, A. 都村敦子 (2000), 'Jidō teate to sedaikan rentai' 児童手当と世代間連帯 [Child allowances and intergenerational solidarity], *Shūkan Shakai Hoshō* 週間社会保障 [Social security weekly], 2091: 24–7.

Tsuruta, R. 鶴田立一 (2003), 'Kōteki shishutsu no keizai hakyū kōka – Chiiki sangyō renkan bunseki ni yoru kōsatsu' 公的支出の経済波及効果―地域産業連関分析による考察 [The ripple effects of public expenditures: Findings based on regional input output analysis], *Chiiki Seisaku Chōsa* 地域政策調査 [Regional policy studies], No. 15. Tokyo: Development Bank of Japan.

Uchiyama, T. 内山哲朗 (2004), 'Kaidai: Sādo sekutā no dōtai to shakaiteki kigyō' 解題 サードセクターの動態と社会的企業 [Translator's afterword: Third sector dynamics and social enterprises] in C. Boruzaga, J. Dufuruni *Shakaiteki kigyō koyō/fukushi no EU sādo sekutā* 社会的企業 雇用・福祉のEUサードセクター [Japanese translation of C. Borzaga. and J. Defourny (eds) *The emergence of social enterprise* (London: Routledge, 2001)], Tokyo: Nihon Keizai Hyōronsha, 501–28.

Uzuhashi, T. 埋橋孝文 (1997), *Gendai fukushi kokka no kokusai hikaku: Nihon moderu no ichizuke to tenbō* 現代福祉国家の国際比較―日本モデルの位置づけと展望 [Contemporary welfare states in cross-national comparison: How to locate and envisage the Japanese model], Tokyo: Nihon Hyōronsha.

Uzuhashi, T. 埋橋孝文 (1999), 'Kōteki fujo seido no kokusai hihaku – OECD nijūyonkakoku no naka no Nihon no ichi' 公的扶助制度の国際比較―OECD二四カ国のなかの日本の位置 [An international comparison of public assistance systems: Japan's ranking among 24 OECD nations], *Kaigai Shakai Hoshō Kenkyū* 海外社会保障研究 [Journal of Overseas Social Security Research (National Institute of Population and Social Security Research)], 127: 72–82.

Uzuhashi, T. 埋橋孝文 (2002), 'Sengyō shufu (katabataraki) setai e no "seisakuteki hairyo" – Ōsutoraria, Doitsu, Nihon, Suēden, Igirisu, Amerika rokkakoku no zei, shakai hoshō seido' 専業主婦(片働き)世帯への「政策的配慮」―オーストラリア・ドイツ・日本・スウェーデン・イギリス・アメリカ6カ国の税・社会保障制度' ['Policy considerations' given to male breadwinner households in six nations – Australia, Germany, Japan, Sweden, the UK and the US – in tax and social security systems], *Keizaigaku Ronkyū* 経済学論究 [The Journal of Economics of Kwansei Gakuin University], 56(3): 47–65.

Yamada, A. 山田篤裕 (1999), 'Shotoku hojo, shakai kikin' 所得補助・社会基金 [Income support and social funds], in S. Takegawa 武川正吾 and Y. Shionoya 塩野谷祐一 (eds) *Igirisu* イギリス [The United Kingdom]. Senshin shokoku no shakai hoshō 先進諸国の社会保障 [Social security in developed nations series], No. 1. Tokyo: University of Tokyo Press, 199–225.

Yamada, A. 山田篤裕 (2005), Koyō to nenkin – kōreiki ni okeru kinrō shūnyū no shotoku kakusa, teishotokuritsu e no eikyō 雇用と年金―高齢期における勤労収入の所得格差・

低所得率への影響 [Employment and pensions in old age: The effects of wage income earned by older people on income disparity and the low income rate], in *Wagakuni no shotoku, shisan kakusa no jisshō bunseki to shakai hoshō no kyūfu to futan no arikata ni kansuru kenkyū: Heisei 16-nendo sōkatsu kenkyū hōkokusho: Heisei 16-nendo Kōseirōdō kagaku kenkyūhi hojōkin (seisaku kagaku suishin kenkyū jigyō) kenkyū hōkokusho.* 我が国の所得,資産格差の実証分析と社会保障の給付と負担の在り方に関する研究: 平成16年度総括研究報告書: 平成16年度厚生労働科学研究費補助金(政策科学推進研究事業)研究報告書 [Empirical research on income and asset differentials and social security benefits and contributions in Japan: 2004 summary report on the results of studies funded through the Ministry of Health, Labour and Welfare's 2004 research grants under the 'policy science research promotion program'], 135–55.

Yamada, A. 山田篤裕, Shikata, M. 四方理人,Tanaka, S. 田中聡一郎 and Komamura, K. 駒村康平 (2008), 'Hinkon kijun no kasanari: OECD sōtaiteki hinkon kijun to seikatsu hogo kijun no kasanari' 貧困基準の重なり、ＯＥＣＤ相対的貧困基準と生活保護基準の重なり [Overlapping Standards of Poverty: How Interchangeable are the OECD Relative Poverty Standard and Japan's Public Assistance Standard], Shakai Seisaku Gakkai dai-111 kai taikai hōkoku 社会政策学会第117回大会報告 [Panel session presentation of the 117th Annual Conference of the Society for the Study of Social Policy].

Yoshinaka, T. 吉中季子 (2007), 'Nihon ni okeru munenkin, muhoken setai no jittai to kadai' 日本における無年金、無保険世帯の実態と課題 [Issues and evidences on Japanese households without pensions or health insurance], in H. Fukuhara 福原宏幸 (ed.) *Shakaiteki haijo/hōsetsu to shakai seisaku* 社会的排除／包摂と社会政策 [Social exclusion/inclusion and social policy], Kyoto: Houritsu Bunka Sha, 153–76.

Zaimushō 財務省 Ministry of Finance (2003), *Zaisei no genjō to kongo no arikata* 財政の現状と今後のあり方 [The current state of public finances and recommendations for the future], http://www.mof.go.jp/jouhou.shukei/sy014.htm.

Zaimushō 財務省 Ministry of Finance (2006), *Nihon no zaisei o kangaeru* 日本の財政を考える [Thinking about Japan's public finances].

Zaimushō 財務省 Ministry of Finance, Policy Research Institute (2002), *Todōfuken no keizai kasseika ni okeru seifu no yakuwari: seisan kōritsu, koyō sōshutsu kara no kōsatsu* 都道府県の経済活性化における政府の役割―生産効率・雇用創出からの考察 [The role of government in stimulating economy on prefectural levels: Production efficiency and job creation]. Available at www.mof.go.jp/jouhou/soken/kenkyu/zk059/zk059dl.htm.

Zenkoku shichō kai, Zenkoku chōson kai, Kokumin kenkō hoken chūōkai 全国市長会・全国町村会・国民健康保険中央会 Japan Association of City Mayors, National Association of Towns and Villages and the All-Japan Federation of National Health Insurance Organizations (2005), *Kōsei rōdōshō, iryō seido kōzō kaikaku shian ni tsuite* 厚生労働省・医療制度構造改革試案について [Comments on the Ministry of Health, Labour and Welfare's proposal to restructure the health care system], 26 October.

Index

Note: page numbers in **bold** refer to figures and tables.

Abe, Shinzō 150–1, 160, 162
ability-to-pay principle 67, 170–1
accident compensation insurance 68, 140, 175
Advisory Council *see* Prime Minister's Advisory Council on the Social Security System
ALMPs (active labour market policies) 24, 90, 185n3
altruism 33
Angel Plan 60–1, 116 *see also* New Angel Plan
Asian currency crisis 38, 65
Asō, Tarō 1, 160
assistantialismo 177
Australia: elder care in 114; net burden of households 102; non-regular workers in 96, 98–9; unpaid work in 91; welfare regime in 13, 17–18

Basic Law for a Gender-Equal Society 68–9, 125
Basic Pension (Japan) 49–50, 124, 128–9
Basic pension identification number 142, 150
Belgium, non-regular workers in 96
benefits: cash 32, 66, 87, 102, 114, 165–6, 168–9; indexation rate of 127–8; in kind 87, 114; take-up rate of 120
Beveridge Plan 8–10
block generation *see* Japan, baby boom generation in
Bretton Woods system 11–12, 36–8

Canada: ALMP in 90; minimum wage in 139; unemployment in 147; unpaid work in 91; welfare regime in 13

capability approach 26–7, 29
caring labour 179
CEDAW (Convention on the Elimination of All Forms of Discrimination Against Women) 53
CGM (Consorzio Gino Mattarelli) 176–8
child allowances: Japanese private 72; Japanese state 52–3, 68; level of 168; in Scandanavian model 14; in three welfare government scheme 166; in work/life balance model 24
child care: choice in services 61, 67; and social cooperatives 177; as universal service 167, 173
child-rearing: burden of 2, 10, 12, 64, 82–3, 159; and commodification of labour 16; in social democratic systems 14; social support of 61 *see also* household production
Child Welfare Act 65, 67
children: in Beveridge report 10; income transfers to 14, 166; and poverty 84, **123**, 138–9
China: reforms in 13; savings in 184; unemployment in 147
co-production 179
Cold War 12–13
collective bargaining 7, 94, 140 *see also* labour unions
collectives *see* workers' cooperatives
communities, sustainable 166
company men 58–9
compensation, performance-based 57
Comprehensive Survey of Living Conditions 83–4, 141, 162, 188n9
construction government *see* Japan, public investment in

216   Index

consumer cooperatives 6, 93–4, 176, 180–1
consumption tax 65, 87
cooperative organizations 5, 8, 173
corporate social responsibility (CSR) 158, 180
corporate tax 170
corporatism 15, 48
Council for Gender Equality 62–3, 124–5
Council on Economic and Fiscal Policy (CEFP) 124, 138, 189n8

de-commodification 14–16, 19, 22, 185n2
de-familialization 19, 23, 61, 68–9
deferred adjudication 151
Denmark: inequality in 139; non-regular workers in 96; pensions in 103; social economy in 174; social security contributions in 99
dependence 34, 58
developed countries 7, 11–13, 23, 30
developing countries 11–12, 23, 26, 30, 44–5
developmental strategies, pro-poor 38
devolution 126
disabled persons 108, 178–9
discrimination, indirect 154, 189n23
distribution: indeterminacy of 31–2; primary 16
divorce: no-fault 79; and pensions 112; and suicide 159
DPJ (Democratic Party of Japan) 1, 131–2, 138

economic crises: cycle of 22, 36–7; and economic policy 38–9; effects of by country **39**; factors triggering 183–4
economic growth: in Japan 135; policy for 7; and social inclusion 181–3; as substitute for welfare 17; and suicide 159; and trickle-down effect 38
economic policy, autonomous 12
Economic Security Index (ESI) 94
education, as universal service 167
EHI (Employees' Health Insurance) 48–9, 63, 149, 186n6
elder care 69, 114, 133, 161
employee benefits 24, 75–6
employees: 'multi-tracking', 70; non-regular **73**; political rights of 36; precarious 44, 169; real incomes of 135–6, **136**; wives of 50–1, 53
Employees' Health Insurance *see* EHI
Employees' Pension Funds (EPF) 49

Employees' Pension Insurance *see* EPI
employer federations 7, 94
employment: full 14; lifetime 47–8, 69–70, 153; long-term 40, 70, 72; non-regularization of 129, 145, 153, 155; precarious 44; public sector 86
employment insurance 48, 68, 148–9, 190n9
employment performance 16–17, 48, 59, 85, 101, 185n3
employment policy 7, 31, 185n1
employment protection 187n10; *see also* lifetime employment
employment protection security index (EPSI) 94–5
EPA (Economic Planning Agency) 91, 162
EPI (Employees' Pension Insurance) 48–50, 74–6, 127, 129, 132, 140–3, 149–51, 154, 169, 190n9
Equal Employment Opportunity Law (Japan) 53, 125, 153–4
equality of opportunity 179
Esping-Andersen, Gøsta 13, 15–16, 18–20, 22–3, 48, 51, 55, 97–8, 129, 178, 186n1
Europe, social economy in 173–4
European Union: social exclusion and 41–2, 179; unemployment in 97
exchange rates: fixed 11; floating 12, 36–7

families: dissolution of 55; dual-career 83; formation of 53, 57, 81, 85; and livelihood security 7–8, 51, 120; support for 85
family allowances 19, 72, 163
family values, traditional 131
family wage hypothesis 10, 23, 31
feminist economics 33
FILP (Fiscal Investment and Loan Program) 143, 153, 207
financial liberalization 22, 36–8
Finland: consumer cooperatives in 180; employment security in 95; inequality in 139; non-regular workers in 96; pensions in 103; social economy in 21, 93, 174
Fiscal Investment and Loan Program *see* FILP
fiscal reconstruction 65
France: employment practices in 96; government spending in 87; inequality in 43; public sector in 86, 88; social economy in 21, 174; social security fund in 165; unemployment in 147; welfare regime in 14–15, 40–1

friendly societies 8, 165
Fukuda, Yasuo 158–9
functional equivalents 7, 16–17

gender: and employment protection 48, 59; and inequality 182; and livelihood security 2–3, 24; and pensions 50–1, 104, 113, 129, 131; and power relations 2, 12–13, 116, 133, 153; and recognition of needs 28–9; and social policy formation 45–6; and utility 29; and wages 32 *see also* men; women
gender equality: and efficiency 179; in Japan 133, 153; Nordic countries' policies for 24; as objective 20 *see also* Council for Gender Equality; Vision of Gender Equality
gender mainstreaming 63, 128
gender roles 24, 32–3, 67
General Survey on Systems of Wages and Working Hours *see* General Survey on Working Conditions
General Survey on Working Conditions 71, 75, 149
General Survey on Working Conditions 187n10
Germany: ALMP in 90; divorce in 112–13; elder care in 114; government spending in 87; inequality in 43, 139; male breadwinner model in 53; net burden of households 102; non-regular workers in 96, 99; pensions in 112–13; public sector in 86, 88; social economy in 21, 174; social security fund in 165; unemployment in 147; unpaid work in 91; welfare regime in 14–15 *see also* West Germany
Gini coefficient 17, 43, 84, 104, **121**, 159, 161, 182
global financial crisis 1, 143
globalization: and jobless recovery 40; and livelihood security 4; and sovereignty 36
Gold Plan 60–1 *see also* New Gold Plan
goods and services, relations of production of *see* production, relations of
Government Pension Investment Fund (GPIF) 143
Greece 95, 103, 116, 174

Hashimoto, Ryūtaro 62 *see also* Hashimoto administration
Hashimoto administration, Six Major Reforms 57, 62, 64–6, 69, 124, 143
Hata, Tsutomu 60

health care: for older people 134; as universal service 167
health insurance: coverage of 141, 145–7; eligibility for 140; national *see* National Health Insurance (NHI)
honebuto policy 124–7, 131, 135, 153
Hosokawa, Morihiro 60 *see also* Hosokawa administration
Hosokawa administration: 21st Century Welfare Vision 60–1; and electoral reform 60
hotel costs 59, 133–4
household production 33
households: as benefit recipients 60, 62, 66, 68, 131; budgets of 29, 33, 53–4, 80, 83, 85; in economic theory 29; elderly 139, 162, 184; lone mother 52, 83, 87, 116, 155; male breadwinner 104, 112–13, 123, 128–30, 156; net burdens of 102; production within 32
housewives 50
housework: absence of allowances for 10; amount of time spent in 91; burden of 2, 4, 12, 33, 53, 159; and marriage 82–3, 92; in relations of production 30 *see also* household production
housing benefits 71, 87, 169
Hungary 101, 114–15, 159

IMF (International Monetary Fund) 12, 38–9, 182
income insufficiency 26
income interruption 10, 15
income tax 53, 61, 74–5, 102, 119, 125, 169–70
income transfers: in late 20th century welfare state 2, 11–12; outcomes of 18, 45
independence 14, 34, 158
inequality, degree of *see* Gini coefficient
international trade, liberalization of 11
Ireland, non-regular workers in 96
Italy: employment practices in 96; livelihood cooperation in 173, 175–6, 178; non-regular workers in 96; social economy in 5, 93, 173, 175; welfare regimes in 14

Japan: 21st century social welfare reforms in 42–3, 160; 1980s social welfare reforms in 52; 1990s social welfare reforms in 56–7, 60, 68; 2011 earthquake and tsunami in 6; ageing population of 4;

218 Index

Japan (*continued*)
  baby boom generation in 71–2; birth rate in 66–7, 81–2, 132, 157–8; birth rate in *see also* total fertility rate (TFR); child care in 116; classification of welfare regime 19–20, 23; commodity production in 85; consumer cooperatives in 181; corporate benefits in 4–5, 71–2; corporate-centred society of 58, 158; currency of *see* yen; economic security in 94; elder care in 114–16; elder care in *see also* long-term care insurance; electoral system of 6, 60; employment practices in 47–8, 57, 69–70, 74, 94–5; family support in 103; gender of labour force in 48; health insurance system in 48–9; household finances in 53, 80–1; income tax in 52–3, 103, 163; inequality in 43, 83–5, 104, 120, **121**, 123, 139, 153, 162–3, 184; labour costs in 75–6, **76–8**, 99, 149; labour market in 44–5; livelihood cooperation in 180; lone mothers in 119; marriage in 79–80, 159; minimum wage in 139; model pension in 50, 128, 130, 168; non-regular employment in 74, 96, 98, 136, **137**, 140, 148–9; origins of welfare state in 11; pension benefit levels in 50, 112, **130**, 168–70, **172**; pension records scandal in 150–3, 155, 160; pension reserve fund in 143, 170; pension system in 49–51, 85, 103–4, 113; poverty in 5, 85, 139; public assistance scheme in 51–2, 119–21, 166, 168; public investment in 4, 54, 85–8, 93; savings in 183–4; self-employed sector in 88–90, 93; social security contributions in 52, 63–5, 74–5, 85, 99, 101–3, 127–8, 165; social security costs in **154**; social security expenditures in 57, 61, 68, 76, 168; social security fund in 87, 165; status of women in 93, 132–3, 171; structural components of welfare system 47–8; three welfare government proposal for 164–6, **164**, 168; unpaid work in 91–3; wages in 40, 71, 74, 98–9
Japan Federation of Employers *see* Nikkeiren
Japanese Trade Union Confederation *see* Rengō
Japanese economy: booms and busts in 37, 40, 135, **136**, 183; price deflation in 98; restructuring of 1; stagnation of 4; unemployment in 97, 135–6, 147–8
jobless recovery 38, 40

knowledge professions 89, 93
Koizumi, Junichirō 124, 131–2, 149–50, 159–60 *see also* Koizumi administration
Koizumi administration: economic policies of 4–5; governmental reforms of 124; health care reforms of 133–5; social policy reforms of 126–7, 154; women in 153
Korea 37, 39, 53, 86, 88, 99–100, 103, 114–15, 137, 199, 208, 212; elder care in 114; financial liberalization in 37; household budgets in 53; nursing homes in 115; self-employed sector in 88; suicide in 159

labour: commodification of 14–15, 34–6; division of 12, 32; domestic 32–4; feminization of 13; organized *see* labour unions; reproduction of 35
labour costs, comparative **100–1**
labour market: active policies *see* ALMP; dualism in 17–18, 47–8, 69, 160, 162; equivalents of welfare state in 16, 36; extra-legality in 44–5, 47, 153; flexibility in 55–6, 116; in Nordic countries 24; regulation of 3, 7–8, 16–17, 23–4, **97**; reintegration into 177; social exclusion in 44
labour reduction 55–6, 98
labour unions: decline in 13; and employment protection 96; legal recognition of 17; and livelihood cooperation 180; and livelihood security 7–8, 165; in post-war period 11; and wage levels 140; and working conditions 16
Law of Fiscal Structure Reform 65
Law on Social Cooperatives (Italy) 173–4, 176–7
LDP (Liberal Democratic Party) 1, 6, 11, 60, 64–5, 131–3, 157–8, 164
lifestyle neutrality 128, 132
lifestyle restoration 124, 126
livelihood: inadequate 2; satisfaction of needs for 3
livelihood cooperation 2, 5, 158, 173, 179–81
Livelihood Protection Scheme (Japan) *see* Japan, public assistance scheme in
livelihood security: for the elderly 75; evolution of approaches to 7–8; for non-workers 36; provision of 7, 28; recognition of needs 46; use of term 2

livelihood security systems: dysfunctional 22, 26; reverse functioning of 3, 45, 47, 85, 123, 155, 157; types of 3, 8, 13, 23, 31 (*see also* male breadwinner model; work/life balance model; market-oriented model); universal requirement for 34; use of term 2, 7
loans, nonperforming 126
local governments: in Japan 42–3, 165; and livelihood security 8; as organs of self-governance 165, 172–3
Local Governments' National Health Insurances 145–6
long boom 11–12
long-term care insurance 59, 61, 64–6, 68–9, 76, 114–15, 133, 155
Luxembourg 114

macro-economic indexation 127
male breadwinner bias 18–19
male breadwinner model: in Beveridge Report 9; characteristics of 23–4; dominance of 2, 4, 12; Esping-Andersen's explanation of 16; in Europe 97; in Japan 4–5, 47, 50, 53–4, 58–9, 61–2, 68, 72, 85, 124–5, 128, 131, 153, 156, 168; in Netherlands 56; and post-industrialization 56; and social exclusion 41; weakening of 13
market-oriented model 3, 8, 13, 24
markets, need for social safety net 34–5, 181–2
marriage, delaying 82–3
men: age-wage profile of 71–2; unemployment of 97
Miyamoto, Tarō 11
Miyazawa, Kiichi 57
Miyazawa administration, Five-Year Plan for Building A Lifestyle Superpower 57–9
Mori, Yoshirō 132
Murayama, Tomiichi 60
'muscular economic structure', 4, 6, 125, 135, 137–8, 153
mutual aid 8, 41, 49, 93–4, 140–1, 174, 180

Nagatsuma, Akira 138
national burden *see* Japan, social security contributions in
National Health Insurance (NHI) 49, 134, 140, 145–6, 165
National Lifestyle Council 58
National Pension Plan (Japan) 49–50, 62–3, 140, 144, 165

NCSS (National Commission on Social Security) 155, 157–8, 160–1, 163–4, 189–90n9
needs: definition of 27, 168; recognition of 28–9
NEETs (not in education, employment or training) 42, 186n3
neoliberalism 4, 55
Netherlands: elder care in 114; labour reduction route in 56; non-regular workers in 96, 98–9; social security contributions in 99
New Angel Plan 116
New Gold Plan 60–1
new household economics 33
New Kōmeito 131
'new public commons' 180
New Zealand: elder care 114; non-regular workers in 96; welfare regime in 17
NICs (newly industrializing countries) 18, 38
Nikkeiren 69–71, 79
non-commodities 30, 86
non-governmental organizations (NGOs) 158, 180
Nordic countries 13, 21, 24, 55
Norway: non-regular workers in 96; nursing homes in 115; pensions in 103
not-for-profit organizations *see* NPOs
NPOs (non-profit organizations) 2–3, 7–8, 20–4, 30–1, 54, 174, 180, 185n4
Nuita, Yōko 62
nursing care: burden of 10, 169; choice in services 67; expenses of 59; in free market 126; as personal service 33; and social cooperatives 177; support for 24, 32, 53, 61, 165; as universal service 167, 173; unpaid 12; value of 31

Obuchi, Keizō 65
occupational health and safety 7, 16–17, 94
OECD, report on Japan 43, 161–2
oil prices 40, 183
oil shocks 12, 48
Ōkōchi, Kazuo 16–17
Old-age Health Scheme 75
old age pensions *see* pension regimes; pension reform; retirement
older people: care of *see* elder care; health care for 134

parents: prospective 81; taking care of *see* elder care; time use of 92
pension indexation 61, 154

220   Index

pension reforms: in Japan 61, 125, 127–30, 132, 150, 153–4, 164; in Western Europe 11, 113
pension regimes: coverage of 141–2, **142–3**; financing of 11; public **105, 107–11**; unified 168–9, 171–2
pension splitting 112–13, 128–31, 170–1
Pension Working Group 127–31
pensions: age of eligibility for 61; benefit levels of **112**; contributions to 50, 75, 108, 127, 144–5, 151, 154; and non-regular employees 128, 130
placement system 42, 67
Plaza Accord 37
Poland 95, 101
Policy Coherence for Development (PCD) 47
Portugal 52, 96, 103, 116, 123, 174
post-industrialization 3–4, 22, 55–6
poverty: among employed persons *see* working poor; incidence 17; indicators of 41; reduction of 18, **122**
privatization 38, 126, 153, 181
production: participation in 32; relations of 30–1, **31**, 33, **54**, 85–6, 93–4
productivist state 18, 68
promotions: 'multi-tracking' of 70; performance-based 57
property rights, protection of 36, 181
public assistance: bodies providing 8; and gender 2; means-testing of 15; stigma of 13–14
public burden *see* Japan, social security contributions in
Pulisoft 178–9
purchasing power 27–8, 31, 34, 99, 101

redistribution: effects of 4; importance of 16; inter-household 112; in Japan 163; labour demands for 11; negative 116, 119, 123, 155–6; and public investment 88
relative poverty: definition of 120; in Japan 5, 120–1, 123, 138–9, 153, 155, 157, 162–3; measurements of 43, 138, 162; of older people 103–4; and single parents 119
Rengō 161
reproduction 33–5
retirement, and social insurance 9–11, 15
retirement allowances 75–6
risk, redistributing 9

safety net, definition of 186n1
satellite accounts 90

savings 80, 168–9, 183–4
self-employed 30–1, 49, 54, 88–90, 93, 119, 148, 166, 170
Sen, Amartya 26–9, 33, 44
service provision *see* social services, provision of
service sector 13, 22, 89, 93
services: definition of 27–8; personal 32–3, 89
sex workers 32
skill obsolescence 10, 22
slaves 27, 30–2, 35
small producers 27, 35
SMEs (small and medium enterprises) 40, 48, 70
social cohesion 182
social cooperatives 5, 158, 173–80
social economy: definition of 20; employment in 21; intermediary nature of 30; in Japan 93–4; role of in welfare regimes 3, 21, 23; and social exclusion 42
social enterprise 24, 43
social exclusion: awareness of 4; in developing countries 44; evolution of concept 40–1; and global fluctuations 36; Japanese examples of 26, 43, 45, 149, 161; and the welfare state 3
social inclusion: in Japan 42; and livelihood security 3; and market economy 5, 181–2; means of 43; need for 35; unfavorable 44
social institutions 60, 182
social insurance: in Beveridge Report 9–10; contribution base of 14, 30, 49, 52, 56, 74–5, 149; costs of 15; coverage of **141**; eligibility for 23, 48, 140; establishment of 165; evasion of payments in 149, 153; levels of 14; of non-regular workers 144; premiums 81, 128, 139, 149, 154–5, 165, 169; role of in welfare state 2; segmentation of 48–9, 129, 149
Social Insurance Agency 144, 150–3, 155
social investment 55
social isolation 44
social policy: effectiveness of 46; evolution of 3, 26–7; process of formation *see* welfare, production of; use of term 7
social profits 179
Social Protection Committee (European Union) 41–2
social risks 3, 19, 22, 42, 56, 186n1

social security: definition of 9; compulsory systems of 8; in late 20th century 2
social security contributions: comparative **100–1**; and social cooperatives 175
social services: design of 12; provision of 5, 7, 21, 173, 175
social solidarity 171, 180
social stratification 15, 19
Social Welfare Act (Japan) 42
socially disadvantaged people 175–6, 178
South Korea *see* Korea
Soviet Union 11–13, 37, 181
Spain: non-regular workers in 96; social economy in 174
spousal allowances 63, 72
Stiglitz, Joseph 37–8
structural adjustment programs (SAP) 39
subsidiarity 14, 19, 51–2, 120, 168
suicide 157, 159
Survey on Time Use and Leisure Activities 33, 91–2
survivor's pension 108, 171
Sweden: ALMP in 90; consumer cooperatives in 180; income of women in 93; inequality in 139; male breadwinner model in 13; net burden of households 102; non-regular workers in 96, 99; pensions in 103, 112, 129, 168–70; social economy in 174
Switzerland, elder care in 114

Taiwan 93, 104
Takagi, Tsuyoshi 161, 163
tax burden 86, 102, 121, 154
tax deductions 19, 53, 102
tax system reform 125, 170
Ten-Year Strategy for Health Care and Welfare for the Elderly *see* Gold Plan
Thailand 37
third sector *see* social economy
Time Dollars system 179
total fertility rate (TFR) 81, 116, 157–8
Turkey 52, 99, 103, 119, 138

unemployment: duration of 136–7, **138**, 147; indicators of 41; mass 9–10, 12, 166; risks of 16–17, 59, 97; structural 41, 44; and suicide 159
unemployment benefits 68, 87, 140, 147–8, **147**, 189n15
Unipol 177
United Kingdom: net burden of households 102; pensions in 113, 168; public sector in 86–8; social economy in 20–1, 174; unemployment in 147; welfare regime in 17–18
United States: benefit take-up rate in 120; current account deficit of 37; economic crisis in 183; elder care in 114; health insurance in 24, 183; minimum wage in 139; net burden of households 102; off-shoring of manufacturing 38; pensions in 113; public sector in 86; relative poverty in 162; unemployment in 147; welfare regime in 13–14, 20
universal services 158, 164, 166–7, 169, 172–3
universalism 5, 14, 166–7
unpaid work 12, 34, 44, 54, 90–3, **92**
utility 27, 29, 33

Vision of Gender Equality 62–4

wage labour 27, 30, 32, 34–5, 85–6, 90, 94
wages: minimum 7, 16, 36, 139–40, 166, 185n3; seniority system of 47–8, 70–1
Washington Consensus 38–9
welfare: definition of 23, 25; community 42–3; production of 34, **45**, 46–7; proportion of GDP spent on 52
welfare politics 185n1
welfare regimes: Esping-Andersen's theory of 8; theory of 19; typology of 8, 13–23, 55
welfare state: 20th century model of 2–3, 7–9; blind spots of 10; dysfunctional 4, 22, 36; origin of term 9; power relationships in 11–12; and social inequalities 116
West Germany, social security in 11, 53, 61 *see also* Germany
White Paper on Health and Welfare 65–8, 82
White Paper on International Trade 135
White Paper on Welfare and Labour 71
widowers 109, 113
widows 51, 104, 112–13, 128, 131, 188n4
women: autonomy of 19, 132; caring for relatives 66; in cooperatives 94, 176; elderly 87, 133, 155; exclusion from labour force 55–6, 137; exclusion from livelihood security 157; and global economy 184; and marriage 79–83, 159, 171; non-regular employment of 72–3, **73**, 83, 98, 135–6, **137**, 148; participation in labour force 4, 13, 70; and pension insurance 141; and poverty 83–4; self-employment of 88–90;

women (*continued*)
  underpayment of 71; and unemployment 97, 137, 148; unpaid work of 12, 54, 64, 90–1, 93; and pensions *see* gender, and pensions
Women's Association for a Better Aging Society 66
work/family reconciliation 116, **117–18**
work/life balance 3–4, 69, 116, 125, 132; model of livelihood security 8, 13, 23–4, 50, 125
workers *see* employees
workers' compensation insurance 48
workers' cooperatives 30–1, 35, 93, 181
working hours, regulation of 7
working poor 10, 139, 161
workplace health *see* occupational health and safety
World Bank 37–8, 182

yen, appreciation of 37
young people: employment of 84; exclusion from livelihood security 157

ROUTLEDGE INTERNATIONAL HANDBOOKS

Routledge International Handbooks is an outstanding, award-winning series that provides cutting-edge overviews of classic research, current research and future trends in Social Science, Humanities and STM.

Each *Handbook*:

- is introduced and contextualised by leading figures in the field
- features specially commissioned original essays
- draws upon an international team of expert contributors
- provides a comprehensive overview of a sub-discipline.

Routledge International Handbooks aim to address new developments in the sphere, while at the same time providing an authoritative guide to theory and method, the key sub-disciplines and the primary debates of today.

If you would like more information on our on-going *Handbooks* publishing programme, please contact us.

Tel: +44 (0)20 701 76566
Email: reference@routledge.com

www.routledge.com/reference

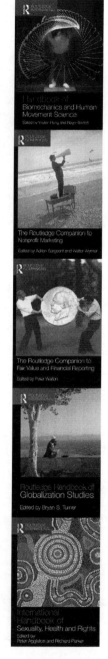

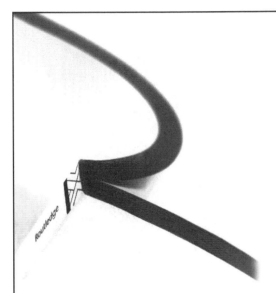

Routledge Paperbacks Direct

Bringing you the cream of our hardback publishing at paperback prices

This exciting new initiative makes the best of our hardback publishing available in paperback format for authors and individual customers.

Routledge Paperbacks Direct is an ever-evolving programme with new titles being added regularly.

To take a look at the titles available, visit our website.

www.routledgepaperbacksdirect.com

ROUTLEDGE Revivals

Are there some elusive titles you've been searching for but thought you'd never be able to find?

Well this may be the end of your quest. We now offer a fantastic opportunity to discover past brilliance and purchase previously out of print and unavailable titles by some of the greatest academic scholars of the last 120 years.

Routledge Revivals is an exciting new programme whereby key titles from the distinguished and extensive backlists of the many acclaimed imprints associated with Routledge are re-issued.

The programme draws upon the backlists of Kegan Paul, Trench & Trubner, Routledge & Kegan Paul, Methuen, Allen & Unwin and Routledge itself.

Routledge Revivals spans the whole of the Humanities and Social Sciences, and includes works by scholars such as Emile Durkheim, Max Weber, Simone Weil and Martin Buber.

FOR MORE INFORMATION

Please email us at **reference@routledge.com** or visit: **www.routledge.com/books/series/Routledge_Revivals**

www.routledge.com

An environmentally friendly book printed and bound in England by www.printondemand-worldwide.com

This book is made entirely of sustainable materials; FSC paper for the cover and PEFC paper for the text pages.